Education for Liberation

Education for Liberation

The Politics of Promise and Reform Inside and Beyond America's Prisons

Edited by Gerard Robinson and
Elizabeth English Smith

ROWMAN & LITTLEFIELD
Lanham • Boulder • New York • London

Published by Rowman & Littlefield
An imprint of The Rowman & Littlefield Publishing Group, Inc.
4501 Forbes Boulevard, Suite 200, Lanham, Maryland 20706
www.rowman.com

6 Tinworth Street, London SE11 5AL, United Kingdom

British Library Cataloguing in Publication Information Available

Library of Congress Cataloging-in-Publication Data

Names: Robinson, Gerard, 1966– editor. | Smith, Elizabeth English, 1992– editor.
Title: Education for liberation : the politics of promise and reform inside and
   beyond America's prisons / edited by Gerard Robinson and Elizabeth English Smith.
Description: Lanham, Maryland : Rowman & Littlefield, [2019] | Includes
   bibliographical references and index.
Identifiers: LCCN 2018042842 (print) | LCCN 2018053066 (ebook) | ISBN
   9781475847765 (electronic) | ISBN 9781475847741 (cloth : alk. paper) |
   ISBN 9781475847758 (pbk. : alk. paper)
Subjects: LCSH: Prisoners—Education—United States. | Criminals—Rehabilitation—United States.
   | Prisoners—Deinstitutionalization—United States.
Classification: LCC HV8883.3.U5 (ebook) | LCC HV8883.3.U5 E48 2019 (print) |
   DDC 365/.6660973—dc23
LC record available at https://lccn.loc.gov/2018042842

♾™ The paper used in this publication meets the minimum requirements of
American National Standard for Information Sciences—Permanence of Paper
for Printed Library Materials, ANSI/NISO Z39.48-1992.

Printed in the United States of America

Contents

Foreword

Newt Gingrich and Van Jones

> *But if man is without education, although with all his latent possibilities attaching to him, he is, but a pitiable object; a giant in body, but a pigmy in intellect, and, at best, but half a man. Without education, he lives within the narrow, dark and grimy walls of ignorance. He is a poor prisoner without hope. The little light that he gets comes to him as through dark corridors and grated windows. . . . Education, on the other hand, means emancipation. It means light and liberty. It means the uplifting of the soul of man into the glorious light of truth, the light only by which men can be free.*

> —Frederick Douglass, "Blessings of Liberty and Education," September 3, 1894

Few government efforts fail us more thoroughly than our prison system.

Our current inability to support people behind prison walls and upon their return to communities across America is demonstrated by astronomical recidivism rates. More than 75 percent of people who have spent time in prison are rearrested within five years, and many do not make it six months before facing another run-in with the law.

In this way, the prison system betrays both victims and perpetrators of crime in addition to society at large by failing to enhance public safety. There is little evidence that prison is deterring or correcting anyone—or making any lives better.

Additionally, in an era of budget consciousness at all levels of government, Americans must reexamine their priorities and give every one of our spending items a long, hard look. Every wasted dollar represents one less dollar for the taxpayers or efforts that actually prevent crime from being committed, like education or mental health treatment. Sometimes our failures are so deep and entrenched that whole ways of doing things must be scrapped and rethought.

Under this lens, our prison system is decidedly not living up to its intended purpose and needs to be completely overhauled.

Our prisons and jails are often called a "revolving door," but that analogy is too narrow. Disturbingly, the conditions in these institutions further traumatize people and leave them with fewer opportunities to succeed upon release.

Meanwhile, people in prison can face barbaric physical and sexual violence. Gangs and drugs are rampant in many facilities, putting all those inside—those who live there and those who work there—at risk.

Since prisons are shut away behind fences, and often hundreds of miles from major cities, most people give little thought to the consequences of these desperate places. But the impact is real—on the incarcerated men and women inside, on the formerly incarcerated outside, and on their loved ones. The situation seems hopeless, even for those committed to working toward a better life.

And this is where famed abolitionist and statesman Frederick Douglass strikes a true note: ignorance and powerlessness of the mind strips away hope.

Today, our justice system leans too heavily toward punishment and fails to actually address the underlying reasons why people are committing crime in the first place or offer them opportunities to rehabilitate. As a result, there are 2.3 million people incarcerated in our local, state, and federal detention facilities—too many of whom have little hope of achieving productive, prosperous lives. This situation must change.

The United States has an obligation to offer prisoners hope and, along with it, the promise of greater public safety and prosperity to all. Each year, more than six hundred thousand people are released from state and federal prisons and become "returned citizens" in search of work, family, and new homes. One way to ensure that they have true second chances (or even a first chance) to achieve their potential is to assist them while they are behind prison walls.

That is why this book is so important.

As two leaders from different philosophical and ideological poles, we can agree that empowering people in prison through greater access to quality educational opportunities is a worthy effort to increase public safety, strengthen our democratic institutions, and grow our economy.

Sadly, most of those in prison never received a quality education in the first place. According to some estimates, between 60 and 75 percent of people in prison are functionally illiterate,[1] and many prisoners score well below average in quantitative and literacy testing.[2] But some are highly capable individuals who simply never had access to robust, formal education.

This education gap has a real-world impact, both inside and outside the wire.

Research shows that the recidivism rate for those who receive educational help in prison drops dramatically compared to those who do not. Similarly, some GED[3] and Adult Basic Education programs also reduce rates of recidivism and re-incarceration for participants.

Additionally, an effective prison education model is vocational training.[4] Formerly incarcerated people were more likely to obtain gainful employment if they participated in job training programs while inside.

New models using tablets and other secure forms of technology promise to deliver even more quality educational tools to those behind bars. These resources, some of which are available for free on the outside, are slowly transforming our learning models and hold immense potential to revolutionize in-prison programming at a fraction of current costs.

Yet educational programs are largely unavailable, oversubscribed, or poorly matched to the needs of individuals in many correctional facilities.

We must do better. To improve the lives of these individuals, their families, and the public, policy makers and advocates should improve access to high-quality in-prison educational programming.

This book shows, through the work of experts, researchers, real-world practitioners, and returned citizens, that these programs do something powerful: they give hope and dignity to the incarcerated.

Education is empowering and has astounding positive impacts on future earnings, mental and physical health outcomes, and interpersonal relationships worn down by time in prison.

Solid educational programs are also cost effective. Today, California spends more money to house and secure an inmate in notoriously dangerous conditions than it costs to send a student to Harvard for a year.[5] By contrast, prison education programs improve in-prison conditions—especially inmate and correctional officer safety[6]—while delivering a remarkable return on investment. For each dollar spent on prison educational programming, the government saves between $4 and $5 on future incarceration costs during the first three years post-release.[7]

Those dividends must be multiplied by the benefits to family cohesion, economic growth, and reduced reliance on government assistance. We must also consider the impact of reducing violence, property crimes, and drug abuse on society as a whole.

The good news is we are turning a page on our approach to how we treat prisoners and returned citizens. Educating prisoners has the power to help them return to purpose-filled, productive lives on the outside.

More than 95 percent of prisoners will eventually come home. Isn't it best that we prepare them well for life on the outside?

We believe that high-quality, well-delivered in-prison educational opportunities can enable us to give incarcerated individuals the tools and skills they will need to return to communities and succeed. This would leave us all better off.

NOTES

1. Michael Sainato, "US Prison System Plagued by High Illiteracy Rates," *Observer*, July 17, 2017, http://observer.com/2017/07/prison-illiteracy-criminal-justice-reform/.

2. National Center for Education Statistics, "Literacy behind Prison Walls," October 1994, https://nces.ed.gov/pubs94/94102.pdf.

3. John Esperian, "The Effect of Prison Education Programs on Recidivism," *Journal of Correctional Education* 61, no. 4 (2010): 316–34, https://www.jstor.org/stable/23282764.

4. RAND Corporation, "Education and Vocational Training in Prisons Reduces Recidivism, Improves Job Outlook" (news release), August 22, 2013, https://www.rand.org/news/press/2013/08/22.html.

5. Associated Press, "At $75,560, Housing a Prisoner in California Now Costs More Than a Year at Harvard," *Los Angeles Times*, June 4, 2017, http://www.latimes.com/local/lanow/la-me-prison-costs-20170604-htmlstory.html.

6. Amanda Pompoco, John Wooldredge, Melissa Lugo, Carrie Sullivan, and Edward J. Latessa, "Reducing Inmate Misconduct and Prison Returns with Facility Education Programs," *Criminology and Public Policy*, May 22, 2017, https://doi.org/10.1111/1745-9133.12290.

7. Lois M. Davis et al., *Evaluating the Effectiveness of Correctional Education: A Meta-Analysis of Programs That Provide Education to Incarcerated Adults* (Santa Monica, CA: RAND Corporation, 2013), https://www.rand.org/pubs/research_reports/RR266.html.

Acknowledgments

The editors thank several individuals for making this volume a reality. First, they would like to thank the authors who contributed so much of their time and talent to this project, particularly those authors who wrote their portions of this book while incarcerated or just upon their release.

The editors thank the staff at the American Enterprise Institute who supported the research conference for this volume and provided edits to the chapters, including Sean Kennedy, Rooney Columbus, Doug Lewis, Moira Griffith, and Farrah Pappa. The editors also thank the staff at the Center for Advancing Opportunity who supported this project and provided edits, including Alma DuVall and Rebecca Feldherr.

Finally, the editors thank the teachers, researchers, correctional staff, program directors, judges, police, policy makers, and advocates who support educational and workforce opportunities for our nation's incarcerated individuals.

Introduction

Gerard Robinson and Elizabeth English Smith

In today's knowledge economy, a quality education serves as one of the first rungs on the ladder to economic freedom and social mobility in the United States. Yet too many of the 650,000 formerly incarcerated men and women who reenter society each year never climb this ladder—or reach for it at all. They often enter through the iron gates of a state or federal prison, lacking a high-quality education and job training, or suffering from socioeconomic or mental challenges that make learning difficult. Once inside a prison cell, the pursuit of an education—be it for a GED, a high school diploma, or a postsecondary credential—can be a daunting journey for inmates as well as the educators who provide it.

Still, thousands of incarcerated men and women grab hold of the first rung of the ladder each day. This journey leads some toward higher education and others toward workforce skills. By reaching for an education while incarcerated, these men and women will minimize the probability that they reenter society woefully underprepared for the world of learning and work, and increase the possibility that their contributions will make communities safer or the families they left behind more stable.

Education offers a pathway toward liberation. How and why are the focus of this book.

It is worth noting that our interest in the lives of incarcerated men and women began during our undergraduate studies at Howard University in the 1980s and the University of Michigan in the 2000s, respectively; however, the journey to find an answer to how and why education matters inside and beyond America's prisons began while we worked at the American Enterprise Institute (AEI). At AEI, we convened conferences with federal lawmakers on the left and right, as well as scholars, reformers, and former inmates who reached different conclusions about the effects of in-prison education on recidivism and employment.

For example, scholars such as Lois Davis at the RAND Corporation shared research that shows a positive return from prison education.[1] Other scholars included David Muhlhausen, then at the Heritage Foundation and now director at the National Institute of Justice, the research and evaluation arm of the US Department of Justice (DOJ), who presented research that shows that the return on investment in prison education programs is weak.[2]

To complement the evidence about what works (or does not) from research and policy meetings in Washington, DC, we began to tour prisons around the country to speak with inmates, correctional officers, and educators. One visit took us to San Quentin State Prison

1

outside of San Francisco, California. There, against barbed wire, against the backdrop of hundreds of men on recreation time—doing pull ups, playing basketball, and making conversation—the one-room trailer offers an education for those lucky enough to attend. In the space occupied by the Prison University Project (PUP), professors from the University of California system teach inmates courses in the humanities, mathematics, and social and physical sciences.

San Quentin has been home to various education programs since the 1960s, though these programs did not always result in an inmate earning a postsecondary credential. In the 1990s, PUP changed this. The program provides college preparatory courses and confers associate's degrees in general studies so students leave prison with something other than a scarlet letter "F"—for felon—to show for their time, providing them with an on-ramp back into the workforce and their communities. With around 300 students currently enrolled, as of 2018, 162 men have received associate's degrees through PUP.[3]

On the other side of the country in the rural South is the medium-security state prison, Burruss Correctional Training Center, in Forsyth, Georgia—about an hour south of Atlanta. Georgia, like California, has begun to come to grips with its bloated prison system in recent years. Between 1990 and 2011, the prison population doubled to nearly fifty-six thousand—meaning one in seventy adults were behind bars in the state—and around 66 percent were African American.

Georgia had the fourth-largest incarceration rate per capita in the nation, and state investment in corrections surpassed $1 billion annually.[4] Leaders in the Republican and Democratic parties decided that the time had come to reform its state's criminal justice system because it was too costly in economic and human terms. By July 2012, the state prison population declined to 52,962, and, for African American inmates, this number was among the lowest levels since the 1980s.[5]

Beginning in 2010, the state enacted a number of criminal justice reform laws that embraced in-prison academic programs as a key driver to lowering recidivism.[6] Lawmakers amended state regulations so an inmate could earn a technical certification as a welder or plumber during his or her time behind bars. As of March 2018, 7,799 inmates had completed vocational certificates through a partnership among the Georgia Department of Corrections (GDC) and technical colleges, the University System of Georgia, and local employers.[7] During fiscal year 2017, GDC awarded 2,371 GEDs to inmates, accounting for 23 percent of all GEDs awarded statewide.[8]

Visits to prisons in Texas, New York, and Maryland and to reentry programs in the District of Columbia and other cities reinforced two themes: a quality education matters to current and former inmates, and access to it remains a challenge. Lack of money and support from university or nonprofit partners serve as the biggest barriers to expanding prison education. Access to technology provides another barrier.

But even when money is available, state regulations, while necessary for the safety of correctional officers and inmates alike, often inhibit the innovative delivery of teaching and learning behind prison walls. While elected officials and entrepreneurs create new solutions to old challenges, let us be mindful that the politics of promise and reform inside and beyond America's prisons is not an unfamiliar story in the history of American criminal justice.

The idea of providing educational instruction to prisoners is not new. In fact, the practice is as old as our nation itself. In 1787, while delegates in New York City enacted the Northwest Ordinance, Benjamin Rush met with public leaders in Philadelphia to discuss crime and rehabilitation to determine how to ameliorate the wretched conditions facing incarcerated men, women, and children inside Philadelphia's Walnut Street Jail.[9]

The group called itself the "Philadelphia Society for Alleviating the Miseries of Public Prisons," and vocational education was part of the society's plan to improve the social conditions of inmates. Shortly thereafter, in the 1800s, Sabbath Schools were used to teach inmates to read the Bible. Education programs in prison later expanded, focusing on secular subjects, including reading, math, and writing.[10]

Prison education during the first half of the 1900s maintained its vocational focus but allowed for innovation. This included the creation of prison libraries, facilities for female inmates, and allowances for inmates to enroll in correspondence courses and extension programs. This era supported larger-scale innovations such as Howard Gill's creation of the nation's first "model prison community" at the Norfolk facility in Massachusetts in the late 1920s.

NORFOLK, MA

The architectural design of the Norfolk facility resembled a college-style quad that facilitated free interaction among inmates and welcomed volunteers from the professional ranks that tutored the men in the sciences, humanities, and art of debate. Between 1933 and 1966, the Norfolk debate team posted a 144–8 record and defeated teams from MIT, Yale, and Oxford.[11]

In the 1960s, President Lyndon Johnson authorized support for prisoner education using Title IV grants under the Higher Education Act of 1965 (HEA). This funding source opened the doors to a host of educational programs for thousands of inmates for the first time. For nearly a decade after HEA's passage, the human improvement through prison education model triumphed over its naysayers.

WAR ON CRIME (shift away from EDU)

'94

But two decades later, President Bill Clinton and a Democratic-controlled Congress moved away from the human improvement through education model with the enactment of the Violent Crime Control and Law Enforcement Act of 1994, embodying the "tough on crime" mentality of the day. This law was not only tough on crime but also tough on educational opportunities for the roughly twenty-three thousand inmates in federal or state prison who were using a Pell Grant to pay for a college education while incarcerated.

In the early 1990s, the United States had some 772 college-in-prison programs in operation in 1,287 correctional facilities.[12] Nine states accounted for two-thirds of all inmates using Pell Grants to support their education—Ohio and New York had more than three thousand students, and Missouri, Texas, Illinois, Massachusetts, Georgia, Alabama, and Virginia each had more than one thousand students. The federal government spent $35 million out of a $6 billion Pell Grant budget on inmates.[13] However, the majority of them closed after the 1994 crime legislation.[14]

'08 Shift back to edu!

The federal government swung the pendulum back toward support for prison education when President George W. Bush signed the Second Chance Act of 2008. The law authorized federal funding for state and local projects seeking to reduce recidivism through mentorship, vocational training, reentry supports, and educational and literacy training for the incarcerated. In 2016, President Barack Obama advanced the human improvement theme one step further with an investment of $30 million in the Second Chance Pell Experimental Sites Initiative, which allows approximately twelve thousand inmates at sixty-five colleges to use a Pell Grant to pay for courses that could lead to a certificate or an associate's or bachelor's degree.[15]

'16 Pell!

Today, under the administration of President Donald Trump, a new era in American politics has painted an unclear picture for what the future holds for education and workforce reentry programs operating inside and outside of prison walls.

One on hand, Trump spoke positively about reform and reentry during the White House Prison Reform Summit held in Washington on May 18, 2018: "At the heart of our prison reform agenda is expanding prison work and the programs so that inmates can reenter society with skills to get a job."[16] On the other hand, the Council of Economic Advisors released a report the same day of the summit that claims that the investment in education programs for inmates is "inconsistent and rates of return more uncertain."[17]

As federal lawmakers, governors, and mayors consider the benefits and challenges of education behind prison walls, they must be mindful of competing schools of thought on the topic and the contentiousness surrounding it. For example, there is strong—and vocal—support behind the idea that felons should not receive federal taxpayer dollars to advance their educations.[18] Supporters believe prisoners forfeited their privilege to receive a taxpayer-funded college education when they committed a crime. Instead, they believe federal money should be spent on those who followed the rules—not those who broke them. Proponents used this line of reasoning to support revoking Pell Grant access to prisoners during debates about the 1994 crime bill, when lawmakers like Senator Kay Bailey Hutchison (R-TX) introduced amendments to restrict educational access to inmates, remarking:

> It is not fair to the millions of parents who work and pay taxes, [who] then must scrape and save and often borrow to finance their children's education. . . . [T]he American people . . . are frustrated and angry by a Federal Government that sets rules that put convicts at the head of the line for college financial aid, crowding out law abiding citizens.[19]

In addition to this debate at the federal level, state lawmakers and governors have debated whether using public funds to educate prisoners is a noble endeavor. Governor William Weld, the Republican leader of Massachusetts in 1991, opposed federal dollars going into higher education when it paid for inmates' education. His belief was that free college does not play well with working families. He remarked during an interview in 1991, "We've got to stop giving a free college education to prison inmates, or else the people who cannot afford to go to college are going to start committing crimes so they can get sent to prison to get a free education!"[20]

Today, the "no-federal-dollars-for-felons" frame of mind is alive and well. But there is another large, and growing, constituency of individuals who argue that providing an education to inmates allows society to correct the many ways our education system failed them in the first place, molding productive, law-abiding citizens in the process.

Undoubtedly, the prison system fails too many today, locking individuals up for long sentences but not providing opportunity for human development and education while serving that time. This is an ineffective approach, considering around 95 percent of inmates will return home at some point, and 2.3 million individuals are behind bars today. Between 1980 and 2015, the United States prison population increased by 500 percent, making the failure to prepare inmates for reentry an increasingly important challenge.

Today, more than 650,000 men and women, around the population of the city of Memphis, return home from prison every year. Oftentimes with little more than some pocket change and a bus ticket, they reenter society and struggle to find work, housing, a supportive social network, and other necessities to successfully transition home.[21] Economic barriers to reentry, the stigma of a felony conviction, and mental health and addiction challenges make reentry a bleak picture, leading many returned citizens to return to a life of crime. A DOJ study of 404,638 inmates in thirty states released in 2005 identified that 68 percent were rearrested within three years and 77 percent within five years of release.[22]

To address how to reform our criminal justice system by better preparing individuals to successfully reenter society, this book compiles chapters written by individuals on the right and the left of the political spectrum, and within and outside the fields of prison education and reentry. Chapters feature the voices of prominent national figures pushing for reform, current and former students who have benefited from an education program while in prison, those teaching or managing educational programs within prison, and researchers, entrepreneurs, and policy influencers.

In chapter 1, Max Kenner, founder and executive director of the Bard Prison Initiative (BPI), lays out the historical development of education inside prison and jails in the United States. This chapter provides context for college-in-prison programs in several states, with a particular focus on California, Texas, and New York. For New York specifically, Kenner describes the work of BPI at six correctional facilities that enroll three hundred incarcerated men and women across a full spectrum of academic disciplines. Kenner argues that college-in-prison programs represent an important experiment in prisoners' self-determination and the beginning of an evolutionary process in postsecondary education.

In chapter 2, Daniel Shoag, an assistant professor of public policy at Harvard Kennedy School of Government, and Stan Veuger, resident scholar at AEI, make an economic assessment of the effects of incarceration on inmates' return home from prison as they struggle to find employment, housing, health insurance, and other basic necessities to allow them to be productive members of society. Barriers to reentry are real; yet the design and implementation of many reentry programs have produced mixed results. In this chapter, Shoag and Veuger address various arguments about impediments to reentry and offer reform suggestions for lawmakers.

In chapter 3, Andrea Cantora, assistant professor in the School of Criminal Justice at the University of Baltimore, addresses the Obama administration's Second Chance Pilot Program—its impetus, rollout, and status today. Cantora has worked directly with incarcerated populations since 2005, and most recently she has developed and oversees the University of Baltimore's Second Chance College Program at Jessup Correctional Institution. Cantora shares the backstory of her project and the pilot writ large, and she addresses the benefits, challenges, and lessons of the initiative.

In chapter 4, Nancy La Vigne, vice president of justice policy at the Urban Institute, answers the million-dollar question: Do reentry programs *work*? La Vigne outlines some of the key evaluations of prison education and reentry programs to date, addresses the strengths and challenges of using random control trials versus other evaluation methods, and discusses why asking these questions is critical to the viability of the field. La Vigne ends the chapter with reflections on lessons learned and proposes a better approach for evaluation for future research.

In chapter 5, Ames Grawert, senior counsel in the Brennan Center's Justice Program, chronicles prisoners' legal battles for access to an education and other basic human rights while serving time. Prisoner-advocates began to advance their cause through wins in federal and state courtrooms after years of attempts to bring change through the legislative process produced few results. In this chapter, Grawert addresses what can be learned from these early court debates, how they are relevant to current debates on this topic, and the limitations of using the courts for this goal.

In chapter 6, Linda Gibbs, a principal for social services at Bloomberg Associates and a senior fellow with Results for America, addresses the institutional dynamics that will shape the delivery of private-sector investments into education and reentry programs for inmates. Specifically, Gibbs discusses how private entities partnered with the state of New York and city leaders to invest in a social impact bond to support the Rikers Island reentry program. Although the program did not deliver intended results, she reflects on lessons learned and examines best practices other cities should keep in mind for effective reentry.

In chapter 7, Renita L. Seabrook, associate professor in the School of Criminal Justice at the University of Baltimore, examines the impact that the rise in the number of incarcerated women in America has on the families they leave behind. Although men account for the vast majority of federal and state inmates, incarcerated women are oftentimes the economic breadwinner and sole parent, making female incarceration particularly difficult for children. Seabrook relies on scholarship and insights on how to help women and the children left behind by our justice system.

In chapter 8, Will Heaton, vice president of policy and government affairs at Just Leadership USA, outlines what it takes for returning citizens to successfully clear barriers to obtain meaningful, lasting employment after serving time. Although he believes access to employment is important to post-incarceration life, preparing inmates—who are accustomed to living regimented lives without a lot of free choice—to enter the free world and function within a new set of rules for economic advancement is challenging.

In chapter 9, Thomas Stewart, president of John F. Kennedy University Online, a regionally accredited institution located in Pleasant Hill, California, shares some of the lessons learned from social entrepreneurs who are using innovative technologies to improve outcomes for those in prison and those returning home after serving time. He builds upon interviews with Silicon Valley and Bay Area entrepreneurs to showcase advancements in criminal justice reform over the last half decade.

In chapter 10, five former inmates shed light on what it is like to attend school in prison in Indiana, Maryland, New York, and Texas. This is important to any conversation about prison reform because, despite reformers' emphasis on improving conditions and opportunities for those in prison, the voices of the incarcerated are almost always left out of public policy conversations. Their stories, told as personal memoirs, provide a rare view into the lives of the people these programs impact, and what policy makers can do to improve, sustain, and expand quality programs behind bars.

The education of prisoners could very well be the next frontier in higher education. Not by simply offering degrees or workforce certificates as the single answer to reentry and recidivism but also as a mechanism for building self-empowerment for inmates and creating a better future for the incarcerated, their families, and their communities. Prison education, if done correctly, has the potential to encourage entrepreneurship and dynamism in a sector that is lacking both, and it can provide a mechanism for prisoners to take a commanding role in their education and lives.

But to realize this promise, much more work needs to be done. This volume intends to examine whether we can get there and, if so, how.

Successful reentry must start at the point of prison entry and extend throughout the reentry process. Providing education to prisoners, and making reentry supports available in communities upon their release, holds great promise in theory, but it also surfaces a variety of challenges and questions that must be addressed if programs are to work as intended. Despite the important developments in the criminal justice reform community over time, many in the field are still unfamiliar with prison education and reentry programs, the barriers to reentry returned citizens face, and how those factors affect communities and families.

This is a critical time in American history when it comes to prisoner rehabilitation and reentry programs. To forge a path forward, exchange in the free market of ideas, and expand opportunities for prisoners, we believe this volume is a necessary addition to the criminal justice reform landscape today. We trust you will find it as useful a handbook as we have in distilling how policy and civil society can together restore human dignity, bolster education and employment opportunities, and make communities safer.

Ultimately, reform must begin with treating returned citizens as human assets, not liabilities, and giving those ready for a second chance a fresh start at life through the redemptive power of education.

NOTES

1. Lois M. Davis et al., *Evaluating the Effectiveness of Correctional Education: A Meta-Analysis of Programs That Provide Education to Incarcerated Adults* (Santa Monica, CA: RAND Corporation, 2013).

2. David Muhlhausen, *Studies Cast Doubt on Effectiveness of Prisoner Reentry Programs*, Heritage Foundation, December 15, 2015, https://www.heritage.org/crime-and-justice/report/studies-cast-doubt-effectiveness-prisoner-reentry-programs.

3. Prison University Project, https://prisonuniversityproject.org/what-we-do/education/.

4. Special Council on Criminal Justice Reform for Georgians, *Report of the Special Council on Criminal Justice Reform for Georgians*, 2011, https://dcs.georgia.gov/sites/dcs.georgia.gov/files/related_files/site_page/2011-GA-Council-Report-FINALDRAFT.pdf.

5. Michael P. Boggs and Carrie A. Miller, *Report of the Georgia Council on Criminal Justice Reform*, CSG Justice Center, February 2017, https://csgjusticecenter.org/wp-content/uploads/2017/02/JR-in-GA_Report-of-the-Council-on-CJ-Reform.pdf.

6. Gerard Robinson, "The Peach State's Civil Society Approach to Criminal Justice Reform," *AEI Ideas*, http://www.aei.org/publication/the-peach-states-civil-society-approach-to-criminal-justice-reform/.

7. Georgia Department of Corrections, "Vocational Certificate Completions Surpassing Goal for FY 18," May 23, 2018, http://www.dcor.state.ga.us/NewsRoom/PressReleases/vocational-certificate-completions-surpassing-goal-fy18.

8. Georgia Department of Corrections, "Vocational Certificate Completions."

9. David J. Rothman, "Perfecting the Prison: United States, 1789–1865," in *The Oxford History of the Prison: The Practice of Punishment in Western Society*, edited by Norval Morris and David J. Rothman (New York: Oxford University Press, 1998), 103; and Ellen Condliffe Lagemann, *Liberating Minds* (New York: New Press, 2016), 114–15. See also Negley K. Teeters, *The Cradle of the Penitentiary: The Walnut Street Jail at Philadelphia, 1773–1835* (Philadelphia: Pennsylvania Prison Society, 1955).

10. Pennsylvania Prison Society Records, 1787–1966, Historical Society of Pennsylvania, https://hsp.org/sites/default/files/legacy_files/migrated/findingaid1946prisonsociety.pdf.

11. Gerard Robinson and Elizabeth English, "Life after Prison: Innovative Prison Education Programs Are a National Necessity," *U.S. News & World Report*, June 20, 2016, https://www.usnews.com/opinion/articles/2016-06-20/innovative-prison-education-is-a-national-necessity; and Adam M. Bright and Natasha Haverty, "Stories from the Norfolk Prison Debate Team," *Public Humanist*, April 14, 2011, http://masshumanities.org/ph_stories-from-the-norfolk-prison-debate-team/.

12. Lagemann, *Liberating Minds*, 9.

13. United States General Accounting Office, "Letter to the Honorable Harris Wofford," August 5, 1994, http://www.gao.gov/assets/90/84012.pdf.

14. Lagemann, *Liberating Minds*, 9.

15. The Vera Institute for Justice, *Second Chance Pell Experimental Sites Initiative Update*, October 24, 2018, https://www.vera.org/publications/second-chance-pell-experimental-sites-initiative-update.

16. Remarks by President Trump at White House Prison Reform Summit, May 18, 2018, https://www.whitehouse.gov/briefings-statements/remarks-president-trump-white-house-prison-reform-summit/.

17. Council of Economic Advisors, *CEA Report: Returns on Investments in Recidivisms-Reducing Programs*, May 18, 2018, https://www.whitehouse.gov/briefings-statements/cea-report-returns-investments-recidivism-reducing-programs/.

18. Federal funding for GED and vocational training is more tolerable to this school of thought than its use for college-in-prison programs.

19. Keesha M. Middlemass, *Convicted and Condemned: The Politics and Policies of Prisoner Reentry* (New York: New York University Press, 2017), 117.

20. Joshua Page, "Eliminating the Enemy: The Import of Denying Prisoners Access to Higher Education in Clinton's America," *Punishment & Society* 6, no. 4 (2004): 358.

21. Elizabeth English, "What Trump Can Do to Help Cities," *U.S. News & World Report*, November 29, 2016, https://www.usnews.com/opinion/civil-wars/articles/2016-11-29/donald-trump-can-fix -cities-by-helping-prisoners-re-enter-society.

22. Matthew R. Durose, Alexia D. Cooper, and Howard N. Snyder, *Recidivism of Prisoners Released in 30 States in 2005: Patterns from 2005 to 2010*, Bureau of Justice Statistics Special Report, April 2014, https://www.bjs.gov/content/pub/pdf/rprts05p0510.pdf.

1

The Long History of College in Prison

Max Kenner

College-in-prison is among the most electric, divisive, and overlooked subjects in American criminal punishment. It cuts directly to these questions: What are prisons for? Do they exist purely to punish? Do they add positive value to the social fabric? The answer to each question has implications far beyond prisons. At its core, college-in-prison raises questions about the purpose of education in American society and who should be entitled to what kind of knowledge.

In the late 1990s, the country was in the throes of the tough-on-crime frenzy. I was an undergraduate at Bard College in New York. It seemed like the college had resources to offer, that some kind of productive relationship could be forged between a college and the nearby prisons surrounding it. After making some rounds and speaking to anyone knowledgeable who would meet with me, someone suggested I watch a film, *The Last Graduation*. It revealed a long, rich history of partnership between these kinds of institutions that had, only recently, come to an abrupt end.

The tragic story this film told was repeated often by those in the field. It went something like this: Following the siege at Attica Prison in 1971, a consensus emerged that American prisons had become too violent, too hopeless, and too cruel. The scrutiny following those events, and the advocacy of the men who had survived, led to the establishment of college programs within American prisons. As I understood it, this happened first in New York, and then across the country.

College became a central part of what happened in prisons. It imbued the institutions with a sense of meaning and hope, and social scientists found that education did more to reduce recidivism than anything else. Despite all that, the Violent Crime Control and Law Enforcement Act of 1994, signed into law by President Bill Clinton, effectively eliminated college opportunity from prisons nationwide when it made incarcerated people ineligible for federal Pell Grants.

The suggestion that Attica led to a more enlightened or progressive period in American corrections was counterintuitive. The years since the early 1970s were a time of unchecked growth in American prisons. But the evidence about the power of college education inside prison was compelling enough to convince me that there was a role my college could play in regional prisons that was timely and of crucial importance.

In 1999, we began in New York with the establishment of the Bard Prison Initiative (BPI). Our focus was on institution building, not history. However, much of the foundational myth told in *The Last Graduation*—that college-in-prison arose during the post–civil rights era and was demolished when the Clinton crime bill made incarcerated people ineligible for federal scholarships—informed our understanding of the work.[1]

In 2017, nearly twenty years later, my colleague Jed Tucker published a terrific article in the *Journal of African American History*. Rooted in archival detail, it describes the process by which Malcolm X sought and thrived in college during his incarceration in Massachusetts in the late 1940s and early 1950s. For those of us invested in college-in-prison, Jed's article represents an astounding example of how unfamiliar we are with the history of it.

Contrary to what we generally assumed, college-in-prison is not a recent phenomenon born in the era of mass incarceration and the establishment of federal Pell Grants. If Malcolm X—perhaps the most celebrated incarcerated American of the twentieth century—could have enrolled in college during his incarceration, how much more of this history might be hiding in plain sight?

This chapter is an attempt to organize what is known about college-in-prison's past and origins. It is essentially an institutional history of colleges, prisons, and the ideas that informed their partnerships. If successful, it will encourage the study of the achievements, disappointments, and excitement that students enrolled in these programs experienced over a long period of time. It is the accomplishments of those alumni that ultimately will be the measure of this field's success.

Prisons are vexing subjects for historians. On the one hand, they represent an unusual opportunity to examine lives and events within them, almost like nowhere else. On the other hand, there is no "prison system" in the United States. There are fifty-one prison systems, countless local jails, and other carceral administrative regimes. Sources are fragmented and dispersed from state to state and prison to prison, and they are often difficult to access.

Any serious investigation into the reality of American prisons tends to zero in on one correctional system or, more likely, one prison. By observing the history of mass incarceration through in-prison college programs, we may understand their stories in a way that better honors local actors, the decisions they made, and aspirations they held.

FROM POSTWAR OPTIMISM TO A CYNICAL CONSENSUS

The Second World War, and the ambitious domestic reforms that followed, transformed the American social landscape. The GI Bill of 1944, for example, was a statement of the country's belief that education was the best investment that governments could make in the future. With funds in hand, millions of veterans enrolled in postsecondary institutions nationwide, and their presence on college and university campuses helped democratize those institutions. This widespread faith in education slowly began to impact prisons in the postwar era, creating the conditions for the development of college-in-prison programs.

An increasing number of prison systems began offering some kind of education through high school equivalency; however, there were more incarcerated Americans eager to improve their lives by pursuing education beyond the secondary level. Prison administrators seeking to make prisons more humane, less destructive, and more focused on the future began creating opportunities to do so.

Before the war, incarcerated people used correspondence coursework to accumulate credits and complete degrees. After the war, colleges and university systems began to offer "extension" academic programs. Many were fully accredited, in-person classes taught by qualified instructors off campus, typically enrolling students part time.[2] Other prisons offered on-site educational programs.

At the Norfolk Penal Colony in Massachusetts, the prison from which Malcolm X enrolled in college, leadership worked to make the prison amenable to learning. Architects built and designed Norfolk in the heady spirit of the Progressive Era because they believed that its pioneering physical characteristics would help men change their lives. Over time, it featured a significant academic library and competitive debate society, as well as an absence of prison uniforms and the ubiquitous emblems of American confinement—prison bars. Leadership also worked to facilitate higher learning through correspondence coursework and invited academics, artists, and teachers to work on site.[3]

Malcolm X knew about Norfolk's programs and petitioned the state for years to be relocated there. After arriving in 1948, Malcolm took advantage of what the prison had to offer. This included the comradery of other incarcerated men with similar interests and ambitions. In his autobiography, Malcolm called Norfolk "the most enlightened form of prison that I have ever heard of."[4]

Norfolk was unique in many ways; however, other states were beginning to adopt its inclination toward education. In the 1950s, Southern Illinois University at Carbondale introduced academic degree programs in the state prison system. The federal prison at Leavenworth in Kansas began sporadic college coursework in one of its units. The University of Maryland started offering courses at the Maryland State Penitentiary.[5] Twenty years after the GI Bill, a dozen college-in-prison programs had emerged across the country thanks in part to American optimism about education.[6]

In the 1960s, an increase in federal investments, coupled with private grant making, was about to make formal higher education a more common, though still rare, feature of American prison life. For example, when President Lyndon Johnson signed the Higher Education Act of 1965 (HEA), the Great Society's effort to make college available to as many Americans as possible, prison inmates benefited from it as well. Title IV of HEA featured the Basic Education Opportunity Grant, which would evolve into the Pell Grant Program. And Johnson's home state of Texas is where one of the early college-in-prisons began.

The Texas Department of Corrections (TDC) was run by an outsized figure named George Beto. Intellectual and formidable, Beto earned a PhD in divinity and another in educational administration.[7] Described as "a reactionary and a reformer," Beto is said to have "walked down the hall with a bat in one hand and a bible in the other."[8] Few executives in the history of American corrections did more to protect funding for education within a state prison system.

While most of Beto's efforts concentrated on primary and secondary education, he also began recruiting colleges to enroll students from within TDC.[9] In 1966, for example, Beto partnered with Lee College to create and maintain perhaps the longest-standing program in the country.[10] Beginning with five academic courses, Lee would over time offer an increasing number of subjects, certifications, and degrees across an array of Texas prisons. At the same time, another experiment was in the works in a large state on the West Coast.

In 1965, the dean of the School of Criminology at the University of California, Berkeley, rallied the state and potential funders "to develop a new departure in correctional rehabilitation through the creation of an accredited four-year college program within a correctional system."[11] He was inspired by Milton Kotler, an "oddball" based at the Institute for Policy Studies, who had the idea that prisons were the place to begin reforming American education.[12]

Before long, the Ford Foundation invested approximately $100,000 for the planning of a new college at San Quentin Prison to be run by Berkeley. "The significance of this proposed grant," wrote Christopher Edley, the first African American officer at the Ford Foundation, "lies in its impact on correctional systems across the United States."[13]

For Edley, the value of collaboration between California's premier public university and San Quentin Prison was its significance as a demonstration project to be replicated nationwide. He described the California prison system as "the best and most progressive in the nation . . . well-financed, professionally operated, receptive to research and innovations."[14] The project was funded on the condition that it launch immediately.

Only after committing to the project did Edley learn of college programs at federal prisons in Leavenworth and Illinois.[15] In fact, even within San Quentin, the idea of ambitious education within American prisons was not an entirely new idea. As early as 1914, college faculty had established opportunities for advanced learning within the expansive perimeters of San Quentin itself.[16]

Meanwhile, the idea of college-in-prison was organically appearing across the country. According to one count, by 1967 there were as many as forty-six prisons across the country offering some kind of college opportunity.[17] A state on the East Coast was part of it.

In 1967, Green Haven Correctional Facility, one of New York's largest and most foreboding maximum-security prisons, hired an ambitious Methodist chaplain named Edwin Muller to establish an array of reform-oriented educational interventions. Within a year, Muller secured an alliance with the former governor of Rhode Island, William Henry Vanderbilt III, who provided access to the highest echelons of philanthropy and the best government contacts. Vanderbilt also appointed Muller executive director of South 40, his recently established charitable organization to, in part, support Muller's work at Green Haven.

With considerable funding, and no certainty that it was possible to successfully enroll men incarcerated at Green Haven in higher education, Muller began to recruit local colleges to participate. Most were initially allergic to the idea, but in 1968, South 40 aligned with Dutchess County Community College and established, perhaps, the first college-in-prison program in the history of New York.

Over time, South 40 was able to secure a generous matching agreement with Law Enforcement Assistance Administration (LEAA), a subdivision of the US Justice Department. For every dollar Vanderbilt would pledge or raise from the private sector, LEAA offered $4. With this commitment in hand, Muller and Vanderbilt raced to create a wide array of pioneering reforms within the seemingly indomitable Green Haven.[18]

Stories about the founding of an in-prison college program in Texas, California, and New York reflect an ongoing tension regarding the definition of success. Meaning, each program was established with social and educational aspirations in mind. And each program, over time, struggled with the question of how to define success: be it in narrow correctional terms or in some broad and ambitious ways.

In New York, for example, Muller's pursuit was to create a collaborative and engaging process through which people in prison could redefine their time, and the institutions themselves was the core reason for the program. South 40's public documents, nevertheless, point to reductions in recidivism as a core reason for the program.[19] A similar clash of visions was occurring back in California and Texas.

The Ford Foundation cited recidivism as a central justification of the work at San Quentin in California, but the practitioners defined program goals more broadly; thus, they began to worry about "a trap."[20] In Texas, the administration at Lee College, Director Beto at TDC, and Milton Kotler envisioned the benefits of its college opportunity to extend far beyond incarceration rates. If recidivism was reduced, that would be, in Kotler's words, "a happy coincidence."[21]

The consequences of this tension turned out not to be trivial. The quietly growing field of college-in-prison during the late 1960s was caught up with increasingly pernicious crosscurrents of its time. While social scientists and funders demanded to measure and to know what "worked" in addressing "deviance" or improving American prisons, advocates, reformers, and radicals called for a comprehensive rethinking of the response to crime that eschewed recidivism as the sole measure of success or, in some cases, prison altogether.

One casualty of this clash of visions was Project NewGate in Oregon. It was the largest, most ambitious, and innovative college-level prison program of the era. After receiving funding from the federal Office of Economic Opportunity (OEO) in 1967, NewGate set out to support rigorous learning environments in prisons across states. Perhaps its most unprecedented feature was an ongoing commitment to incarcerated students after they returned home. Upon release, students were encouraged to enroll in community-based colleges and offered ongoing counseling while doing so.[22] This approach operationalized what would become known as "reentry" years later.[23]

Another unique aspect of NewGate was that inmates enrolled full time in courses and were not expected to maintain additional work assignments. NewGate campuses aspired to offer curricula on par with the standards and rigor of a traditional campus, and its stated objective of "not adapting content" for these particular students was a core principle.[24]

By the end of the decade, OEO was funding NewGate programs in five states. Despite its aspiration to provide students with an experience liberated from the vocabulary of criminology, in the end it served too many masters to succeed. Historian Stephen Duguid, director of Simon Fraser University's Prison Education Program between 1984 and 1993,[25] identifies two primary factors in NewGate's demise.[26]

First, NewGate failed to realize the purely educational experience suggested by its emphasis on academic standards and autonomy. According to Duguid, NewGate acquiesced to the dominant "medical" model of the day and became, in effect, a prison treatment program. It expected a "prisoner's desire to change his patterns of behavior" to figure in admission decisions, required "intensive therapy and counseling," and, despite a commitment not to tailor curricula, frequently reiterated its mission to help "prisoners achieve a non-criminal lifestyle." These compromises blurred the distinction between college and prison.

Second, NewGate linked its fortune to an assessment regime for which it was unprepared.[27] Like programs elsewhere, NewGate emphasized to funders that the reduction of recidivism was its central reason for being. Ultimately, however, the measurement of recidivism is more fraught than it may first appear. Foremost, recidivism is a result of public policy as much as it is of individual behavior.

Furthermore, NewGate did not have at its disposal the kind of sophisticated longitudinal study that could establish the certainty of any kind of outcome. When a 1972 evaluation conducted only three to five years after programs launched failed to demonstrate an impact lowering recidivism rates, OEO allowed funding to expire.[28] However, there is little to no evidence that NewGate did not reduce recidivism or improve public safety. According to its evaluators:

Despite some methodological problems inherent in the original research design, i.e., the absence of a longitudinal perspective, and in some of the hypotheses to be tested, this study has produced some very clear conclusions which have far-reaching implications. The study demonstrates that prison college programs can have significant impact on their participants, namely, in significantly reducing alcohol and drug use, in raising participant aspirations and occupational goals, and in increasing occupational achievement and academic achievement.[29]

Nevertheless, NewGate failed to pass muster in the "what works" spirit of its day.

In the end, OEO expected concrete, criminological measures of impact to justify its support. While NewGate was the outstanding program of the time, it failed to meet funders' criteria for success. The promise of effecting recidivism, and it alone, haunted the NewGate evaluations in just the ways that Milton Kotler had predicted five years before. By 1973, New-Gate faded as the next era of prison education began. Some of its franchises adapted to survive; others disappeared. All of its programs in reentry closed with the end of OEO support.[30]

The demise of NewGate was emblematic of increasingly contentious debates about the American criminal justice system in general, and as the political movements of the 1960s escalated toward their own conclusions, life within American prisons became more explicitly politicized than ever.

The American Friends Service Committee, for example, argued in the book *A Struggle for Justice* that our system of criminal justice magnified inequality "not only because of bias on the part of police or prosecutors but because the substantive content of the law affects those who are not social equals in quite different ways."[31] The Lutheran Church's Board of Social Ministry issued a damning report of its own, and the *Washington Post* issued a special report titled "The Shame of Prisons."[32]

Meanwhile, the furious voices of incarcerated people escaped the confines of prison and reached the general public. Formerly incarcerated authors and activists had joined forces with radical movements of the time, providing firsthand critiques of corrections writ large. In November 1970, men incarcerated at Folsom State Prison issued a series of demands to authorities. That August, George Jackson, the prominent author and de facto leader of the Black Panther Party's incarcerated cadre, was killed in circumstances that authorities described as an escape attempt. Two weeks later, the siege at Attica consumed the prison there and the national media along with it. Inmates issued a statement echoing the Folsom Manifesto:

> We, the men of Attica Prison, have been committed to the N.Y.S. Department of Corrections by the people of society for the purpose of correcting what [have] been deemed social errors in behavior. Errors which have classified us as socially unacceptable until programmed with new values and more thorough understanding as to our value and responsibilities as members of the outside community. . . . The programs which we are submitted to under the façade of rehabilitation, are relative to the ancient stupidity of pouring water on a drowning man, inasmuch as we are treated for our hostilities by our program administrators with their hostility as a medication.[33]

Within the academy, particularly among those intellectualizing about crime, a sense that the state could accomplish nothing good through confinement, or nothing good at all, spread rapidly. The totality of the disruption was captured in a catchphrase promulgated by a sociologist based at the City College of New York, Robert Martinson. Before moving to the East Coast, Martinson had been a long-term graduate student at Berkeley, had run for mayor as a socialist, and had been a Freedom Rider in Mississippi, spending just over a month imprisoned there.

In New York, Martinson joined a team of researchers commissioned by the state to perform an enormous literature review of scholarly articles measuring the impact of prison programs designed to curb recidivism. His pitch—"nothing works"—influenced readers and officials of an extraordinary variety.[34] Martinson commented that the tumult reflected "growing disgust with what inmates regard as the hypocritical fakery of treatment."[35]

In the *New Republic* the following April, Martinson declared that the "long history of 'prison reform' is over. On the whole, the prisons have played out their allotted role. They cannot be reformed and must be gradually torn down."[36] Martinson later split from the research team that hired him and began to pursue media attention independently.

Without the constraints of a team, Martinson promoted his own ideas with remarkable success. He was featured on *60 Minutes*, in *People* magazine, the neoconservative *Public Interest*, and the left-wing *Nation*. The cry "nothing works" appealed to radicals, neoconservatives, and the public at large. However, the phrase was weaponized in the opposite way from which he intended: it amplified skepticism about anything good, but not a desire to mitigate the bad, inside prison.

At the same time, "nothing works" and calls for prison abolition collided with a new commitment to punishment.

In particular, a dark, unforgiving view of human nature, articulated by James Q. Wilson and fellow neoconservatives, captured the public policy debate sometime in the first half of the 1970s. Wilson, the era's intellectual champion of American punishment, belittled the idea that "programs" or "education" possibly lead to a significant change in people's behavior.[37] He focused on the other side of the ledger, insisting, as my colleague Ellen Lagemann writes, that "incentives should be changed, with punishment becoming ever more strict and immediate."[38]

The concurrent prominence of prison abolitionism, and neoconservative calls for a renewed commitment to punishment, can be explained as a conflict between competing visions of society. It can also be accurately understood as a perverse consensus across a fraught political spectrum. Exhausted by the pitched battles of the late 1960s and early 1970s, ideological combatants gave up on the hope of making prisons better or more effective at increasing safety.

Some social scientists and liberals abandoned their focus on the state, education, and governance. Some conservatives absolved themselves of the pretense that prisons should have a purpose other than retribution. Punishment became a facet of American life where state intervention was the one, best answer. The most essential feature of public safety, it was argued, was that punishment be "certain." This cynical consensus left a vacuum leading to unforeseen growth of American prison systems.

Prisons themselves, increasingly filled with Hispanic and African American men, became symbols of the shortcomings of integration and the failures of the New Deal and Great Society. Uprisings in Watts, Newark, and cities nationwide, coupled with the presidency of Richard Nixon and, ultimately, the siege at Attica, brought these tensions to the forefront of the public imagination. Despite all this, the postwar period was in fact a time of relative stability in American criminal justice. Nationally, roughly two hundred thousand people were incarcerated in prisons or jails in 1970. The Texas state prison system held 14,331, California imprisoned roughly 25,033, and 12,059 people were incarcerated in the New York state system.[39] That was about to change.

THE ERA OF MASS INCARCERATION

What is now called the era of mass incarceration is the period during which the United States embarked on an experiment of investing in prisons at an unprecedented scale. Americans began locking up more people, for longer periods of time, at younger ages, often for smaller and smaller infractions of the law. And, perversely, the more people we incarcerated, the more we also made the prisons people were confined in less livable, less hopeful, and less oriented toward creating a better future for anyone.

Mass incarceration is divided into three stages. The first begins with the start of the relentless rise in prison populations and the "War on Drugs" in 1972 and closes with the Clinton crime bill of 1994. The second begins with the implementation of the crime bill in 1995 and extends to 2008. The third begins in 2009 and ends in 2018.

The First Stage of Mass Incarceration (1972–1994)

In 1972, the number of people in prison in the United States began a relentless uptick that continued for a generation. As the incarcerated population began to skyrocket, so, too, did the number of college programs. By the end of the 1970s, there would be nearly 350 of them.[40] The increase was not the result of central planning. Rather, the spread of community colleges, coinciding with the growth of prison systems and the authorization of Pell Grants, created a demand and a means for funding programs nationwide.

In New York, with pressure mounting following the public hearings about Attica, the state office of education seized the initiative. The new Higher Education Opportunities Program (HEOP), dedicated to increasing college enrollment of academically and economically excluded students, began recruiting colleges to establish programs within a handful of the state's most formidable institutions.[41]

HEOP sought first to expand the college at Green Haven, then reached out to colleges that had not previously participated.[42] To the leaders of South 40, who had a difficult time engaging schools just a few years earlier, it became clear that there was a new calculus driving the decision making of college administrators. Pell had changed the paradigm. Also, Attica made the work more timely, pressing, and, to the cynical among us, more in vogue than before.[43]

For Dutchess Community College, there was suddenly competition for students within Green Haven. Marist College, a private liberal arts college, entered the prison with the willingness to enroll considerably more men and the ability to confer a bachelor's degree. North of Albany, along the Vermont border, HEOP was successful in recruiting Skidmore College to enter the prison at Comstock.[44]

In October 1973, the State University of New York announced its intention of opening a "liberal arts prison college" in a facility for women in Bedford Hills.[45] And, in western New York, HEOP organized a network of three postsecondary institutions—Niagara University, Canisius College, and Daemen College—to create what would become the Niagara Consortium. It began enrolling students in Attica in 1975. Pell support was supplemented by state-level Tuition Assistance Program (TAP) grants and, often, by additional funds from HEOP.[46] By 1980, there would be college presence in virtually every prison in the state.[47]

The experience in New York was not uncommon. Pell Grants, often combined with state-level tuition grants, enabled colleges to fund and operate college-in-prison programs nationwide.

In Ohio, the growth of the prison system, and of college within it, was particularly pronounced. While some programs in Ohio dated as far back as 1964, with Pell the programs expanded dramatically. Analogous to New York, incarcerated Ohioans were eligible to receive a state-level, need-based Ohio Instructional Grant to pay for postsecondary education. By 1975, every prison in Ohio hosted a college. In the years that followed, the incarcerated population jumped from under eight thousand to more than fifty thousand. At its peak, the Ohio prison system enrolled more than five thousand students through seventeen separate colleges and universities.[48]

By the 1980s, college opportunity had become a central tenet of American criminal punishment. The number of programs increased from the dozens to the hundreds. The dramatic increase in prison populations had left correctional administrators with an urgent need to "keep people busy."

While people who manage prisons are commonly assumed to be hostile to college, and some are, it was often prison staff who sought out colleges to participate. In some instances, wary administrators became supportive of programs after seeing the impact they had on morale and safety.[49] Over time, many correctional officials came to view college as a core activity within the prisons. Meanwhile, for many community colleges, engaging incarcerated people became a central way to increase enrollment and revenue.

Bad Quality

Unfortunately, oversight of academic quality in prison college programs was lackluster. The dumbing down of coursework, "no-fail" policies, faculty absenteeism, and missing course books all figure in reports of the worst abuses. If anyone should have been responsible for regulating standards, it was not clear who. The college? Prison administration? State policy makers? Philanthropists? In some states, educators and correctional officials collaborated to provide governance, or to create an oversight regime, most prominently in Ohio and New York. These organizations were exceptions, not the rule.[50]

In the mid-1980s, the college programs began to face resistance after years of unabated growth. At first, murmurs about the abundance of low-quality academics or abuse of government funding raised concerns. Prison-based education was hardly unique in this. Nonetheless, reports of abuse of the Pell program grew in number over the period and exploded into genuine scandal in 1993.[51] However, concern over quality was not what would lead to the demise of many college-in-prison programs. In the end, the persuasion that these programs were morally wrong, and their students undeserving, carried the day.

'82 Limiting Pell in Prison

In 1982, Congressman William Whitehurst proposed legislation limiting the use of Pell Grants in prison to a cap of $6 million per year. This was the first of what became annual attempts by members of congress to limit or eliminate Pell funding within prisons.[52] At the same time, the cost of college began to rise while government tuition aid started a fast decline. By 1986, the College Board reported increases, over a five-year period, of 12 percent to 26 percent for annual tuition while federal financial aid dropped nearly 20 percent.[53]

Elected officials' skepticism about the Pell program and tough-on-crime measures began to merge.

The Drug Free Workplace Act of 1988, for instance, required "anyone who receives a Federal grant" to "pledge that he will not be involved in drug-related activities." Pell Grant recipients on campuses had to take an "anti-drug oath."[54] Massachusetts governor Bill Weld claimed that if the Pell program continued in prison, "people who cannot afford to go to college are going to start committing crimes so they can get sent to prison to get a free college education!"[55]

60 Minutes ran a feature in which Governor Weld told Morley Safer that Boston University should make its program available "to poor, law-abiding citizens who have committed no crime" and that incarcerated students could become reacquainted with "the joys of making small rocks from big rocks."[56] Back in Washington, North Carolina senator Jesse Helm convinced Congress to pass his amendment banning anyone serving a life sentence from receiving

Pell, although earlier legislation introduced in 1991 intended to eliminate Pell for all people in state and federal prison regardless of sentence.[57]

Toward the close of the year's congressional session, Texas senator Kay Bailey Hutchison introduced Amendment 1158 to eliminate Pell Grant eligibility for people in prison. It passed the Senate with little debate or resistance. By the spring of 1994, the lower house was debating the extensive legislation—a debate intended to demonstrate the Democratic Party's ability to address the crime issue.   *Myth:*

The most frequent and false claim in the increasingly contentious debate about Pell for prisoners is the assertion that a Pell Grant issued to an incarcerated person meant a Pell Grant was taken away from someone else. In November 1993, Senator Hutchison addressed her colleagues to garner support for her amendment:

> What has happened is that because prisoners have zero income, they have been able to step to the front of the line and push law-abiding citizens out of the way to get these grants for college educations . . . this amendment will . . . free-up the $200 million dollars that was going to prisoners to have their educations funded and it will now go to the children of these low income families for whom the Pell Grants were originally intended.[58]

Hutchison exaggerated the cost of Pell in prison by nearly 600 percent, inflating $35 million to $200 million. More important, cutting the program did not "free up" monies to help pay for college for students anywhere. The inaccuracy of the argument was lost in one-sided "debates." This occurred, for instance, on April 19, 1994, when NBC's *Dateline* aired a segment presenting the Pell issue as a competition between conventional and incarcerated undergraduates.

When asked whether he thought "more students could get a Pell Grant if you took them away from prisoners," Democrat representative Bart Gordon of Tennessee replied, "There's no question that they could."[59] The morning after the *Dateline* broadcast, Representative Gordon, along with two other lawmakers, proposed an amendment to make incarcerated people ineligible for Pell. In the House, one representative took a lonely position defending the programs. Albert Wynn of Maryland modestly suggested that the program be extended for two years while the federal government measured its success.[60] He was unsuccessful.

To some, the public's animosity for Pell came as a surprise, as Pell providers were entirely unprepared for the political backlash and, subsequently, the possible loss of federal funding. The Niagara Consortium was a unique exception and had been squirreling away savings for years. At first, the forward-looking financial approach reflected concern about the possibility of another prolonged shutdown at the prison and the need to pay core staff when financial aid might temporarily disappear. By the early 1990s, the consortium was putting away money because of a different fear: due to public hostility, federal grants and state scholarships (or both) could evaporate.

That August, New York's college providers met in the Hudson Valley for their annual retreat. The gathering was scheduled months in advance, before it was clear that this meeting might be the last. Over the summer, the state had been sending delegations to Washington to oppose Pell revocation. Every college working in the state system attended, along with some correctional personnel, roughly a hundred people in total.

In Washington, the provision to eliminate Pell had made its way into the final version of the bill, which had already passed the House. On August 25, 1994, while the conference of college providers was in session, word came from the Capitol that the crime bill had passed the Senate, 61–38. The corrections officials in attendance knew that the scope and purpose of their work was going to change immediately, perhaps forever. Representatives of colleges

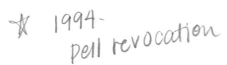
1994 - pell revocation

and universities understood their programs would not last long. Virtually all were shuttered within the academic year.[61]

ultimate demise

On September 13, leaders from Congress and law enforcement gathered in the Rose Garden for the signing ceremony of the Violent Crime Control and Law Enforcement Act of 1994. President Clinton assured leaders that "the laws of the land will be brought back into line with the values of our people and begin to restore the line between right and wrong."[62] In the twenty years since Folsom, Attica, and Robert Martinson, the problem of prisons had grown worse. But it no longer inspired intense intellectual debate; liberals looked the other way while conservatives championed expensive, big government solutions.

Paradoxically, during this period, prisons became a site for the establishment of hundreds of new little colleges. Whether one considers these schools to be "correctional" or "rehabilitative" is a matter of semantics: education anywhere is the cultivation and development of a person. Within American prisons, the establishment of "programming" that was not coercive represented a quiet watershed. Unfortunately, college practices did not resemble the "treatment" of the "medical" era that leaders at Folsom and Attica specified in their list of grievances.

Rather than being vehemently opposed by them, the colleges were championed by incarcerated people, families, and advocates. Eddie Ellis was in Attica during the uprising and Green Haven through the golden years of the college programs. He was perhaps the most influential formerly incarcerated advocate of his generation. In his words, "Prisoners, very early, recognized that they needed to be better educated—that the more education they had the better they would be able to deal with themselves, their problems, the problems of the prison, the problems of communities from which most of them came."[63]

In the end, all prisoners became ineligible for a Pell Grant. While in-prison college programs began to close across the country, the crime bill earmarked $7.5 billion toward the construction of new prisons.[64] Enough to maintain funding of the Pell program for incarcerated Americans for more than two hundred years.[65]   Edu ↓   Incarc. ↑

The Second Stage of Mass Incarceration (1995–2008)

The passage of the Clinton crime bill marked the end of the first period of mass incarceration. As Ian Buruma has written, this change in public policy represented a shift in governments' approach from being "tough on crime" to "tough on criminals."[66] It removed the pretense of "rehabilitation" or "correction" from American prisons at precisely the moment that they had become a more central part of our societal fabric than ever before.

The end of Pell decimated the college programs. Nationally, enrollment dropped 40 percent in the first year and more in the years immediately following. A national survey of correctional education directors found that nearly half reported the elimination of Pell "completely changed" their systems.[67]

In the 1990s, the cynicism of the 1970s turned into outright government hostility toward those ensnared in the criminal justice system and toward young people in general. A protégé of James Q. Wilson, John DiIulio Jr., popularized the phrase "superpredators" to describe a generation of children. In 1995, DiIulio published a highly influential essay in the *Weekly Standard* and was subsequently welcomed at the Clinton White House to expand on it.[68]

Meanwhile, prison officials were not uniformly supportive of the new, single direction in which policy was moving. A spokesman for the American Correctional Association declared that "the pendulum is swinging too far" toward harsh measures and that it "is not the politicians" who have to contend with the fallout from their bad decisions.[69] At the same time, state governments nationwide debated eliminating funding or outright banning college programs within prisons.

In New York, George Pataki was inaugurated governor and quickly moved to revoke state-level TAP grants. The change took effect immediately, compounding the loss of Pell and eviscerating programs statewide.[70] While Pataki repeated the false claim that college-in-prison made college access more difficult for conventional students, he also moved to cut financial aid for students on campuses across New York. The priorities were clear: punishment was a good investment, education less so. In 1998, the Center on Juvenile and Criminal Justice reported:

> Whereas New York spent more than twice as much on universities than on prisons in 1988, the state now spends $275 million more on prisons than on state and city colleges. The 1997–98 figures represent only the corrections operating cost, and do not include the $300 million approved for the construction of 3,100 new prison spaces approved in the state budget for that year.[71]

In other state capitals, results were less predictable.

In Texas, with its tradition and commitment to prison education dating back to the directorship of George Beto in the 1960s, legislators did not succeed in eliminating the $7 million line item for college in the state budget. Unlike New York, Texas found a compromise to keep programs running, though it featured a drastic 50 percent budget cut.[72] In North Carolina, a formalized relationship between the Department of Corrections and the Community College System insulated programs from revocation of Pell funds.

In Ohio, where prominent members of the state senate vehemently opposed the programs, the head of the state corrections department told his team to "get ready to fight."[73] Why? The corrections department had documentation to show its programs reduced recidivism. Ultimately, it succeeded, but only to a point. State funding continued, under two extraordinary conditions: the study of the liberal arts—history, mathematics, science, and literature—had to be excluded, and college study in Ohio prisons could never culminate in a college degree.[74]

Across the country, in a hostile environment, educators and correctional officials were forced to make difficult decisions and forge uncomfortable compromises to keep any degree of education going.

The elimination of Pell was the most dramatic and important moment in the history of the field. It exemplified the punitive national mood and had a drastically effective impact. However, the decisions of legislatures in these states proved that Pell was not in fact the alpha and omega of college-in-prison—state and local funding was essential to its existence.[75] They also demonstrated that college-in-prison does not operate on a conventional left/right political axis. Still, advocates in legislatures, corrections, and communities continued to lobby for government funds to pay for in-prison education, even through the worst times.

While allies in government preserved as much of the programs as they could for the post-Pell era, incarcerated people, religious communities, undergraduates and graduate students, and private citizens created new initiatives. Gradually, diversely funded efforts restored the presence of college on a small scale and functioned as a reminder to the country that better things were possible within its enormous systems of punishment. New York and California offered examples.

At Bedford Hills, the maximum-security prison for women in New York State, incarcerated women organized and successfully reestablished a college program there.[76] At Sing Sing, inmates and allies followed suit, establishing a program for men. This would come to be called Hudson Link. It established franchises with various academic partners across New York State.

At Bard College, fellow undergraduates and I petitioned the college to enroll incarcerated people and negotiated access into the state prison system, creating BPI.

In California, after exceptional college faculty and correctional staff attempted to keep something intact within San Quentin, Jody Lewen, a graduate student at the time, took charge of the floundering remains of the college program and built a lasting institution that became the Prison University Project (PUP) in 2003.[77] Thirteen year later, she accepted the National Humanities Medal from the president of the United States on behalf of PUP.

Hudson Link, PUP, and BPI were in-prison college programs that share a common theme: private funding was the immediate-term path to survival. Proximate to Manhattan and San Francisco, fundraising was more viable than elsewhere. Still, none of the programs had financial guarantees in the early years, so success was not inevitable.

If anything, none of them would have come to be if not for the enthusiastic commitment of the administrative leadership at prisons like Bedford Hills, Eastern, and San Quentin. In essence, these initiatives for the post-Pell era became analogs to the demonstration projects of the 1960s programs. They were established on the historical premise described at the start of this chapter, that Pell revocation was the field's Armageddon, and until it returned, small-scale initiatives with private funding were the only option.

Whatever the level of support at the local level, politically, BPI were very much in the wilderness. Until 2005, our understanding was that we were tolerated by the political leadership so long as we worked in secret. From California, when I asked Jody Lewen to describe the field at the time, she replied, "The thing I think of, just that it was incredibly small. It felt like that there were five of us, it was like us and Bob Hausrath: very isolated, very committed people digging their own trench." And, without any aspiration or hope of statewide or national initiatives, "it was very focused on quality."

Reflecting on his forty-one years directing the Niagara Consortium, Bob Hausrath describes "the last 20 years [as] the most difficult . . . I felt like I was alone in corrections and that I had a target on my back." We worked with the feeling that the field was infinitesimally small and that we were, essentially, alone.[78]

In 2005, a white paper issued by the Institute for Higher Education Policy suggested otherwise. It reported that during the 2003–2004 academic year more incarcerated people had enrolled in college than prior to the end of Pell. By 2004, more than 20 percent of North Carolina inmates were enrolled in some form of postsecondary education.[79] Federal Incarcerated Youth Offender (IYO) grants, along with state funding and private philanthropy, were being used to cobble together new educational programs and to maintain older ones, in reduced form.

Strikingly, courses available to people in prison were now overwhelmingly vocational, not academic. The authors note that "prison inmates are not earning college degrees, even at the associate's level, in any significant numbers."[80] As had happened in Ohio and other states, the breadth and choice of coursework, and the option to complete a college degree in prison, had been all but eliminated from American prisons. However, there were exceptions.

In Texas, Lee College soldiered on with some state and federal funding. Indiana, a state that hosted almost no programs during the Pell era, became a hotbed of college-in-prison. And, in western New York, the Niagara Consortium managed to keep on by spending down savings, and then enjoying brief success with philanthropy. Also, support from a liberal, city-based assemblyman and a conservative, rural state senator, helped the consortium keep its doors open.

Throughout this period, the politics of the issue gradually improved. The existence of outstanding demonstration projects, the dramatic national decline in crime, and the emergence of new groups of advocates for prison reform all contributed to the change. By 2008, a generation of formerly incarcerated advocates coalesced into the makings of a genuine social movement. Some of these people were young enough to have been precisely the individuals that John DiIulio was referring to when he popularized concern about "superpredators."

A growing body of research also contributed to the change in public opinion and contextualized the investment in punishment. For instance, one set of researchers found that, in some of New York's poorest neighborhoods, governments were spending more than $1 million per year to incarcerate residents of single urban blocks. The "million-dollar blocks" provoked debate about how taxpayer money could be put to better use.[81] For college-in-prison, the second stage of mass incarceration was defined by retreat and resilience. Programs vanished, reemerged (often in secret), and gradually reentered the national conversation on new terms.

During this period, populations inside American prisons soared from the now quaint numbers of 1972. In New York, the population of the state prison system peaked around 72,000, while Texas surpassed 150,000, and California approached 175,000.[82] Nationally, the number of incarcerated people inched toward 2.3 million. However unpopular the work was thought to be, or how easily legislators made a scandal out of it, college-in-prison was never more imperative than under the new regime and extraordinary scale of American incarceration.

The Third Stage of Mass Incarceration (2009–2018)

During this third stage of mass incarceration, there are modest decreases in prison populations, though rates remain extraordinarily high by any measure. After peaking in 1991, the national crime rate has steadily decreased, and the violent crime rate has fallen nearly 50 percent.[83] After years of perpetual growth, the number of incarcerated people in the United States did not increase in 2009. Nevertheless, as this is written, well over six million Americans are without voting rights. More African Americans are legally denied the franchise today than prior to the Voting Rights Act.[84]

The financial crisis of 2008 was followed by another series of cuts in government spending for college-in-prison.[85] The life cycle of some of the oldest programs has come to a close. Simultaneously, a groundswell of small, independent programs has created grassroots communities of providers who are aligned with a growing network of formerly incarcerated advocates and a bipartisan coalition committed to a transformation of American criminal justice.

In Texas, legislative budget cuts in 2011 coincided with the expiration of federal funding. IYO, which buoyed many holdouts from the Pell era, was eliminated in 2011. In a single year, Lee College lost 72 percent of its support for prison work. The combination devastated, but did not destroy, programs in Texas. Instead, there was a predictable casualty: programs in the liberal arts, the humanities, and coursework designed to be transferable to four-year degree programs. Professional coursework and certifications continue to this day.[86]

In Indiana, the simultaneous end of federal IYO and state funding led to a precipitous decline.[87] Indiana is peculiar in that there was not widespread college-in-prison during the Pell era, but in the late 1990s, with IYO and some state investment, it became one of the richest environments for higher education in prison nationwide. Through the first decade of the twenty-first century, Indiana issued an ever-increasing number of college degrees in prison until funding was pulled in 2011. At its peak, the programs in Indiana led to the conferral of more than eight hundred associate's degrees and nearly three hundred bachelor's degrees a year.[88]

Not long before, BPI had entered the business of recruiting other colleges and universities across the country to join this line of work. Following a *60 Minutes* feature in 2007, philanthropy approached us with questions about how to do more.[89] In contrast to the large bureaucracies of corrections, education within prisons is best offered at a human scale. Rather than franchise BPI in different states, the best thing to do with more resources was to share our expertise among dedicated colleges and universities.

By 2011, BPI had made significant investments in new programs at Wesleyan University in Connecticut, Grinnell College in Iowa, and Goucher College in Maryland. With this in mind, Daniel Karpowitz set out to see whether anything could be salvaged from the legacy in Indiana. After some work, he recruited the University of Notre Dame and Holy Cross College to collaborate in restoring college-in-prison in the state.

With the participation of the most influential university in the state, the Indiana Department of Corrections agreed to collaborate and provide public funding. The state's contribution was miniscule as compared to the recent past, but it was far more than trivial in the new climate. It led to the establishment of the Moreau College Initiative (MCI), which now confers bachelor's and associate's degrees every spring.

This moment of crisis in higher education generally provides colleges of every variety an opportunity to rethink "mission" and access. Louis Nanni, a vice president at Notre Dame, has said of college-in-prison:

> There are few engagements more meaningful to our faculty and speak more deeply to the soul of this University. The void of educational opportunities extended to those in prison is alarming. We need to expand our efforts and invite more partners to join [the effort] to make a lasting difference.[90]

Of the new era's demonstration projects, the University of Illinois Urbana–Champaign has made a particular contribution; the Freedom Education Project of Puget Sound in Washington State enrolls women in degree-granting programs; Goucher College's contribution in Maryland offers bachelor's degrees; and efforts in Maine, New Jersey, Arizona, and Massachusetts have taken a variety of forms depending on funding mechanisms.

Some elite universities—reluctant to dilute the market value of their transcripts—have established partnerships with local community colleges to offer associate degree programs. Others have been more forthcoming, including Washington University in St. Louis and New York University, which have established small but robust degree-granting programs.

Meanwhile, the sole holdout from the Pell era, the Niagara Consortium in New York, finally closed without fanfare in 2016. Its director of forty-one years, Bob Hausrath, who had quietly persevered through the toughest times, reflected on the meaning of his work in Attica and elsewhere: "I think the legacy is that we understand that it is ideas that change men's lives. Usually through the liberal arts . . . ideas change lives."[91]

Voters and decision makers are coming to agree with him. In 2013, national philanthropy, led by the Ford Foundation, partnered with Republican governors attempting to reestablish programs in New Jersey, North Carolina, and Michigan. In 2014, New York governor Andrew Cuomo announced his intention to restore state funding. While the proposal failed in the face of traditional, visceral opposition, for the first time public polling was conducted on the issue, and the results surprised many of us. The data showed that the public favored Cuomo's proposal by a double-digit margin.[92]

At the same time, two different political movements working behind the scenes at the grassroots level gained influence and prominence. First, conservative thought leaders whose *conservative movement for edu* [handwritten]

discomfort with mass incarceration was first articulated in private, and then in relative obscurity, burst into mainstream conservative debate. What had originated with Chuck Colson's brief incarceration and the long advocacy of his deputy Pat Nolan, now involved former speaker Newt Gingrich, the libertarian-leaning Koch brothers and their network, and an active Texas-based think tank, Right on Crime, which served as a nerve center for policy cultivation and implementation.

These efforts gradually turned criminal justice reform into perhaps the single issue in contemporary American political life with promise for bipartisan action and agreement. The leader of Right on Crime, Marc Levin, recently described conservative thinking on the specific question of college-in-prison, saying that there are two central policy concerns dominating conservative thought on higher education.

The first is that government tuition aid, like Pell Grants or the state-level equivalents, have the counterintuitive effect of driving up the cost of college. The second is that not enough resources are directed toward teaching as opposed to the production of obscure scholarship. The absence of either of these considerations in our context, he suggested, leaves room for support in the new climate of criminal justice reform.

During Barack Obama's second term, the administration turned to address criminal justice in an increasingly serious and focused way. The pivotal moment came in October 2015. The Federal Interagency Reentry Council, an innovation of Attorney General Eric Holder, and later continued by the Trump administration, invited a group of formerly incarcerated advocates to lead a discussion. This followed years of grassroots efforts to ensure that people with direct experience of incarceration have a place of influence and prominence in policy debate.

Eight leaders, women and men, arrived from Alabama, California, North Carolina, and New York. They addressed a room of roughly forty senior government officials. Each of them described the work they were doing in their home communities: housing advocacy, voting rights, ban-the-box, criminal justice reform in the South, education, and leadership development. At the conclusion of the presentation, the director of the Federal Bureau of Prisons rose and declared, "I will never do my job in the same way again."

Individuals directly impacted by mass incarceration had been released, paid their dues, created organizations, done advocacy, and, now, stunned a room of officials who were tasked with rethinking American justice policy. One fact hit home with the leadership of the council: nearly every one of the eight leaders present went to college in prison. They each spoke about the place of education in their lives and in solving the most vexing social problems we face as a country.[93]

CONCLUSION

The legend represented in *The Last Graduation* is, in part, a setup. It is the story of a losing, Manichean battle between large forces and small people: Bill Clinton, Congress, and white supremacy versus inmates, educators, and correctional officials. The truth is that more of the outcome is determined at the local level—within states and prisons themselves—than we generally knew.

Moreover, the battle is not all or nothing. The greatest and least recognized conflict in this story pertains to the question of what kind of knowledge people in prison should have. More precisely, what knowledge of history, mathematics, or science should members of America's

local level [handwritten]

most forgotten class be entitled to receive? This question of the character and quality can get lost in attempts to count the number of programs or participants.

For those seeking metrics or context, the literature that exists provides some certainty: college-in-prison does reduce recidivism; it increases the likelihood of meaningful employment for people returning home; even when people are unsuccessful in finding work, they are less likely to return to prison; and education also reduces violence in the prisons and increases public safety outside of them.[94]

In other words, it accomplishes all the things that the optimistic or genuine practitioners of the "treatment" regimes sought to do. But college is not done coercively *to* people in prison but practiced collaboratively *with* or *by* them. As Vivian Nixon, one of those eight leaders who visited the Reentry Council in 2015, recently told me:

> There is extraordinary support [for college] among incarcerated and formerly incarcerated people. Very little of it has to do with public safety or recidivism. It is about giving people the capacity and the tools to make independent and informed decisions about what they want to do with their lives and lifting the bar, raising the ceiling of what's possible to them. It's not about the "system"; it's about themselves and their life capacity.[95]

College-in-prison "works" for precisely the same reason that it is controversial: because it treats people in prison with dignity, because it provides something desirable, and because it looks forward to a promising future rather than backward to a contentious past.

NOTES

1. While I cannot recall how I initially encountered the film, one of the three women who produced *The Last Graduation* was instrumental in the very early years of BPI and helping me navigate the field very early on. Benay Rubenstein had been a program director for Marist College, then a director of the college program at Bedford Hills. All of us at BPI are exceptionally indebted to her.

2. Stuart Adams, "Higher Learning behind Bars," *Change* 5, no. 9 (1973): 45–50, https://doi.org/10.1080/00091383.1973.10568589.

3. Jed B. Tucker, "Malcolm X, the Prison Years: The Relentless Pursuit of Formal Education," *Journal of African American History* 102, no. 2 (March 1, 2017): 184–212, https://doi.org/10.5323/jafriamerhist.102.2.0184.

4. Malcolm X and Alex Haley, *The Autobiography of Malcolm X* (New York: Grove Press, 1965), 160–61.

5. Walter Silva, "A Brief History of Prison Higher Education in the United States," in *Higher Education in Prison: A Contradiction in Terms*, ed. Miriam Williford (Phoenix, AZ: Oryx Press, 1994), 25; Adams, "Higher Learning Behind Bars," 46.

6. Joshua Page, "Eliminating the Enemy: The Import of Denying Prisoners Access to Higher Education in Clinton's America," *Punishment & Society* 6, no. 4 (October 1, 2004): 357–78, https://doi.org/10.1177/1462474504046118; G. V. Richardson to Christopher Edley, Ford Foundation Records, Rockefeller Archive Center, July 29, 1965; and J. T. Willingham to Christopher Edley, Ford Foundation Records, Rockefeller Archive Center, July 29, 1965.

7. Paul M. Lucko, "Beto, George John," *Handbook of Texas Online*, June 12, 2010, www.tshaonline.org/handbook/online/articles/fbenm.

8. Donna Zuniga (Lee College), discussion with the author, February 28, 2018.

9. Bob Evans (Lee College), discussion with the author, March 5, 2018.

10. Donna Zuniga, *Special Regents Briefing* (Baytown, TX: Lee College, 2015).

11. Sanford S. Elberg to Christopher Edley, "Prison College Proposal," Ford Foundation Records, Rockefeller Archive Center, July 20, 1965.

12. Christopher Edley to Paul Ylvisaker, Ford Foundation Records, Rockefeller Archive Center, May 11, 1964.

13. Christopher Edley, *Docket Excerpts: University of California (Berkeley) Planning of a Prison College*, Ford Foundation Records, Rockefeller Archive Center, July 12, 1965.

14. Edley, *Docket Excerpts*.

15. G. V. Richardson to Christopher Edley; and J. T. Willingham to Christopher Edley, Ford Foundation Records, Rockefeller Archive Center, July 20, 1965.

16. Thom Gehring, "Post-Secondary Education for Inmates: An Historical Inquiry," *Journal of Correctional Education* 48, no. 2 (1997): 46–55.

17. John F. Littlefield and Bruce I. Wolford, "A Survey of Higher Education in U.S. Correctional Institutions," *Journal of Correctional Education* 33, no. 4 (December 1982): 14–18.

18. Ed Muller, in discussion with the author, March 2, 2018. For a contemporaneous description of South 40's work, see Linda Charlton, "'South 40' Tries to Aid Convicts," *New York Times*, April 23, 1972, www.nytimes.com/1972/04/23/archives/south-40-tries-to-aid-convicts-education-program-and-rehabilitation.html.

19. Charlton, "'South 40' Tries to Aid Convicts"; Lee College, "Second Chance," November 2012, www.lee.edu/publications/wp-content/blogs.dir/11/files/2012/02/secondChance-2012-11.pdf; and *The Last Graduation*, directed by Barbara Zahm (1997; New York: Deep Dish TV, 2005), DVD.

20. Edley, *Docket Excerpts*.

21. Milton Kotler, Prison College Conference, Ford Foundation Records, Rockefeller Archive Center, November 5, 1966.

22. Marjorie J. Seashore and Steven Haberfeld, *Prisoner Education: Project New Gate and Other College Programs* (New York: Praeger, 1977), 2–5.

23. Rex Herron and John Muir, *History and Development of Project NewGate—a Program of Post-Secondary Education for Incarcerated Offenders—Final Report*, National Institute of Justice, 1974, www.ncjrs.gov/pdffiles1/Digitization/74550NCJRS.pdf.

24. Stephen Duguid, *Can Prisons Work?* (Toronto, Canada: University of Toronto Press, 2000), 100.

25. Allen Tung, "Capping off an Illustrious Teaching Career," *Simon Fraser University News*, March 10, 2016, www.sfu.ca/sfunews/stories/2016/meet-the-2015-sfu-excellence-in-teaching-award-winners/stephen-duguid-humanities.html.

26. Duguid, *Can Prisons Work?*

27. Marjorie J. Seashore et al., *Additional Data Analysis and Evaluation of "Project NewGate" and Other Prison College Programs*, Marshall Kaplan, Gans and Kahn, March 1975, www.ncjrs.gov/pdffiles1/Digitization/45655NCJRS.pdf.

28. It's worth pointing out the near impossibility of measuring recidivism in relation to programs that had only been established three to five years prior. The number of students who could have completed college coursework, been released, and remained out of (or returned to) prison, all in a period of only three years, could not have been substantial enough to draw any reliable conclusions about the efficacy of programs in reducing recidivism.

29. Seashore et al., *Additional Data Analysis*.

30. Duguid, *Can Prisons Work?*, 105.

31. American Friends Service Committee, *Struggle for Justice: A Report on Crime and Punishment in America* (New York: Hill & Wang, 1971), 15.

32. Ben Bagdikian, "The Shame of Prisons," *Washington Post*, January 29, 1972–February 6, 1972.

33. L. D. Barkley, "The Attica Liberation Faction Manifesto of Demands," *Race & Class* 53, no. 2 (September 2011): 28–35, https://doi.org/10.1177/0306396811414338.

34. Jessica H. Neptune, "The Making of the Carceral State: Street Crime, the War on Drugs, and Punitive Politics in New York, 1951–1973" (PhD diss., University of Chicago, 2012), 396–409.

35. Adam Humphreys, "Robert Martinson and the Tragedy of the American Prison," *Ribbon Farm*, December 15, 2016, www.ribbonfarm.com/2016/12/15/robert-martinson-and-the-tragedy-of-the -american-prison/.

36. Robert Martinson, "The Paradox of Prison Reform—IV, Planning for Public Safety," *New Republic* 166, no. 18 (April 29, 1972): 23.

37. For example, he writes characteristically, "It requires not merely optimistic but heroic assumptions about the nature of man to lead one to suppose that a person, finally sentenced after (in most cases) many brushes with the law, and having devoted a good part of his youth and young adulthood to misbehavior of every sort, should, by either the solemnity of prison or the skillfulness of a counselor, come to see the error of his ways and to experience a transformation of his character." James Q. Wilson, *Thinking about Crime* (New York: Basic Books, 1975), 170.

38. Ellen Condliffe Lagemann, *Liberating Minds* (New York: New Press, 2016), 130.

39. Patrick A. Langan et al., *Historical Statistics on Prisoners in State and Federal Institutions, Yearend 1925–86*, US Department of Justice, May 1988, www.ncjrs.gov/pdffiles1/digitization/111098ncjrs.pdf.

40. Littlefield and Wolford, "A Survey of Higher Education," 14; and Silva, "A Brief History of Prison Higher Education in the United States," 28.

41. Robert Hausrath (director, Consortium of the Niagara Frontier), in discussion with the author, February 28, 2018.

42. Hausrath, discussion.

43. Skidmore College, *Commemorative Book of Reflections: University without Walls*, May 2011, www .skidmore.edu/odsp/documents/UWWReflections.pdf.

44. Skidmore College, *Commemorative Book of Reflections*.

45. Adams, "Higher Learning behind Bars," 49.

46. New York State Higher Education Services Corporation, "Appendix E: New York's Tuition Assistance Program—a History," n.d., www.hesc.ny.gov/partner-access/financial-aid-professionals/ programs-policies-and-procedures-guide-to-grants-and-scholarship-programs/appendix-e-new-york-s -tuition-assistance-program-a-history.html.

47. T. A. Ryan and Joseph Clifton Woodard Jr., *Correctional Education: A State of the Art Analysis*, University of South Carolina, July 7, 1987, https://eric.ed.gov/?id=ED325718.

48. Jerry McGlone (former superintendent of Ohio Prison Schools), in discussion with the author, December 6, 2017; and General Accounting Office, *Pell Grants for Prison Inmates*, August 1994, www .gao.gov/products/HEHS-94-224R.

49. Hausrath, discussion; and McGlone, discussion.

50. Hausrath, discussion; McGlone, discussion; and Linton, discussion.

51. "The Pell Grant Mess," *Washington Post*, October 30, 1993, www.washingtonpost.com/ archive/opinions/1993/10/30/the-pell-grant-mess/2b23c0dc-8c57-430b-a984-eae29eb6511a/?utm_ term=.43455cc45a9a.

52. Gehring, "Post-Secondary Education for Inmates," 48.

53. "How Student Financial Aid Has Become a Barrier to Education," *New York Times*, October 18, 1986, www.nytimes.com/1986/10/18/opinion/l-how-student-financial-aid-has-become-a-barrier-to -education-828986.html.

54. "Campuses Coping with a Drugs Oath," *New York Times*, October 8, 1989, www.nytimes.com/ 1989/10/08/us/campuses-coping-with-a-drugs-oath.html.

55. James Gilligan, *Violence in California Prisons: A Proposal for Research into Patterns and Cures*, Sacramento (Report No. 1026-S), 11.

56. Silva, "A Brief History of Prison Higher Education in the United States," 29.

57. Page, "Eliminating the Enemy."

58. "Senate Session," C-SPAN, US Senate, November 16, 1993.

59. *Dateline*, "Society's Debt?" NBC, April 19, 1994.

60. Page, "Eliminating the Enemy."

61. Hausrath, discussion.

62. *ABC News*, "President Bill Clinton Signs the Crime Bill of 1984" (Washington, DC, September 13, 1994), http://abcnews.go.com/Politics/video/archive-video-president-bill-clinton-signs-crime -bill-38309076.

63. *The Last Graduation*, directed by Zahm.

64. Marc Mauer, *Race to Incarcerate* (New York: New Press, 2006), 22.

65. General Accounting Office, "Pell Grants for Prison Inmates," August 1994, www.gao.gov/ assets/90/84012.pdf.

66. Ian Buruma, "Uncaptive Minds," *New York Times Magazine*, February 20, 2005, www.nytimes. com/2005/02/20/magazine/uncaptive-minds.html.

67. Richard Tewksbury, David John Erickson, and Jon Marc Taylor, "Opportunities Lost," *Journal of Offender Rehabilitation* 31, no. 1–2 (June 29, 2000): 43–56, https://doi.org/10.1300/J076v31n01_02.

68. John J. DiIulio Jr., "The Coming of the Super Predators," *Weekly Standard*, November 27, 1995, www.weeklystandard.com/the-coming-of-the-super-predators/article/8160.

69. Dirk Johnson, "Taking Away the Privileges of Prisoners," *New York Times*, September 8, 1996, www.nytimes.com/1996/09/08/us/taking-away-the-privileges-of-prisoners.html.

70. Emily M. Bernstein, "Pataki's Budget Would Pare College Grants," *New York Times*, December 19, 1995, www.nytimes.com/1995/12/19/nyregion/pataki-s-budget-would-pare-college-grants.html.

71. Center on Juvenile and Criminal Justice, *New York State of Mind? Higher Education vs. Prison Funding in the Empire State, 1988–1998*, December 1998, www.cjcj.org/uploads/cjcj/documents/new_york.pdf.

72. Zuniga, discussion; and Wendy Erisman and Jeanne Bayer Contardo, *Learning to Reduce Recidivism: A 50-State Analysis of Postsecondary Correctional Education Policy*, Institute for Higher Education Policy, November 2005, www.ihep.org/sites/default/files/uploads/docs/pubs/learningreducerecidivism.pdf.

73. McGlone, discussion.

74. McGlone, discussion; and Erisman and Contardo, *Learning to Reduce Recidivism*.

75. Erisman and Contardo, *Learning to Reduce Recidivism*.

76. Robert Worth, "Bringing College Back to Bedford Hills," *New York Times*, June 24, 2001, www .nytimes.com/2001/06/24/nyregion/bringing-college-back-to-bedford-hills.html; and Michelle Fine et al., *Changing Minds: The Impact of College in a Maximum-Security Prison* (New York: Ronald Ridgeway, September 2001).

77. Jody Lewen (executive director, Prison University Project), in discussion with the author, March 7, 2018.

78. Lewen, discussion; and Hausrath, discussion.

79. Erisman and Contardo, *Learning to Reduce Recidivism*.

80. Erisman and Contardo, *Learning to Reduce Recidivism*.

81. Center for Spatial Research, "Million Dollar Blocks," n.d., http://c4sr.columbia.edu/proj ects/million-dollar-blocks; Emily Badger, "How Mass Incarceration Creates 'Million Dollar Blocks' in Poor Neighborhoods," *Washington Post*, July 30, 2015, www.washingtonpost.com/news/wonk/ wp/2015/07/30/how-mass-incarceration-creates-million-dollar-blocks-in-poor-neighborhoods/?utm_ term=.78befa35b52f; and NPR, "Million-Dollar Blocks' Map Incarceration's Costs," October 2, 2012, www.npr.org/2012/10/02/162149431/million-dollar-blocks-map-incarcerations-costs.

82. California Department of Corrections, *Adult Population Projections 2008–2013*, Fall 2017, www .cdcr.ca.gov/Reports_Research/Offender_Information_Services_Branch/Projections/F07pub.pdf; and Texas Department of Criminal Justice, *Statistical Report: Fiscal Year 2008*, 2008, www.tdcj.state.tx.us/ documents/Statistical_Report_FY2008.pdf.

83. Matthew Friedman, Ames C. Grawert, and James Cullen, *Crime Trends 1990–2016*, Brennan Center for Justice, 2017, www.brennancenter.org/sites/default/files/publications/Crime%20Trends%20 1990-2016.pdf.

84. Christopher Uggen, Ryan Larson, and Sarah Shannon, *6 Million Lost Voters: State-Level Estimates of Felony Disenfranchisement, 2016*, Sentencing Project, 2016, http://www.sentencingproject.org/wp -content/uploads/2016/10/6-Million-Lost-Voters.pdf.

85. Michael Mitchell, Michael Leachman, and Kathleen Masterson, *A Lost Decade in Higher Education Funding: State Cuts Have Driven Up Tuition and Reduced Quality*, Center on Budget and Policy Priorities, August 23, 2017, https://www.cbpp.org/research/state-budget-and-tax/a-lost-decade-in -higher-education-funding.

86. Mark Levin, in discussion with the author, March 13, 2018; Evans, discussion; and Zuniga, discussion.

87. John Nally, in discussion with the author, March 18, 2018.

88. Patrick Callahan, e-mail message to the author, March 9, 2018.

89. *60 Minutes*, "Maximum Security Education," CBS, April 15, 2007.

90. Jay Caponigro, e-mail to the author, December 13, 2017.

91. Hausrath, discussion.

92. Robert Harding, "Siena Poll: Majority Supports Cuomo's Plan to Offer College Courses for Inmates in New York Prisons," *Citizen*, March 24, 2014, http://auburnpub.com/blogs/eye_on_ny/siena -poll-majority-supports-cuomo-s-plan-to-offer-college/article_02b576c6-b372-11e3-88ae-0019 bb2963f4.html.

93. Vivian Nixon, in discussion with the author, March 13, 2018.

94. Daniel Karpowitz and Max Kenner, *Education as Crime Prevention: The Case for Reinstating Pell Grant Eligibility for the Incarcerated*, Bard Prison Initiative, 2003, www.prisonpolicy.org/scans/ crime_report.pdf; Annette Johnson, *Testimony Concerning the Positive Correlation Between Inmate Education and Reduction of Recidivism* (December 4, 2000) (internal document); Fine et al., *Changing Minds*; Lois M. Davis et al., *Evaluating the Effectiveness of Correctional Education: A Meta-Analysis of Programs That Provide Education to Incarcerated Adults* (Santa Monica, CA: RAND Corporation, 2013), www.rand.org/content/dam/rand/pubs/research_reports/RR200/RR266/RAND_RR266.sum .pdf; Miles D. Harer, *Prison Education Program Participation and Recidivism: A Test of the Normalization Hypothesis*, Federal Bureau of Prisons, May 1995, www.bop.gov/resources/research_projects/ published_reports/recidivism/orepredprg.pdf.

95. Nixon, discussion.

2

The Economics of Prisoner Reentry

Daniel Shoag and Stan Veuger

There are perhaps as many as sixty-five million people in the United States who have been arrested and/or convicted of criminal offenses,[1] more than ten million of whom are of working age and have been convicted of a felony in the past.[2] To place these numbers in perspective, just over 160 million people were in the labor force in August 2017. Individuals who have passed through the criminal justice system represent an enormous economic resource. If these individuals are not in a position to develop their abilities and participate in the free exchange of goods and services, the loss to both them and society as a whole is significant, making prisoner reentry an area of interest to economists as well as criminologists, sociologists, and other social scientists more traditionally focused on the issue.

On a macro level, estimates suggest that the reduced likelihood of employment of former prisoners decreases the overall male employment-to-population ratio by as much as three percentage points.[3] This permanent reduction is similar in size to the Great Recession's drop in the male employment-to-population ratio. Such a reduction in labor force participation has important negative consequences for overall output and the sustainability of social insurance programs.

In addition to these society-wide implications, limits on the ability of individuals to accumulate human capital, find employment, start businesses, and otherwise realize their full economic potential have starkly negative private consequences. The private returns to education, for example, are large and have grown dramatically over the past few decades. Schooling increases earnings, opens up job opportunities that offer a greater sense of accomplishment, and is associated with better health outcomes.[4]

In this chapter, we analyze the challenges and opportunities associated with enabling prisoners to rejoin society productively and avoid incurring these losses to the extent possible. We begin, in the first section, with a discussion of the economic theory and empirics of crime and punishment focused on the perceived costs and benefits of crime to the individual. We explain that public policy can influence this trade-off through law enforcement and criminal justice; by helping (former) prisoners maintain and build human capital; and through active labor market policies.

While deterrence and incapacitation are obviously important tools in the policy maker's arsenal, the focus of this book is on reentering the world outside prison. Our focus is therefore not on the front-end questions of how and why we should or should not reduce the number of people entering prison. We focus instead on what we can expect public policy to accomplish if we take individuals' incarceration as given.[5]

The rest of the chapter therefore analyzes various aspects of human capital development and labor market policies. To offer a sense of what we can hope to accomplish, the second section gives an overview of what we will refer to as the reentry labor market. We first provide some key demographic characteristics of the prisoner population. We then look at the labor market outcomes of workers with similar characteristics in terms of age, gender, and education and compare these to the labor market outcomes of released prisoners.

We find that while the labor market outcomes of the set of comparable workers without a history of incarceration are not necessarily great, they are significantly better than those of the group of workers we are interested in here. This result serves as a benchmark of what type of outcomes we can hope to see under ideal reentry circumstances.

Some examples of pre-release policies that can help meet such levels of success are presented in the third section. To maintain some level of realism, we emphasize the difficulties inherent in attempts to meet even these downward adjusted expectations. There are, unfortunately, a number of reasons to expect that otherwise similar individuals without criminal records will be more successful, not merely just as successful.

Many professional and social skills decline if not used regularly, while spells of solitary confinement can do lasting damage, and social networks fade away without maintenance. To address these concerns and a number of others, we turn from active pre-reentry policies to damage control and explain the value of criminal justice reform and guarantees of basic prison health and safety standards.

This mixed message on the feasibility of maintaining or even fortifying prisoners' human capital prior to reentry leads us to shift focus toward the second substantive set of policies discussed in this chapter: active labor market policies targeted at workers with criminal records or the low-skilled labor market more generally, which is the subject of this chapter's fourth section. Perhaps the best known in the first category are so-called Ban the Box policies, which do away with questions about an applicant's criminal history in the early stages of the job recruiting processes.

While effective in accomplishing their declared goal, such policies effectively distribute opportunities away from workers without criminal records toward workers with them. Similar dynamics come into play when governments increase the minimum wage, a policy commonly applied in an attempt to help low-skilled workers. We explain the pros and cons of these types of regulatory redistribution before suggesting a number of alternatives that can help certain vulnerable groups of workers without inflicting as much harm on other such groups.

A fifth and final section that contains a brief discussion of our central findings and recommendations concludes the chapter. We emphasize here that the costs of current levels of crime and the rates of incarceration associated with them will likely remain high, but significant room for improvement remains.

THE ECONOMICS OF CRIME AND PUNISHMENT

The economic approach to crime and punishment is, in principle, straightforward. It develops from the idea that potential criminals decide whether to commit crimes by calculating the expected utility of doing so.[6] This idea, associated with Nobel laureate Gary Becker's work from the late 1960s, is an early example of economists applying their way of thinking to questions outside those of traditional political economy. No longer limiting themselves to attempting to explain why inflation is high, whether free trade is good, or how to organize production processes, economists started paying attention to questions that had traditionally been under the purview of sociologists, lawyers, educators, and even doctors.

The perspective economists bring to these questions is typically based on notions of rational expectations and decision making through utility maximization. A natural implication of thinking along these lines is that incentives matter: if expectations are set rationally and decisions are based on the careful weighing of pros and cons, policy makers can influence the behavior of individual actors by influencing their expectations or changing their payoffs.

Now, the simple idea of potential criminals maximizing their expected utility allows for plenty of nuance if properly understood, and it is the framework within which we will operate here. An expected utility calculation is not dissimilar from a cost-benefit analysis: it involves choosing the path of action that maximizes the happiness and flourishing perceived by the individual.

To set the stage for understanding the economics of crime and punishment, think of the decision to engage in a criminal act—theft, for example. On the one hand, there is a clear gain to the potential thief from committing theft: he acquires something he presumably desired. On the other hand, there is the opportunity cost of his time and effort, and, in addition, there is a chance he will get caught and be punished.

The more likely punishment is, the less attractive committing the crime becomes, and if the punishment is more severe, the crime becomes less attractive as well. Note that we are not making claims about how the perceived utility cost of committing a crime varies with the likelihood and severity of punishment yet—such claims are better derived from empirical analysis than from introspection and a priori modeling.

The potential thief's counterpart, the potential victim, sustains harm when the thief decides to engage in thievery. In general, the reason why certain activities have been criminalized is that they are perceived as costly to the rest of society. We are of course using a broad notion of cost here: in many cases, activities are criminalized because they are expected to cause utility losses in the future if normalized, because they could have caused utility losses, or simply because they trigger moral outrage among particular segments of society.

In designing public policy focused on managing crime and recidivism, the economic approach suggests weighing the damage done by criminals (after netting out their gains, if one is so inclined) against the social cost of law enforcement. Depending on specific modeling choices, precise optimality conditions can be derived, but even just organizing our thoughts in this manner immediately suggests areas of focus for public policy.

If we think about the individual potential criminal's optimization problem, at least four ways to reduce crime become apparent: limiting the gains from criminal activity, increasing the odds of getting caught, making punishments more severe (conditional on conviction), and adding to the opportunity costs of engaging in criminal activity. The most obvious way to add to the opportunity costs of engaging in criminal activity is to increase the potential criminal's legal-market wages.

A recent study by Crystal Yang, for example, finds that such increases have sizable effects on recidivism rates.[7] She reaches this conclusion through examination of administrative prison records collected by the Bureau of Justice of four million ex-offenders released from state prison to more than two thousand counties in forty-three states between 2000 and 2013. After controlling for certain factors such as policing and corrections behavior, Yang identifies that a wage increase in a local market with low-skill workers reduces the risk of recidivism by 2.3–4.0 percent.

Note that improved labor market opportunities affect the attractiveness of committing criminal acts in at least two ways: by creating a better alternative to criminal activity as a career, and by raising the opportunity cost of time spent incarcerated. Increasing a former prisoner's legal-market wages can be done pre-release or post-release by adding to his or her human or social capital, or through active labor market policies that redistribute opportunities toward him or her. We discuss examples of both types of policies later in the chapter.

Taking the broader view of social welfare optimization, some perhaps more surprising policy considerations force themselves to the foreground. Incarceration—widely used as punishment in contemporary criminal justice systems—does not look particularly attractive at first blush. Not only does it make it very difficult for the prisoner himself to be a productive part of society, but it is also likely to reduce his human capital and social network.

In addition, it imposes costs on others, as buildings, guards, and food need to be funded, typically from tax revenue. Fines and restitution, by contrast, are simple transfers that do not reduce the size of the pie or involve waste. But let us recognize for now that incarceration is common, and focus on the opportunities former prisoners face when they reenter society after serving time.

THE REENTRY LABOR MARKET

There is a great amount of variation in the labor market outcomes for various demographic groups in the United States, whether one looks at differences across groups distinguished by age, education, gender, and/or race. The patterns in the data are mostly well known. Older workers—those more than twenty-five or thirty years old—are more likely to work and to enjoy high incomes than younger ones, but that pattern is reversed as workers age into retirement.

Workers with higher levels of education, especially college-educated workers, are more likely to have jobs and high incomes than workers who dropped out of high school or finished high school but never went to college. Labor market outcomes for African Americans and Latinos are worse across the board than for whites and Asians. Finally, while female labor force participation has gotten close to male labor force participation, income levels still lag their male counterparts significantly.

It is reasonable to expect that the labor market opportunities open to reentering prisoners upon release are in large part driven by the same basic demographics of age, education, gender, and race. These basic features of the prison population can be summarized as follows (the overall picture is not particularly controversial).[8] The overwhelming majority of prisoners, at both state and federal levels, is male, at more than 90 percent. Prisoners are significantly younger than American adults overall: a third are under the age of thirty, and another third are between the ages of thirty and forty. And, important for our purposes, prisoners have a much weaker educational background than the overall population. Only around 10 percent have enjoyed any college education, and some 40 percent of prisoners are high school dropouts, compared to more than half and less than 20 percent of the general population, respectively.

We have pretty good information on the labor market outcomes of workers with various characteristics regardless of their criminal history; these workers can serve as an illustration of what successful prisoner reentry policy can hope to accomplish. These outcomes for the various relevant groups are roughly as follows.[9] In 2016, some 30 percent of male adults under the age of thirty without a high school diploma were employed. A little under 70 percent of those with a high school diploma were employed, and almost three out of four of those with at least some college education were employed. The numbers are drastically higher for those between the ages of thirty and forty, and still high but slightly lower for men over forty.

Hourly wages are higher for groups with older workers, and for more highly educated ones. Based on these numbers and the characteristics of the prisoner population, a rough back-of-the-envelope calculation suggests that about two-thirds of released prisoners should be employed. Some support for the idea that this calculation is reasonable comes from recent data on the employment status of incarcerated adults: around two-thirds of the individuals in that group were indeed employed full time or part time prior to their incarceration.[10]

Now, there is no particularly reliable large-scale data on the labor outcomes of reentering prisoners, but it is unlikely that more than half are employed a year after their release.[11] The number is probably closer to a third.[12] This number is comparable to that of high school dropouts under the age of thirty, even though almost 90 percent of the reentering prisoners have a demographic profile usually associated with much higher employment rates. There is a range of explanations for this gap.

First of all, there is stigma associated with a history of incarceration; one of the active labor market policies we will discuss below focuses on dealing with that. Second, certain professions are not accessible at all to felons because of regulatory decisions. And third, as we will see, there is reason to believe that periods of incarceration will, if anything, reduce prisoners' human capital. Not all of these factors can be overcome, but the gap in outcomes between the two groups discussed here shows that there is significant room for improvement if we can get reentering prisoners to perform as well as workers who are at least superficially similar.

PREPARING FOR REENTRY

Teach prisoners skills that will help them when they are released from state custody, one may say. Develop techniques that make them focus their attention on productive, socially acceptable behavior, not criminality, one could recommend. Those are reasonable ideas: if we can change a prisoner's options upon release by improving his labor market opportunities, recidivism will become less likely, and both the prisoner and society will benefit. We know from studies of the impact of variation in labor market tightness that this mechanism is effective: raising market wages reduces recidivism.[13]

In addition, we know that increasing an individual's "human capital," another economic concept popularized by Gary Becker, raises his expected market wages. When a worker's stock of marketable skills grows, demand for his labor services increases. Much like with factories, machines, or software, we can make investments that grow this stock—and we know what such investments look like. And yet employment rates remain low while recidivism rates remain high.

Part of the explanation for this paradox is that politicians often see spending taxpayer funds on education or cognitive behavioral therapy for prisoners as risky. After all, most of the private returns to such human capital investments will accrue to people that society decided to punish. As discussed in the introduction to this volume, this has led to policies limiting educational opportunities in prison such as the Violent Crime Control and Law Enforcement Act of 1994.

President Clinton put it as follows when he made inmates ineligible for Pell Grants through that legislation: "This bill puts government on the side of those who abide by the law, not those who break it. On the side of the victims, not their attackers."[14] As a consequence, released prisoners face the labor market with a level of human capital that is at best as high as it was when the individual entered prison.

This political reality has combined with the fact that we have a limited understanding of interventions that work to produce a situation in which most prisons are not environments conducive to the acquisition of new skills. The following chapters of this book explore those programs that do exist, evaluate their effectiveness, and identify obstacles to the implementation of promising programming.

Prison spells also reduce workers' existing human capital in a number of ways. Time spent unemployed reduces workers' skills and earnings potential outside prison, and there is no reason to believe that hysteresis does not materialize inside prison as well. Prisoners' social capital presumably declines even faster than that of the long-term unemployed, especially for the sizable numbers of prisoners incarcerated far from their home environment. These two types of human capital destruction are probably hard to avoid.

But there is a third category of drivers of the decline in prisoners' human capital during their incarceration that may offer more room for improvement. A history of physical or sexual abuse is somewhat common among prisoners, while around half of the prison population struggles with mental health problems.[15] Overcrowding, violence, solitary confinement, drug abuse, and abusive behavior by state personnel frequently exacerbate these problems.[16]

These types of harsh prison conditions do not appear to reduce recidivism,[17] and it may be more politically palatable to establish lower bounds on incarceration conditions, thereby reducing the escalation of mental and physical health issues that occur while prisoners are effectively wards of the state.

The most obvious way to keep these reductions in workers' existing human capital from happening is, of course, to reduce the time they spend locked up, outside the regular labor force, subject to social isolation, and victims to harsh living conditions. Efforts to reform that aspect of the criminal justice system have made some headway in recent years, but they have focused almost exclusively on low-level, nonviolent offenders. The sheer number of violent offenders limits the effectiveness and scope of this approach.

For example, there are almost two hundred thousand people in prison today just for murder and manslaughter, a number that is similar to the total state prison population just forty years ago.[18] Unless a sudden consensus emerges that long prison sentences are unconstitutional due to their rarity around the time of the Founding, other reentry policies will need to accompany this line of attack.

ACTIVE LABOR MARKET POLICIES

The final layer of prisoner reentry policies is that of labor market policies that attempt to help former prisoners once they have returned to civilian society. Programs that focus on improving employer–former prisoner matches aside, these measures are, by necessity, measures that to a large extent redistribute—as opposed to generate—employment, output, and surplus. The most politically palatable among these measures do so not directly through taxation and spending but through regulatory redistribution. Redistribution generates winners as well as losers, and we will highlight both here in a brief analysis of two leading examples: so-called Ban the Box (BTB) measures and minimum wage legislation.

The box in "Ban the Box" refers to the box job applicants are often asked to check if they have ever been convicted of or arrested for a crime. Advocates have long worried that this line of questioning makes it unreasonably difficult for, among others, former prisoners to find work, as the stigma associated with their criminal background can lead employers to believe that they cannot possibly be productive workers. BTB measures disallow questions about applicants' criminal record in (the early stages of) recruiting processes.

Over the past decade, a wide range of local and state governments, private-sector firms, and even the federal government (for its contractors) have adopted such measures. These measures strive to reallocate labor market opportunities away from individuals without criminal records toward individuals with criminal records and, thus, are a good example of an active labor market policy intended to facilitate successful prisoner reentry. In recent work, we assess how successful BTB measures have been at accomplishing this goal and find that they are an effective way to further the interests of former prisoners.[19]

Using a number of statistical techniques, we evaluate the impact of changes in employee screening procedures that pushed questions about criminal records later on in hiring processes. Using data from both private-sector employers (such as Walmart, the largest private employer in America, which adopted BTB in 2010) and public-sector employers, we find that these policies increase employment of residents of high-crime neighborhoods by as much as 4 percent. This added employment is concentrated in the public sector, which is more commonly subject to BTB measures and where compliance is likely to be greater, and in lower-wage jobs.

This success story comes with an important caveat. It is not obvious that BTB measures place the economy on a different growth path, and much of the seemingly added employment is likely to be reallocated employment. For example, a recent study by Jennifer Doleac and Benjamin Hansen focuses on the heterogeneous impact of BTB measures across demographic groups. It finds that young, low-skilled black and Hispanic men, who are less likely to have criminal records, see their employment decline after BTB measures are introduced. As one would expect, they also find that older black men, who are more likely to have criminal records, see their employment increase. On aggregate, the research conducted by Doleac and Hansen implies that black men's employment opportunities increase somewhat after the introduction of BTB rules.[20]

Amanda Agan and Sonja Starr analyze this phenomenon at the firm level, using fictitious applications by young male applicants with distinctly black and white names; they confirm that young black applicants without criminal records are less likely to be called back under BTB.[21] These findings have made some worry that eliminating observable characteristics such as criminal records leads to increases in so-called statistical discrimination by employers. The logic is as follows: If employers do not like the idea of hiring workers who are likely to commit crimes, they are less likely to hire applicants with criminal records. And if they cannot tell which applicants have criminal records, they will replace the no-longer-available criminal record with applicant characteristics that signal a high likelihood of having a criminal record. But that is not what the combination of negative consequences for young black applicants and positive consequences for older black applicants suggests. After all, older applicants are more, not less, likely to have criminal records. A much more likely explanation, then, is simply that BTB measures lead to redistribution of labor market opportunities from younger black men to older black men—that is, from the group less likely to have a criminal record to the group more likely to have one.

Now, perhaps what drives the concerns is a fear that employers discriminate against young black applicants because they believe they are more likely to end up with a criminal record in the future. While this fear is legitimate, there is no reason to believe that employers would not also engage in this type of racial profiling in a world without BTB measures. It is not obvious that policy makers should punish applicants with criminal records instead of firms that engage in these discriminatory practices.

Instead, it would be of interest to explore whether women, who are also less likely to have criminal records, see their labor market outcomes deteriorate. That should allow us to distinguish between the simple mechanics of redistribution, on the one hand, and racial discrimination, on the other. Regardless of the specifics of which demographic groups lose out, it is important that policy makers consider those groups as well as the former prisoners who stand to gain from BTB rules.

A different labor market policy intended to help vulnerable labor market participants is the wage floor, or minimum wage. There has been a federal minimum wage since the 1930s, and it has been raised on many occasions since. In addition, many states and localities have their own (higher) minimum wage. The declared goal of the minimum wage as currently constituted is to raise the wages of (low-skilled) workers beyond what it would be if left to the outcome of bargaining processes in the free market. As we have seen, many former prisoners are low skilled, and the minimum wage should thus help them: both by rewarding their labor and by drawing them into the labor market through supply-side or even demand-side effects.

There is, unfortunately, a serious downside risk to this policy. Unless the labor market is dominated by employers with monopsony power, even relatively modest minimum wages will generate unemployment effects. While this is a controversial debate among economists and policy makers, there is significant evidence that this downside risk has materialized on certain occasions in the recent past.

A study by Jeffrey Clemens and Michael Wither shows how risky these measures can be.[22] The authors study the increase in the federal minimum wage that took effect in July 2009, in the midst of the unemployment crisis triggered by the financial crisis. This increase, to $7.25 an hour, raised the federal minimum wage in some states but not in those that already had a state minimum wage of at least that amount.

Clemens and Wither find that this increase reduced the employment of low-skilled workers, and increased the likelihood of work without pay among those who continued to be employed. When they extrapolate their findings to the full set of late 2000s federal minimum wage increases (the federal minimum wage went up by some 30 percent over this period), they estimate that these increases reduced the national employment-to-population ratio by 0.7 percentage points, or well over one million workers. Hardest hit are young, low-skilled workers—precisely the most common profile of the prisoner population. Some workers—those who see their wages increase and their jobs survive—did, of course, benefit from these measures, but policy makers should again be cognizant of the distributional choices they make.

CONCLUSION

The hundreds of thousands of individuals who reenter society, and with that the economy, in any given year are a significant potential resource. A non-negligible part of the measured divergence between labor force participation rates in the United States and most other developed economies can be explained by the numbers of potential workers who spend time incarcerated. We have attempted here to give a sense of the magnitude of this phenomenon—of potentially productive areas of focus for advocates, policy makers, and researchers—and of the enormous challenges ahead.

The broader labor market context constrains what policy makers can hope to accomplish on the prisoner reentry front given the human capital levels of the population in question. In this chapter, we have attempted to set expectations for what success would look like by describing the demographics of the reentering population and the typical labor market outcomes associated with workers of similar characteristics regardless of criminal history.

Later chapters will give a broad overview of practices and programs that have been successful in nurturing the human capital of reentering former prisoners. Let us here conclude with a few comments that touch upon basic economic principles.

Policy makers do not have perfect foresight. They need to be aware of the (perhaps unintended) distributional consequences of programs like Ban the Box and policy decisions like minimum wage increases—or at least of the possibility of such unintended consequences. It may be best for society as a whole or for whatever your preferred interest groups are to redistribute through the regulatory system, but it is important to distinguish between policies that mostly do that and policies that genuinely create societal surpluses.

Incentives matter. It may be attractive, for short-term political gain, to punish former offenders in a wide range of ways, but doing so will often reduce their market wages and make both unemployment and recidivism more attractive. For example, amendments to the Higher Education Act that were enacted in 2001 made drug offenders (temporarily) ineligible for federal school aid after their conviction.

Empirical estimates using data from the National Longitudinal Survey of Youth suggest that this legislative change did nothing to reduce crime, while reducing college enrollment among the affected group.[23] Similar problems arise with the wide range of occupational licenses that limit the access workers with a criminal record have to certain professions.[24]

Finally, there are trade-offs everywhere. Parts of the price we pay for the law enforcement and incarceration decisions we make are the destruction of human capital that time spent in prison almost inevitably brings, as well as the differences between the labor market outcomes of reentering prisoners and workers who never spent time incarcerated. It is hard to imagine public policies that undo these negative consequences entirely.

NOTES

1. Michelle Natividad Rodriguez and Maurice Emsellem, *65 Million "Need Not Apply"—the Case for Reforming Criminal Background Checks for Employment*, National Employment Law Project, March 2011, https://www.nelp.org/wp-content/uploads/2015/03/65_Million_Need_Not_Apply.pdf.

2. John Schmitt and Kris Warner, *Ex-Offenders and the Labor Market*, Center for Economic and Policy Research, November 2010, http://cepr.net/documents/publications/ex-offenders-2010-11.pdf.

3. Schmitt and Warner, *Ex-Offenders and the Labor Market*.

4. Philip Oreopoulos and Kjell G. Salvanes, "Priceless: The Nonpecuniary Benefits of Schooling," *Journal of Economic Perspectives* 25, no. 1 (2011): 159–84; and James J. Heckman, John Eric Humphries, and Gregory Veramendi, "Returns to Education: The Causal Effects of Education on Earnings, Health, and Smoking" (working paper 22291, National Bureau of Economic Research, Cambridge, Massachusetts, May 2016).

5. We use the term *prisoner* somewhat loosely throughout this chapter, typically referring to people who spend time in prison as well as in jail. It will become apparent from the context that some of the questions we discuss are relevant to anyone who is merely arrested, while others apply mostly to people who spend significant amounts of time incarcerated.

6. Gary Becker, "Crime and Punishment: An Economic Approach," *Journal of Political Economy* 76, no. 2 (1968): 169–217.

7. Crystal S. Yang, "Local Labor Markets and Criminal Recidivism," *Journal of Public Economics* 147, no. C (2017): 16–29.

8. Schmitt and Warner, *Ex-Offenders and the Labor Market*.

9. Authors' calculations based on the Merged Outgoing Rotation Groups extracts from the Current Population Survey provided by the National Bureau of Economic Research.

10. Bobby D. Rampey et al., *Highlights from the U.S. PIAAC Survey of Incarcerated Adults: Their Skills, Work Experience, Education, and Training*, National Center for Education Statistics, November 2016, https://nces.ed.gov/pubs2016/2016040.pdf.

11. See, for example, Christy Visher and Shannon M. E. Courtney, "One Year Out: Experiences of Prisoners Returning to Cleveland," Urban Institute, April 18, 2007, https://www.urban.org/research/publication/one-year-out-experiences-prisoners-returning-cleveland.

12. Devah Pager, Bruce Western, and Naomi Sugie, "Sequencing Disadvantage: Barriers to Employment Facing Young Black and White Men with Criminal Records," *Annals of the American Academy of Political and Social Sciences* 623 (2009): 195–213.

13. Yang, "Local Labor Markets and Criminal Recidivism."

14. Lydia Emmanouilidou, "Earning a 2-Year Degree While Serving a 6-Year Sentence," NPR, July 7, 2017, https://www.npr.org/2017/07/07/526783435/earning-a-two-degree-while-serving-a-six-year-sentence.

15. Doris J. James and Lauren E. Glaze, *Mental Health Problems of Prison and Jail Inmates*, Bureau of Justice Statistics Special Report, December 2006, https://www.bjs.gov/content/pub/pdf/mhppji.pdf.

16. Craig Haney, "Mental Health Issues in Long-Term Solitary and 'Supermax' Confinement," *Crime and Delinquency* 49, no. 1 (2003): 124–56; Allen J. Beck et al., *Sexual Victimization in Prisons and Jails Reported by Inmates, 2011–12*, Bureau of Justice Statistics, May 2013, https://www.bjs.gov/content/pub/pdf/svpjri1112.pdf; and Richard T. Boylan and Naci Mocan, "Intended and Unintended Consequences of Prison Reform," *Journal of Law, Economics, and Organization* 30, no. 3 (2014): 558–86.

17. M. Keith Chen and Jesse M. Shapiro, "Do Harsher Prison Conditions Reduce Recidivism? A Discontinuity-Based Approach," *American Law and Economics Review* 9, no. 1 (2007): 1–29.

18. John F. Pfaff, *Locked In: The True Causes of Mass Incarceration and How to Achieve Real Reform* (New York: Basic Books, 2017).

19. Daniel Shoag and Stan Veuger, "'Ban the Box' Measures Help High-Crime Neighborhoods" (AEI Economics Working Paper 2016-08, HKS Faculty Research Working Paper Series RWP16-015, September 2017).

20. Jennifer L. Doleac and Benjamin Hansen, "Does 'Ban the Box' Help or Hurt Low-Skilled Workers? Statistical Discrimination and Employment Outcomes When Criminal Histories Are Hidden" (working paper 22469, National Bureau of Economic Research, Cambridge, Massachusetts, July 2016).

21. Amanda Y. Agan and Sonja Starr, "Ban the Box, Criminal Records, and Racial Discrimination: A Field Experiment," *Quarterly Journal of Economics* 13, no. 1 (2018): 191–235.

22. Jeffrey Clemens and Michael Wither, "The Minimum Wage and the Great Recession: Evidence of Effects on the Employment and Income Trajectories of Low-Skilled Workers" (working paper 20724, National Bureau of Economic Research, Cambridge, Massachusetts, December 2014).

23. Michael F. Lovenheim and Emily G. Owens, "Does Federal Financial Aid Affect College Enrollment? Evidence from Drug Offenders and the Higher Education Act of 1998," *Journal of Urban Economics* 81 (2014): 1–13.

24. Michelle Natividad Rodríguez and Beth Avery, *Unlicensed & Untapped: Removing Barriers to State Occupational Licenses for People with Records*, National Employment Law Project, April 2016, https://nelp.org/wp-content/uploads/Unlicensed-Untapped-Removing-Barriers-State-Occupational-Licenses.pdf.

3

The Second Chance Pell Pilot Program

From Policy to Practice

Andrea Cantora

On August 3, 2015, the US Department of Education (ED) announced an Experimental Sites Initiative (ESI) that would allow higher education institutions to provide postsecondary education and vocational training to people incarcerated in state and federal prisons. The Second Chance Pell Pilot Program was established to allow Title-IV-eligible public and private colleges and universities to administer Pell Grants to eligible state and federal prisoners so they can earn a certificate, an associate's degree, or a bachelor's degree.

The announcement of this initiative was quite historic considering the twenty-one-year ban preventing incarcerated men and women from accessing federal financial aid. Prior to 1994, college-in-prison was common across the country. However, during the "tough on crime" era, Congress passed the Violent Crime Control and Law Enforcement Act of 1994, which included a provision to exclude incarcerated students from receiving federal financial aid. This federal law greatly reduced incarcerated students' access to college.

This new Second Chance Pell Program is an opportunity for thousands of incarcerated students to participate in postsecondary education programs. Based on the moral premise of "education for all," and the political notion of being "smart on crime," this experiment has the potential to show real impact on how transforming lives through education can directly impact the prison reform movement. Reducing the number of people who enter, and return to, our criminal justice system should be the objective of every state and the federal government.

Using education as a way to accomplish this goal is a point of agreement for many people on both sides of the political aisle. It is the hope of many that, if successful, the Second Chance Pell Program may lead to the return of Pell Grants to *all* incarcerated people across the nation.

This chapter will include a description of ED's Second Chance Pell Experimental Sites Initiative, information on the participating sites, challenges of administering Pell to incarcerated students, workforce and reentry support, preliminary program participation outcomes, discussion of evaluation needs, and, finally, the political climate on the topic of "Pell for Prisoners."

SECOND CHANCE PELL APPLICATION PROCESS

In August 2015, ED invited colleges and universities to apply for consideration to participate in the ESI. Colleges with existing or new partnerships with federal or state correctional institutions were eligible for consideration. A letter of application from the higher education institution was required by October 2, 2015, to include information on the correctional institution partnership, the type of academic program planned, and brief details for implementation.

On January 21, 2016, a select number of institutions were invited to submit detailed plans by responding to a series of questions, including type of program proposed; plans for academic support services; number of students projected; cost of tuition; and implementation plans. Applicants had to explain to ED how they would assist students with completing the program after release from prison, as well as how they would provide reentry support to their students who reenter the community.

Given the fact that many justice-involved people are barred from entering certain occupations due to state laws and licensing regulations that exclude them from certain jobs, careful consideration was given to colleges and universities that ensured they would offer programs that would prepare students for jobs they can obtain. There are more than twenty-seven thousand licensing restrictions for people with criminal records, and close to thirteen thousand of these are considered "blanket bans," which disqualify people for *any* type of felony.[1] These vary greatly by state, and although there are exceptions to the rule, people with criminal records are often barred from work in health care, education, and law.

Sites also had to be free from any Title IV Higher Education Act (HEA) violations to be eligible to participate. Letters of support from the correctional institution were also part of the process. ED also had several participation requirements for student selection, such as (1) *exclusion* of sex offenders serving an involuntary civil commitment after incarceration; and (2) *prioritization* of students who are likely to be released within five years of their program's start date. Assessing potential release is used by either release date or parole eligibility date (or both). People serving life without parole sentences are excluded.

The final proposal for each site was due to ED on March 20, and sites were selected at the end of June 2016. To kick off the initiative, the *Washington Post* was one of the first news outlets to announce on June 24, 2016, "12,000 inmates to receive Pell grants to take college classes."[2] More than two hundred universities and colleges applied to participate in the experiment, with only sixty-nine selected (sixty-five are currently active).

Fifty-nine percent of the selected sites spent the fall 2016 semester gathering Free Application for Federal Student Aid (FAFSA) documents from students and began awarding Pell Grants in the spring 2017 semester. Forty-one percent were able to start this process earlier and began Pell Grant implementation in fall 2016.[3] The University of Baltimore (UB) in partnership with Jessup Correctional Institution (JCI) is honored to be one of the sites selected by ED to participate in the initiative.

UB faculty have been teaching noncollege courses at JCI since 2014 through the prison's noncredit college program. It was from the positive experience teaching incarcerated students, and more than fifteen years working with reentry populations, that I became interested and motivated to develop a program where students would have an opportunity to earn college credits. ED's initiative opened a door to allow UB to develop a comprehensive program.

UB was instantly excited about the idea and provided internal support to help operationalize their vision. They developed a model targeting a cohort of freshmen who would ideally begin their course work at the prison and complete it at UB. Following UB's standard admissions requirements, they recruited from a pool of 150 incarcerated men who were actively involved in the noncredit college program. They selected twenty-eight students based on UB's admissions criteria, freshman status, parole/release dates, and Pell Grant eligibility, which will be discussed in another section.

UB's program started in August 2016, only two months after being selected. The first two years of the program are designed to offer general education courses that mirror the same required courses offered on UB's campus. Through the university's foundation, UB was able to secure funds to hire a reentry coordinator to assist students approaching release. As of June 2018, UB expanded their program to a total of forty-five students.

The prison has been supportive in their efforts and has dedicated a tier within a housing unit for college students. The UB students share this tier with Anne Arundel Community College (also an experimental site) students. This new college tier has naturally transformed into a "learning community" setting where students are fully occupied with studying and completing class assignments.

OVERVIEW OF THE SITES

The sixty-five schools participating are dispersed across twenty-six states and offer educational programs in more than one hundred prisons. The majority of the schools selected had existing prison college programs already in operation; however, twenty-five (40 percent) new programs were developed through the experiment. Most of the colleges participating are community colleges, with twenty-seven being four-year institutions. In terms of credentials, seventy-three offer an associate's degree, twenty-four offer a bachelor's degree, forty-four offer technical certificates, and thirty-one offer nontechnical certificates.[4]

Several well-known universities are participating in the experiment. This includes California State University, Los Angeles; the City University of New York; Rutgers University in New Jersey; Arkansas State; and Bard College in New York.

One of the largest programs in operation is the Prison Education Initiative at Jackson College in Michigan. Jackson College, a public four-year school, operates in sixteen correctional facilities in the state with an annual enrollment of more than thirteen hundred students currently earning either a certificate or an associate's degree.[5] Jackson College's prison program has been operating since 1967 but ended in the mid-1990s, like other programs, due to cuts in federal funding brought about by the 1994 crime bill.

The Jackson College programs reopened their doors in 2012 through a self-pay method, and in 2013 they received external funding when they became part of the Vera Institute of Justice's Pathways from Prison to Postsecondary Education Project.[6] Today, since Jackson College is an experimental site, incarcerated students in Jackson College programs are able to receive Pell Grant funds to go toward their tuition. This has allowed Jackson College to expand its program even further. Although Jackson College has no current evaluation in place to assess the success of all of their programs, participants at two facilities will be tracked for two years post-release.[7]

Texas has the highest number of colleges and universities of all the states participating in the Pell Pilot. The largest program in the state is Lee College, a public two-year university.[8] Lee College has provided educational programming inside prisons since 1966 through state and private funding sources. It currently has programs operating at six facilities with more than twelve hundred students working toward an associate of applied science degree or a certificate program. Lee College's programs prepare students to work in horticulture, auto mechanics, truck driving, welding, and business management. In 2015, Lee College graduated eighty-seven students with an associate's degree and conferred more than four hundred certificates.[9]

Ashland University, a private nonprofit, four-year college in Ohio, is the third-largest program in the Pell Pilot. With more than one thousand students, Ashland offers certificates and degree programs inside eighteen correctional facilities, including the Louisiana State Penitentiary.[10] Ashland's program operates on state funds and will now use Pell Grant funds to expand. The program offers a range of certificate and degree options in business management, office management, and a bachelor's in multidisciplinary studies. Ashland is one of the few programs that offers both in-person instruction and online courses.[11]

Having access to Pell Grants will allow existing programs to include more students. For some, it will mean expanding into additional correctional institutions. And others—including programs at UB, Indiana University of Pennsylvania, Northeastern Technical College in South Carolina, and Florida Gateway College—were created thanks to the Second Chance Pell Pilot Program.

PELL GRANT FUNDING

A common misconception is the belief that Pell Grants cover the full cost of tuition. In fact, Pell Grants typically do not cover the full amount of a yearly tuition for the eight million non-incarcerated students using them to pay for a college education. In academic year 2017–2018, the maximum annual award a student could receive was $5,920. The amount of Pell awarded is based on a student's expected family contribution, the student's employment status, and the cost of attendance at the school.[12] For most incarcerated students, receiving the maximum award is highly likely due to the incredibly low wages prison jobs pay.

Incarcerated students who work a prison job usually make less than several thousand dollars and typically do not pay taxes. Prison officials consider low pay as part of their debt to society. In Maryland, the average salary of an incarcerated person working in the prison industry ("the shops") is less than $2,000 a year. Jobs separate from prison industries (e.g., maintenance and kitchen work) usually yield a salary of a few hundred dollars. Incarcerated students who report on the FAFSA that they are married, or are considered "dependent" on parents, may not receive the maximum award.

Having Pell Grant funds contribute to student tuition allows for existing programs to expand and new programs to start up. Regardless of the Pell Grant contribution, many programs continue to use other sources of funds to fully support the operation of their program, since Pell Grants usually only cover a portion of it. Many prison college programs existed before the Pell Pilot with private and foundation dollars. Goucher College in Maryland is an example.

Some programs also operated on student self-pay methods, such as Ann Arundel Community College in Maryland. In self-pay models, students are required to pay a portion, or all, of the tuition costs of the program. State funds have also been made available to some programs. For example, students in Lee College's program in Texas receive loans from the state that they must pay back as part of their parole requirement.[13]

CHALLENGES ADMINISTERING PELL
TO INCARCERATED STUDENTS

The challenge for all programs participating in the pilot was completing the federal financial aid process. For instance, the FAFSA application was not designed for incarcerated students.

As part of this experiment, no changes to the FAFSA were made, and no exceptions were granted other than the waiver to allow otherwise eligible state and federal prisoners to apply and receive aid.

Some major roadblocks for programs collecting and processing FAFSAs were students who needed to provide further documentation of eligibility or students who were not eligible at all. This included students who failed to register for selective service, had a prior student loan in default, had social security number mismatches, were in need of parental income verification, or were married students in need of spousal income information. Some of these issues are highlighted below.

Use of the Internet

Figuring out how incarcerated students would complete the FAFSA was one of the initial challenges of the program. Non-incarcerated students have access to the internet and are able to complete their FAFSA online. They have the ability to receive e-mails regarding the status of their application and can submit additional documentation if requested by ED. For incarcerated students, access to the internet is incredibly rare, since most prisons throughout the country do not allow students access for security purposes.

To complete the FAFSA, schools either brought in paper copies to be completed on-site or obtained special permission to bring in laptops to assist students with their applications. For schools who collected paper FAFSAs and mailed them to ED, the time period for processing the documents took several weeks. Some colleges had the financial aid staff enter the required information on behalf of the students. After completion of the application, it is up to the college to collect additional documentation from incarcerated students.

FAFSA Requirements

Another challenge with the FAFSA is that it has many questions that do not apply to incarcerated students. For instance, as mentioned before, most incarcerated students do not pay taxes. But four pages of the FAFSA are dedicated to individual, spouse, or parent financial and tax information. For independent students (i.e., non-married and over the age of twenty-four) who do not pay taxes, the application is not cumbersome to complete.

Considering the fact that incarcerated people with a prison job make a wage far below the poverty line, they likely receive the maximum amount of Pell funds allowed. Married or dependent students may receive less than the maximum, depending on their family income. Students with an annual income less than $24,000 automatically qualify for the maximum amount of Pell.[14]

Incarcerated men and women who indicate they are married on the FAFSA are often selected for verification of their spouse's IRS income tax transcripts. Additionally, young people under the age of twenty-four are required to have their parent/guardian complete a portion of the FAFSA and may be subject to verification of parental income. Obtaining tax information and verification signatures from spouses and parents is often a time-consuming process that may prevent a student from starting a program. Financial aid offices must have all appropriate documentation and verification forms completed before they are able to administer federal student aid.

Financial aid offices have the authority to override a dependent status to an independent student when there are special circumstances surrounding her or his home life. This includes incarceration, hospitalization, institutionalization, or abandonment of an inmate's parent. Dependent students living in abusive households or in foster care may also qualify for independent status. However, dependent students who are incarcerated themselves are not eligible for the override based on the incarceration alone. Often financial aid staff will consider a range of circumstances before authorizing a dependency override.

Default and Loan Rehabilitation

Students who have entered college at any point prior to their incarceration may not be able to receive a Pell Grant if they have outstanding debt from a student loan. When applying for federal student aid, a student may be found ineligible due to having defaulted on a loan. Students who failed to make a loan payment for nine months end up in default. Students are able to get out of default and into deferment after they make nine consecutive monthly payments to rehabilitate the loan. Students who are in prison are permitted to make small $5 payments for the nine months and will have their loan transferred to deferment status after they make consistent payments. Once in deferment status, students become eligible for Pell.

Students are often unaware they owe money to a loan servicer. It is not until they apply for a Pell Grant that they learn about their outstanding debt. Although students may be disappointed they cannot get a Pell Grant for an upcoming semester, if they begin the payment process, they are typically eligible for Pell several months later. Although this is burdensome, incarcerated students who start this payment process while in prison will be able to receive federal financial aid for college attendance once released without any delay.

Selective Service

Early on during this experiment, one of the roadblocks many programs faced was the selective service registration requirement for receiving federal financial aid. Registering incarcerated men between the ages of eighteen and twenty-five for selective service would prevent any delay in receiving federal financial aid for college, as well as other federal government benefits. Men who are over the age of twenty-five and failed to register during that time frame may be denied federal financial aid or have their aid delayed until they submit the proper documentation that explains why they failed to register.

During the implementation of the Pell Pilot in 2016, the program at UB discovered that 50 percent of their incarcerated college applicants did not register for selective service. The students were either incarcerated during the required registration time frame or in and out of the criminal justice system and unaware of this federal requirement. In order to receive federal financial aid, students who failed to register were required to request a status information letter from the Selective Service System (SSS). Students were required to complete this request, explain why they failed to register, and submit proof of incarceration if that was their reason.

The SSS requires this information in order for students to receive a status of information letter that either exempts a student for failing to register (due to incarceration during eligible registration years) or confirms that their failure to register was not willful or knowing. For students who were not incarcerated the entire duration of eligible years, but simply failed to register due to a lack of knowledge and life circumstances, the SSS informs them that the student should

[handwritten: have to show / not on purpose]

not be denied any Federal benefit if he can demonstrate that his failure to register was not knowing or willful . . . [and that] any explanation to justify your failure to register must be made to the agency administering the right, benefit, or privilege you seek . . . the final decision regarding your eligibility is with the authority of that agency.[15]

UB's Financial Aid Office accepted copies of all the documentation students submitted to the SSS. Since the status information letter takes several weeks to generate, the Financial Aid Office used professional judgment to determine whether failure to register was purposeful. All of UB's incarcerated students who failed to register were exempt (due to incarceration during registration years) or did not willfully fail to register and, therefore, were deemed eligible for federal financial aid.

ends up being OK but extra bureau step

Since UB's program was brand new, a lot of the financial aid challenges experienced were new to the financial aid department. Program staff worked directly with financial aid to ensure each and every applicant had the proper documentation submitted prior to the start of the academic semester. Recognizing the length of time it takes to process incarcerated students' financial aid documents, going into the second year, UB was able to start the process months earlier to ensure enough time for collecting and processing paperwork.

All of the challenges addressed in this section are not permanent barriers that prevent students from enrolling in college, but they are barriers that require a lot of staff manpower to overcome. Once students complete the financial aid process and are admitted and enrolled into their program, the focus shifts to providing quality college courses, getting students ready for the workforce, and preparing them for reentry.

WORKFORCE PREPARATION AND REENTRY

As other authors have mentioned, students who participate in postsecondary education programs are more likely to obtain employment and make higher earnings than those who do not participate. A goal of any postsecondary prison program should be to prepare students for high-demand fields in the communities to which they are returning. Expanding on this point, ED purposely stated in their announcement of the initiative that colleges "must ensure students are not enrolled in a program that prepares them for careers in fields where they face legal barriers to employment."[16]

With thousands of licensing restrictions throughout the country, it is necessary to pay close attention to the job market for this population. The Pell Pilot provides a diverse range of certificate to degree programs. Some of the sites, based on their location in the country, specifically target high-demand fields. Table 3.1 illustrates the various programs offered by colleges and universities participating in the Second Chance Pell Pilot Program.[17]

The sites that offer an associate's or bachelor's degree program have developed processes to help students transfer their credits if they do not complete the degree while in prison or if they plan to continue their education. Some programs were intentional about offering liberal arts, or general studies, programs based on the idea that students will be able to transfer their credits once released and apply them toward a bachelor's degree of their choosing.

Reentry Support

Participating in postsecondary education or vocational programs while incarcerated will enhance an individual's skills and education level. It is not, however, enough to simply provide training or education and expect that program participation will lead to reentry success. Program completion and post-release support are needed to ensure success in the community.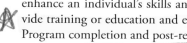

Table 3.1. Types of Certificate and Degree Programs

Certificate Programs	Associate's and/or Bachelor's Degree*
Business administration	Organizational management and leadership
Entrepreneurship	Nonprofit management and community leadership
Marketing	Organizational leadership
Human services	Business administration
Carpentry	Entrepreneurship
Welding	Interdisciplinary studies
Customer service	Liberal arts
Horticulture	Sociology
Hotel management	Heating and air conditioning
Restaurant management	Automotive technology
Office assistant	Construction carpentry
Substance abuse counseling	Criminal justice
Computer service	Hospitality and tourism
Production technologies	
Mechanical design	
Fire technology	
Automotive maintenance	
Automotive technology	
Culinary arts	
Air conditioning and refrigerator technology	
Manufacturing	
Environmental science	
Environmental health and safety	
Construction carpentry	

*Several of these degree programs, such as sociology, liberal arts, and interdisciplinary studies, prepare college students to be critical and creative thinkers, good communicators, and open to a range of perspectives, making them attractive employees to business.

Source: Vera Institute of Justice, *Second Chance Pell: Site Profiles*, 2016.

ED recognized this when it specifically asked site applicants to respond to how the college or university would prepare students for reentry and the workforce. All of the programs in existence today report providing post-release assistance with all or some of the following support services: assistance transferring credits to continue education; reentry preparation prior to release; reentry support in the community; academic and career counseling; and/ or job placement.

Oftentimes when those who have been in prison return to their communities, obtaining employment, securing housing, and taking care of basic life needs are their immediate goals. Education and career advancement are not. We should include education and workforce needs as part of the immediate goals package because failure to do so often distracts a previously motivated student from continuing his or her pursuits begun behind bars. Many incarcerated students will be released before completing their degree (especially a bachelor's program). So support services become incredibly necessary to ensure a continuum of education.

Campus-Based Reentry Support

Many programs work with students to enroll them in courses at the same college that was offering the inside program, or at other schools in the area in which the person is released (e.g., John Jay's College Initiative and Rutgers's NJ-Step Program). Assisting students with the admissions, enrollment, and financial aid process will help ensure continuity from in-prison coursework to on-campus participation. For many programs, like UB, students are already admitted to the college once they are accepted into the prison college program.

The continuity then requires ensuring students become acclimated to the campus, enroll in courses, and receive ongoing support from campus staff. For students who want to transfer to a different college, many prison college programs will assist them with that transfer process.

(handwritten margin note: same college upon release)

College Costs

The cost of attendance is also a barrier for people returning home. Many programs assist returning students with applying for existing scholarships to help support their tuition. Programs should explore ways to develop new scholarship opportunities and on-campus work opportunities. Creating work opportunities on campus would certainly benefit students who don't have immediate employment established for when they return.

Some programs are able to employ their returning students in administrative office jobs on campus. Students returning home might qualify for Federal Work Study—a way to pay student workers for campus employment. Partnering with workforce programs in the local community will also help fill the need for addressing their immediate employment gap. Although UB has not had any students released and enter campus, they do plan on implementing many of these strategies to ensure that students are able to continue their education.

Ban the Box

Additionally, supporting policy changes to college and job applications that exclude criminal history questions will reduce some of the barriers that criminal-justice-involved people experience when trying to obtain work and apply to college. Criminal justice questions on applications may deter individuals from applying or may result in discriminatory decision making based on prior history.[18] In 2016, ED released a fifty-page guide that provided data on the use of criminal justice information during the college admissions process, recommendations on how to alter admission policies, and resources on how to support students with criminal histories after they are enrolled.[19]

This report, in addition to ED's campaign to get higher education institutions to move "beyond the box," was part of the larger Obama administration agenda to expand educational opportunities for justice-involved people. Many colleges and universities signed Obama's Fair Chance Higher Education Pledge, including prestigious universities like Howard, Columbia, and Cornell. Signing the pledge means each institution will develop a plan to expand education access (including removing criminal history questions from admissions applications) for people with criminal records.[20]

Over the past few years, California and New York removed the criminal history questions from public college admission applications. In Louisiana, the 90–1 passage of Louisiana House Bill 688 removed the criminal history question on public college admission applications in the state. This bill was signed into law at the end of June 2017.[21] Other states, including Maryland, have also drafted bills to remove the criminal history question. While Maryland's bill passed both the house and the senate, Governor Larry Hogan vetoed the bill in spring 2017. Advocates of the bill hoped the senate and house would choose to override the veto in the 2018 legislative session, which they did.

TECHNICAL ASSISTANCE AND PROGRAM OUTCOMES

The Vera Institute of Justice was selected by ED to serve as the technical assistance provider to the selected sites. Vera's key role is to help sites successfully implement high-quality education and vocational programs in correctional institutions. Following the selection of the sites, Vera hosted an inaugural convening on July 19, 2016, in Washington, DC. Three representatives from each site were invited to participate in a day-long event that included opening remarks from then US Department of Education secretary John King and US deputy attorney general Sally Yates.

The event focused on developing strong correctional partnerships, implementing effective programming, and providing details on how to administer Pell Grants and assist incarcerated students with the FAFSA process. Several research groups were present and discussed ways to collaborate with Second Chance Pell sites to conduct impact evaluations of their programs. The research groups included RAND, Urban Institute, George Mason University, and RTI International, among others.

As this experiment enters its third year, no known impact evaluation is currently under way. Funding for a large-scale evaluation has not been made available by the federal government, and no foundation funds have been secured. This is recognized as a shortfall, and efforts to work with the sites on a data collection strategy are being discussed.

While a core objective of the pilot is to provide postsecondary education to incarcerated students prior to their release, therefore reducing their likelihood of recidivism, other objectives of interest to ED are also being evaluated. These include (1) examine how providing Pell Grants to incarcerated students influences their participation in educational opportunities and academic outcomes; and (2) examine any challenges or obstacles to an institution's administration of Title IV HEA programs to incarcerated students.[22]

With this in mind, ED does collect individual student data from the sites. This includes the following: enrollment status (full time, part time, etc.); direct costs for the student (e.g., tuition, fees, books); indirect costs (e.g., health insurance, parking, library fees); amount of Federal Work Study funds awarded regardless of whether funds were disbursed to students; other federal and nonfederal aid awarded; and credits attempted and earned during the award year and cumulatively. ED also collects data on whether students have graduated or discontinued the program, and whether they are still incarcerated or released.

Vera gathers participation data from the sites. This includes the number of students who completed FAFSAs, barriers to completing the FAFSA, the number of students awarded Pell, and how many students enrolled in courses. A recent Vera webinar provided an overview of the first year process-level outcomes.[23] During the spring 2017 semester, 4,097 students received Pell to participate in a postsecondary prison college program.

More than sixteen hundred courses were offered to Second Chance Pell students during the 2016–2017 academic year. While the majority of students are actively enrolled in their postsecondary program, 458 students graduated from a prison education program via the Pell Grant, with the majority receiving a certificate. Notably, 356 students graduated inside the prison, and fifty-five participated in graduation ceremonies on their home campuses.

Over the past year, Vera has also visited sites around the country to understand the challenges of implementing Pell and postsecondary correctional education in general. Sites from similar states or regions have been convened to discuss challenges with implementation. These meetings have been a way for sites to learn from one another and share best practices. Vera has also hosted a series of webinars for site participants. Webinar topics have covered challenges administering FAFSA, supporting student success while in prison, and supporting students on-campus, post-release.

Some programs that were operating prior to the implementation of the Pell Pilot do track student outcomes. Individual programs, if they have the capacity, are able to keep track of students as they continue their education in the community and after graduation. Outcomes tracked often include graduation rates, employment, and/or recidivism. For example, participants of Bard's Prison Initiative have very low rates of recidivism: those who graduate the program have a 2 percent recidivism rate, while those who take some classes but don't graduate have a 5 percent rate.[24]

Other prison college programs report similar rates. Roosevelt University in Chicago, Illinois,[25] has graduated more than five hundred students who were formerly incarcerated. They have been able to track recidivism rates for their graduates and report a 6 percent recidivism rate, notably lower than the state average of 31 percent.[26] New York's Hudson Link program currently has 575 active students, 690 alumni living in the community, and 534 college graduates. They report a 4 percent recidivism rate.[27]

PROGRAM-LEVEL EDUCATIONAL OUTCOMES

Although no large outcome evaluation has been conducted since the Pell Pilot began, several sites have reported some program-level outcomes related to educational success. For example, at Jackson College, incarcerated students make up 3 percent of the entire college population but account for 46 percent of the school's part-time dean's list. Their success at completing developmental math is close to 100 percent, compared to 54 percent of on-campus students.[28]

UB also experiences high rates of developmental math completion with twenty-nine out of thirty passing in one semester. After completing three semesters (or twenty-four credits), twenty-two out of thirty students in UB's program had a 3.5 GPA and qualified for the Honor Program.

Program administrators and instructors often argue that students participating in prison postsecondary education programs exceed expectations. One might expect the need for enhanced remedial support for participants in these programs based on the research that shows that incarcerated people have lower levels of educational attainment than the general public.[29] While these statistics imply the need for enhancing adult basic education and GED programs, opportunities to develop college-level programming should not be overlooked.

Most prison college programs provide the same quality of instruction that students in on-campus programs receive. Many programs do focus heavily on college preparatory coursework before a student moves into a college program. Support services are often provided at the prison through student and adult volunteers who assist with tutoring in math and writing. The main difference between on-campus and in-prison programs is the lack of technology available to incarcerated students.

This barrier often makes instruction more challenging and resources fewer. However, students still manage to excel in their courses. While many programs are able to provide students with computer access for typing assignments, only a few states have more advanced technology capabilities (e.g., online instruction and course material on tablets).

FUTURE EVALUATION SUGGESTED

Plans for evaluating the Second Chance Pell sites should include an implementation and outcome evaluation. Vera is collecting some implementation data (e.g., how programs are operating and barriers to delivering college inside prison), including data on the number of students participating, the number of courses and credentials offered, and challenges to completing the FAFSA. This information will certainly be useful to ED and all the sites that still struggle with gathering financial aid documents and administering Pell.

Additionally, and beyond Pell administration, understanding how the different programs have been implemented and operate (especially new programs), and the challenges they've faced, will be useful to other colleges interested in developing a new program.

Understanding implementation issues will also help inform any outcome evaluation that shows negative or positive results. Implementation barriers are often the reason programs "fail," and understanding both the barriers and the successes will allow program administrators to learn best practices. Participating sites should absolutely track post-release outcomes. Many programs that have been operating for years prior to the Pell Pilot independently keep track of outcomes such as academic achievement, employment, and recidivism, but all sites should be encouraged to keep and maintain data on program participants.

Data should include whether students continue their education, graduate, obtain employment, and remain free from further criminal behavior. Data should also capture in-prison outcomes, including whether students engage in prison misconduct during the course of their participation in postsecondary education and after they complete the program. Measures of other prison outcomes, such as overall level of prison violence and misconduct as well as correctional officer outcomes (e.g., job stress and morale) may also be useful in understanding how postsecondary education programs impact the prison environment.

While a major limitation of the Pell Pilot is the current lack of an outcome evaluation, there are ways to ensure that data is being collected from all the participating sites. Having all sites collect similar participation-level measures would allow future evaluators the ability to review data previously gathered and match it with outcome data (i.e., recidivism). For example, participation-level data might include keeping track of individual attendance records.

This type of data collection may already be collected by the prison, instructors teaching classes, or both. At UB, students are required to sign in when they enter our study hall sessions in the prison library. Students also sign out laptops during study hall. Since this type of data is already collected, it would be relatively easy to link participation-level data to outcome data once students are released.

Other data points sites could easily keep track of include (and some of these are collected by ED) course completion; grade point averages; program retention rates and reasons why students do not continue; length of participation; and completion rates. Like many colleges, UB already keeps track of these data points. They could also easily begin to track the reasons students withdraw from courses, do poorly (or excel) in certain courses, and overall perceptions of what aspects of our program work well and what do not.

Students openly discuss these aspects with program staff. Documenting these data points would not necessarily take up too much staff time. Still, developing a systematic way to track qualitative data—and training staff to collect it—would require an effort that some sites might not have the expertise or capacity to develop.

THE POLITICAL RESPONSE

As an Obama administration initiative, this Second Chance Pell Program followed several other important criminal justice reform efforts at the federal level. Restoration of Pell Grants in 2014 for young people incarcerated in juvenile justice facilities, local detention centers, or both opened new possibilities for educational access. My Brother's Keeper was another initiative launched in 2014 to reduce the achievement and learning gap among young men of color.

Communities across the country were encouraged to develop mentoring and support programs to help young boys enter the school system ready to learn, reach their appropriate reading level, and obtain a quality education that would prepare them to enter and complete college and career training programs.

Criminal justice reform efforts in the past decade have been centered on using evidence-based science, or "what works" research, to inform crime and justice policies. The Second Chance Pell Pilot fits well within that framework. The evidence-based literature on correctional rehabilitation programs emphasizes targeting eight changeable risk factors (i.e., criminogenic needs), which include improving an offender's employability and education levels. Programs that address risk factors will more likely see reductions in recidivism than those who do not target them.[30]

Correctional administrators and governors are often strong supporters of in-prison programming that set incarcerated people up for employment once released. Along the same lines, thoughtful conservative policy makers recognize the importance of providing education and vocational opportunities so people do not return to crime. Studies have shown that correctional education, including postsecondary programs, reduces recidivism.[31] As long as the funding for the Pell Pilot continues, and a large-scale evaluation is established, this experiment will hopefully be another important example of the effectiveness of in-prison college and vocational programs.

State-level efforts around the country to expand educational access for incarcerated students are also taking shape. In New York, Governor Andrew Cuomo announced that he would award $7 million for colleges to offer prison education programs to approximately twenty-five hundred prisoners. Funding for this initiative would not come from the state budget; instead, it would come from a Manhattan district attorney's large bank settlements.[32]

In California, the passage of Senate Bill 1391 in 2014 removed barriers to allow community colleges to offer college courses to incarcerated students housed in state prisons. Previously, students were permitted to participate in correspondence college programs. This bill will allow students to participate in a pilot program where four community colleges provide on-site instruction with coursework leading to an associate's degree or certificate. This pilot will run for three years and will include an evaluation of its effectiveness.[33]

Additionally, there are twenty colleges in the state of California currently providing college courses at thirty-four different prisons. Incarcerated students enrolled in courses through the community colleges are eligible for tuition waivers (i.e., a CA Promise Waiver) that non-incarcerated, low-income students are eligible to receive. Students enrolled in courses through California State University, Los Angeles, have their tuition covered by Pell Grants and through a grant from the Opportunity Institute, a nonprofit organization.

As New York and California lead the country in expanding correctional education opportunities, other state-level reforms are needed to ensure the sustainability of prison college programs.

The future of federal financial aid is uncertain, but states could ensure the longevity of this pilot if prison education and recidivism reduction become state priorities. Ensuring sustainability through state legislative action is one way to maintain and expand college-in-prison.

Texas, a state with one of the largest number of students engaged in prison college programs, is a good example of how state funds are "loaned" to incarcerated college students. Students who enroll in college while in prison receive a loan from the state and are required to pay it back once released. Although not a perfect model (due to potential inability to pay the loan back and accruing debt), this approach would certainly expand opportunities if adopted in other states and would also remove the negative perceptions around providing college at no cost to incarcerated people.

OPPOSITION

Providing Pell Grants for incarcerated people is a controversial topic. The elimination of Pell Grants in the 1990s was primarily due to the tough-on-crime perspectives that shaped criminal justice policy of that time. Today, some of the early views opposing "Pell for Prisoners" continue to influence conservative viewpoints. Some people simply do not believe in second chances and feel that prisoners do not deserve "free college." Everyday citizens may hold animosity toward the idea of allowing people in prison to attend college at little to no cost when they struggle to afford college for themselves and their children.

Another argument against "Pell for Prisoners" is that federal funding allocated to this effort takes away Pell funds for law-abiding students. This is simply not true. Pell Grants provide low-income students who would otherwise not afford college with the opportunity to get a college education. The funding allocated to the experiment is just a sliver of federal financial aid funds available nationally. In 2015–2016, the Pell Grant supported 7.7 million students with $28.5 billion in funds.[34] The funding for this experiment is only $30 million (less than 1 percent of the entire budget).[35]

Awarding Pell to incarcerated students does not take away funds from low-income students in the community. An individual student's Pell eligibility is individualized based on family income. Allowing incarcerated students access to Pell Grants does not mean other eligible students are denied access—it simply means more federal student aid spending. Still, the misconception exists that awarding Pell to an incarcerated student means that funds are taken away from law-abiding students.

While these viewpoints and misconceptions do exist, the research on the positive outcomes of those who participate in postsecondary education has influenced more conservatives to support the idea that access to higher education is a smart recidivism reduction strategy.

CONCLUSION

The Second Chance Pell Pilot has certainly created a level of excitement among prison education advocates and students who are benefiting from the pilot. The Pell Pilot has led to a national expansion of prison education programs across twenty-seven states. The importance of this experiment is in expanding the knowledge base that access and participation in higher education and vocational programs while incarcerated will greatly increase reentry success, future education access, and prevent future crime.

While many view this effort as the morally right approach on expanding educational opportunities to low-income people living in prison, a stronger, more compelling argument is the public safety benefit and cost savings generated by providing postsecondary education to people in prison. As this Pell Pilot currently provides educational access to thousands of incarcerated students, it is the hope that, if successful, hundreds of thousands of men and women behind bars will also be afforded the opportunity to shine.

NOTES

1. Michelle Rodriguez and Beth Avery, *Unlicensed & Untapped: Removing Barriers to State Occupational Licenses for People with Records*, National Employment Law Project, April 26, 2016, www.nelp.org/publication/unlicensed-untapped-removing-barriers-state-occupational-licenses/.

2. Danielle Douglas-Gabriel, "12,000 Inmates to Receive Pell Grants to Take College Classes," *Washington Post*, June 24, 2016, www.washingtonpost.com/news/grade-point/wp/2016/06/24/12000-inmates-to-receive-pell-grants-to-take-college-classes/?utm_term=.ad3ddebd3eab.

3. Vera Institute of Justice, "Supporting Formerly Incarcerated Students on College Campuses," webinar, September 20, 2017 (internal document).

4. Vera Institute of Justice, "Expanding Access to Postsecondary Education in Prison: One Year Later," Vera Institute internal meeting, August 19, 2017.

5. US Department of Education, "Institutions Selected for Participation in the Second Chance Pell Experiment in the 2016–2017 Award Year," news release, July 7, 2016, https://www2.ed.gov/documents/press-releases/second-chance-pell-institutions.pdf.

6. Vera Institute's Pathways from Prison to Postsecondary Education Project is a national demonstration project operating in fourteen prisons in Michigan, New Jersey, and North Carolina; and Jackson College, "Prison Program Helps: Students Graduate to a New Future," We Are Jackson College Newsletter, Fall 2015, www.jccmi.edu/wp-content/uploads/2015/10/PEI_article.pdf.

7. Leanne Smith, "Jackson College's Pathways from Prison Program Producing Dean's List Students," M Live Media Group, July 28, 2015, www.mlive.com/news/jackson/index.ssf/2015/07/jackson_colleges_pathways_from.html. This work is funded by Vera's Pathways Project.

8. US Department of Education, "Institutions Selected for Participation in the Second Chance Pell Experiment in the 2016–2017 Award Year."

9. "The Story of Lee College Offender Education Program," *Second Chance* 3, no. 1 (Winter 2015), www.lee.edu/publications/files/2012/02/Second-Chance-Feb-2015.pdf.

10. US Department of Education, "Institutions Selected for Participation in the Second Chance Pell Experiment in the 2016–2017 Award Year."

11. Vera Institute of Justice, *Second Chance Pell: Site Profiles*, 2016 (internal document).

12. Spiros Protopsaltis and Sharon Parrott, *Pell Grants—a Key Tool for Expanding College Access and Economic Opportunity—Need Strengthening, Not Cuts*, Center on Budget and Policy Priorities, July 27, 2017, www.cbpp.org/research/federal-budget/pell-grants-a-key-tool-for-expanding-college-access-and-economic-opportunity.

13. Abner Fletcher and Maggie Martin, "Prison Education: How Programs Are Taking Education beyond Bars," Houston Public Media, July 27, 2017, www.houstonpublicmedia.org/articles/news/2017/07/27/227534/prison-education-how-programs-are-taking-education-beyond-bars/.

14. Protopsaltis and Parrott, *Pell Grants*.

15. This statement is included on the status information letters issued by the Selective Service System. See generally https://www.sss.gov/Registration/Status-Information-Letter.

16. See US Department of Education Federal Register notice: https://www.federalregister.gov/documents/2015/08/03/2015-18994/notice-inviting-postsecondary-educational-institutions-to-participate-in-experiments-under-the.

17. Vera Institute of Justice, *Second Chance Pell: Site Profiles.*

18. Marsha Weissman et al., *The Use of Criminal History Records in College Admissions*, Center for Community Alternatives, November 2010, www.communityalternatives.org/pdf/Reconsidered-criminal-hist-recs-in-college-admissions.pdf.

19. US Department of Education, *Beyond the Box: Increasing Access to Higher Education for Justice-Involved Individuals*, May 9, 2016, www.aascu.org/BeyondtheBox/.

20. Juleyka Lantigua-Williams, "Giving Students a Second Chance," *Atlantic*, June 10, 2016, www.theatlantic.com/politics/archive/2016/06/fair-chance-education-pledge/486518/.

21. Gretel Kauffman, "College after Prison? New Louisiana Law Makes It Easier," *Christian Science Monitor*, July 5, 2017, www.csmonitor.com/EqualEd/2017/0705/College-after-prison-New-Louisiana-law-makes-it-easier.

22. US Department of Education, "The Department of Education's Experimental Sites Initiative, Second Chance Pell: Pell for Students Who Are Incarcerated," webinar, July 28, 2016, https://experimentalsites.ed.gov/exp/pdf/SecondChancePellSlides.pdf.

23. Vera Institute of Justice, "Supporting Formerly Incarcerated Students on College Campuses."

24. Ellen Condliffe Lagemann, *Liberating Minds: The Case for College in Prison* (New York: New Press, 2016).

25. Roosevelt College was initially selected as a Pell site but later dropped out of the experiment.

26. Vera Institute of Justice, *Second Chance Pell: Site Profiles.*

27. Hudson Link, "Hudson Link: Changing Lives One Degree at a Time," www.hudsonlink.org/what-we-do/fact-sheet.

28. Lindsay Vanhulle, "Michigan Colleges Leaders in Offering Pell Grants to Prisoners," *Crain's Detroit Business*, August 6, 2016, www.crainsdetroit.com/article/20160806/NEWS/160809877/michigan-colleges-leaders-in-offering-pell-grants-to-prisoners?X-IgnoreUserAgent=1.

29. Caroline Wolf Harlow, *Education and Correctional Populations*, Bureau of Justice Statistics, January 2003, www.bjs.gov/content/pub/pdf/ecp.pdf.

30. Don Andrew, James Bonta, and Stephen Wormith, "The Recent Past and Near Future of Risk and/or Need Assessment," *Crime & Delinquency* 52, no. 1 (2006): 7–27.

31. Lois M. Davis et al., *Evaluating the Effectiveness of Correctional Education: A Meta-Analysis of Programs That Provide Education to Incarcerated Adults* (Santa Monica, CA: RAND Corporation, 2013), www.bja.gov/publications/rand_correctional-education-meta-analysis.pdf.

32. Jesse McKinly, "Cuomo to Give Colleges $7 Million for Courses in Prisons," *New York Times*, August 6, 2017, www.nytimes.com/2017/08/06/nyregion/cuomo-to-give-colleges-7-million-for-courses-in-prisons.html.

33. Dennis Pierce, "California Expands Partnerships between Community Colleges, Prisons," American Association of Community Colleges, September 10, 2015, www.aacc21stcenturycenter.org/article/california-expands-partnerships-between-community-colleges-prisons/; and California Legislative Information, Senate Bill No. 1391, September 27, 2014 (Cal. 2014), http://leginfo.legislature.ca.gov/faces/billTextClient.xhtml?bill_id=201320140SB1391.

34. Protopsaltis and Parrott, *Pell Grants.*

35. Douglas-Gabriel, "12,000 Inmates to Receive Pell Grants to Take College Classes."

4

Reentry Programs, Evaluation Methods, and the Importance of Fidelity

Nancy La Vigne

Promoting the successful reentry of people leaving correctional confinement remains a critical public safety challenge for criminal justice stakeholders and policy makers. Despite recent criminal justice reforms, the United States continues to incarcerate more people than any other developed country in the world.[1] In 2015, well over six million people were under the purview of the US criminal justice system, including 4.6 million people on probation or parole supervision, another 728,800 incarcerated in local jails, and 1.5 million in state or federal prison.[2]

Importantly, the vast majority of people behind bars ultimately reenter the community.[3] In 2014, 641,100 adults were released from prison into the community,[4] and another eleven million cycle through the nation's jails on an annual basis.[5] Regrettably, the prospects of success following release from correctional confinement are relatively slim. Most analyses find that two-thirds of people are returned to custody within three years of their release from prison,[6] although recent research suggests that the people who do return to custody are oversampled, and thus recidivism rates may be considerably lower.[7]

Regardless of the differences in measurement, the factors that contribute to recidivism are well documented. Most people enter and exit incarceration with significant challenges, such as untreated trauma,[8] limited education and marketable job skills, lack of stable housing,[9] chronic physical and behavioral health issues,[10] and fragile support networks.[11] Research suggests that successful reentry depends largely on the degree to which these multiple hurdles are surmounted.[12]

This begs the question: What are the most effective strategies to meet these reentry challenges and promote the critical public safety goal of successful reintegration from correctional confinement? Ask any number of experts—caseworkers, parole officers, service providers, public officials, and, importantly, the formerly incarcerated themselves—and odds are the most common answers would be acquiring education and securing employment. Indeed, the most frequently cited needs reported by men participating in a large federally funded reentry initiative were education (94 percent), job training (82 percent), and employment (80 percent).[13]

Employment has been established as particularly vital to reentry success, often serving as a requisite for stable housing and food security. It is also a commonly required condition of post-incarceration supervision. Studies indicate that unemployment corresponds to an increased risk of recidivism;[14] joblessness also tends to hasten reoffending.[15] But finding people jobs—particularly for those with limited education, the "scarlet letter" of a criminal record, and considerable time out of the workforce due to incarceration—is not easy. Few people with histories of incarceration have the education or training to secure employment and earn a decent living.[16]

Understanding what works and what does not work in educating and preparing incarcerated people for employment and helping them obtain—and retain—jobs on the outside requires a thorough culling of the evaluation literature and a careful assessment of its limitations. This chapter explores that literature in detail, first providing an overview of the various forms of research evidence, and then describing the balance of that evidence specific to programs designed to enhance education and promote employment among correctional populations. This evidence is critiqued from two perspectives: evaluation methodology and program design. The chapter concludes by presenting a new, improved "platinum standard" model of research methodology, discussing how both evaluation utility and program fidelity can be enhanced, in tandem, through an emphasis on implementation evaluation and the use of an action research approach.

In summary, this chapter makes the case that examining evaluation findings, whether in isolation, in a compiled meta-analysis, or in a research synthesis, fails to deliver to the field what it truly needs: a thorough understanding of the nuances of research findings and limitations of research to date that can point to better application of reentry programs, more accurate documentation of their impact, and a detailed understanding of program implementation failures that can guide improvement in practices and, ultimately, enhancement of public safety.

DEFINING "EVIDENCE"

The notion of an "evidence-based practice" has firmly taken root in the context of corrections in recent years. It is embraced equally by academics, practitioners, and "good government" advocates, who argue that taxpayer dollars should be dedicated to programs that work. In fact, a culling of the state-level reform efforts in the past decade finds that more than one-third (ten out of twenty-eight)[17] included measures designed to ensure that corrections programs are grounded in evidence and, thus, most likely to yield a return on investment.[18] However, requiring the delivery of evidence-based reentry programs, while inarguably sensible, becomes clouded by a lack of knowledge of—or agreement about—what accounts for "evidence."

In recent years, however, the federal government and the academic community have aligned in agreement that evidence is most persuasive when studies are conducted with the greatest possible methodological rigor. This entails employing either randomized controlled trials (RCTs) or strong quasi-experimental designs (QEDs). In RCTs, subjects are randomly assigned to treatment or control groups, and outcomes are compared over time. With sufficient sample sizes, these two groups are roughly equal at the outset, making the sole difference between them whether or not they are administered the treatment.[19]

RCTs are widely agreed to be at the top of the evaluation design hierarchy. When conducted with sufficiently large-sized samples, RCTs are considered the "gold standard" of evaluation methodologies. This is particularly true in clinical or laboratory settings when both assignment to treatment or comparison group and delivery of the treatment can be conducted with fidelity. (Unfortunately, in the context of the criminal justice system, this is rarely the case—more on that later.)

Rather than using random assignment, QEDs employ a variety of methods to create reasonably comparable comparison groups using statistical controls to simulate equivalence. QEDs are more commonly employed than RCTs for several reasons. For instance, they allow retrospective evaluation (examining outcomes after the program or treatment was delivered), do not require extensive cooperation from program providers, and can be more affordable, particularly when relying on extant administrative data. *selection bias issue...*

 The challenge with QEDs is that they make it very difficult to control for selection bias. Meaning, the factors that lead people to be inclined to participate in a program, or get the most out of it, may differ regardless of whether the participants appear identical to comparators based on their age, criminal history, or other controllable factors.

This cursory overview of evaluation methodologies is offered as a foundation from which to summarize the knowledge base of research on employment and education programs designed to promote successful reentry. But at the risk of spoiling the punch line, the short answer to the question of "What works in reentry?" is that everything works—at least some of the time. Name an intervention—it could be work release,[20] family visitation programs,[21] or even transcendental meditation[22]—and there's at least one evaluation that finds it yields the intended impact. That said, for every type of program that works, there are countless studies that find the same type of program doesn't work. How does one make sense of it all?

SYNTHESIZING THE RESEARCH EVIDENCE

Efforts to sift through, assess, extract, and cull evidence from existing evaluation literature in the criminal justice realm date back several decades. In 1966, in recognition of the absence of evidence on effective rehabilitation programs, the governor of New York commissioned a comprehensive review of existing research. The resulting study yielded the discouraging headline that "nothing works"[23] and prompted a backlash against rehabilitation in favor of punishment for punishment's sake.[24]

This led to a sea change in ideology around punishment and rehabilitation, with conservatives and liberals alike rejecting individual rehabilitation as a failed concept in favor of incapacitation (on the right) and social justice (on the left).[25] It took another two decades for the field to recover from this notion of "knowledge destruction"[26] and to revisit the research evidence. Since then, countless undertakings to summarize the knowledge base on what works in correctional and rehabilitation programming have been executed, taking one of two forms:

1. meta-analyses, which combine findings across studies to generate a statistical average across effect sizes; and
2. systematic reviews, which compile and organize evidence after curating evaluation studies for sufficient rigor.

Lessons from Meta-Analyses

A review of existing meta-analyses and research syntheses on the topic of education and employment programs for people exiting prison or jail yields considerable evidence in favor of such efforts, with educational programs generating stronger and more consistent impacts than employment and vocation programs, on average. For instance, a 2000 meta-analysis reviewing thirty-three studies of correctional, vocational, and work programs administered to adults since 1975 found a significantly lower rate of post-release recidivism among program participants.[27] In particular, adult participation in educational programs such as Adult Basic Education (ABE), General Equivalency Development (GED), or college-level courses reduced recidivism by 11 percent, while vocational education improved employment opportunities but did not necessarily reduce recidivism.[28] A subsequent meta-analysis identified smaller and roughly equal impacts on recidivism among basic education and employment training programs, with 5.1 percent and 4.8 percent lower rates of recidivism, respectively, and a considerably larger 12.6 percent reduction in recidivism for vocational programs.[29]

Yet in the same year, a study of employment programs for incarcerated or recently released populations, which restricted inclusion to only those studies that employed random assignment, found just eight eligible studies published since 1970 and no impacts on recidivism.[30] More recently, a meta-analysis aggregated findings across fifty-eight educational program evaluations published within the past thirty years and concluded that those who participated in educational programs had 36 percent lower odds of recidivating and 13 percent higher odds of securing post-release employment.[31]

These meta-analyses are useful but limited. On the one hand, they demonstrate that, on average, educational and employment programs deliver their intended impacts. On the other, they fall short of describing which programs are most effective, and for whom. This is something that can be more easily discerned from systematic reviews.

Findings from Systematic Reviews

Research findings from the most comprehensive research synthesis of reentry evaluations, the What Works in Reentry Clearinghouse (WWRC),[32] yield similar findings as meta-analyses, with postsecondary education being the most promising intervention to reduce recidivism. Adult basic education programs are more modestly favorable, and vocational, GED, and basic education and life skills program evaluations have resulted in much more uneven outcomes.[33]

Among the three studies of postsecondary education included in the WWRC, each one of them found an impact on recidivism. One of these three studies examined the impact of a variety of postsecondary programs (with the potential to earn various types of certificates, including vocational certificates and associate's and bachelor's degrees) in three states: Massachusetts, New Mexico, and Indiana.

While impact varied from modest to meaningful, all three found lower rates of rearrests among participants.[34] A Maryland-based college program designed to help participants obtain their associate's degree found similarly favorable impacts, identifying a dramatic difference between participants and comparison group members in recidivism—at 27 percent and 58 percent, respectively—even though only one in four earned an associate's degree (the average participant completed 38.1 credit hours).[35]

Vocational training program evaluations all yielded more mixed results, with some showing reductions in recidivism and increases in employment and others finding no effect. For example, a study of a Queensland, Australia, program that offered vocational training in various business, computer, health care, and hospitality fields found significantly lower rates of recidivism, with 23 percent of vocational program participants re-incarcerated within three years versus 32 percent of the comparison group members.[36]

Importantly, this program offered certificates and prioritized participation based on the results of a risk and needs assessment. However, three other studies of vocational programs featured in the WWRC found no impact on recidivism or employment, and one study of vocational training in Ohio found that program participants actually had lower rates of post-release employment.[37]

Similar to vocational training findings, the two studies of GED completion featured in the WWRC found no impact on outcomes of interest. A study of a GED program in New Jersey examined the impact of GED completion on rearrests, finding no statistical differences between treatment and comparison groups.[38] On a more positive note, while a study of a Florida GED program on post-release earnings found no impact among the treatment population overall, the program did benefit non-white participants.[39]

Adult basic education programs, of which two are featured in the WWRC, also yielded mixed findings. With only two programs identified for inclusion in the clearinghouse, a study of a Minnesota basic education program found no impact on any measure of recidivism yet documented a dramatic 59 percent increase in likelihood of employment within three years following release from prison.[40] A study of a Florida basic education program dating several decades earlier found a significant impact on post-release employment rates, yet detected no impact on earnings; the authors did not examine the program's impact on recidivism.[41]

 Across the board, researchers associated with the WWRC review of educational programs observed that program effectiveness is highly dependent on the quality of implementation.[42] One might also conjecture that the nature and content of educational programs, particularly those associated with earning a degree or diploma, are more uniform compared with vocational training programs, which might vary considerably in content and duration. By definition, certificate and degree programs are more regimented and consistent in terms of the standards that must be met in order to successfully complete them. *interesting* ✗

The uniformity in program content associated with degree-earning programs may well explain the more consistently positive impact of GED and ABE programs compared to other, less-well-specified educational offerings behind bars.

The uneven patterns of findings among educational program types described here are mirrored in the WWRC's summaries of individual evaluations of employment-related programs. A variety of program types, including work release, prison industries, and transitional job programs, have been found to reduce recidivism rates or increase post-release employment—at least some of the time. WWRC's reviews of evaluations of these programs found roughly half detected impacts on either recidivism or employment, although few had an impact on both measures.[43]

The jobs program Project Rio, which provided job readiness behind bars and placement services upon release, is one of the better documented successful correctional employment programs in the research literature. Participants were more likely to be employed for longer periods of time during the twelve months following release from prison, and their recidivism rates were considerably lower as well, particularly among high-risk program participants.[44]

An evaluation of a similar program in Minnesota, titled Employ, which placed a strong emphasis on continuum of service provision from prison to the community, also identified statistically significant impacts on both employment and recidivism. Participants worked more hours, earned more wages, and were slower to reoffend than comparison group members.[45] By contrast, a more recent employment reentry program implemented in Chicago, Detroit, Milwaukee, and St. Paul, which placed participants in transitional jobs upon their release from prison, found positive impacts on recidivism but only a short-term impact on employment.[46]

Among work release programs that both reduced recidivism and increased employment, a Florida program found a modest 3 percent decrease in the likelihood of a new conviction and an 11 percent increase in securing employment,[47] while a Minnesota program found a 14 to 17 percent reduction in recidivism and an average of $4,869.13 more in wages than comparison group members.[48] This latter program, however, found alarmingly higher (78 percent) risk of return to prison for technical violations of conditions of post-release supervision.

Among prison industry programs, which vary considerably based on the type of employment experience they offer behind bars, from furniture crafting to agriculture and recycling, the federal UNICOR program is well documented for both recidivism and employment outcomes. Participants have increased likelihood of post-release employment (although no impact on wages), with 71.7 percent of the treatment group employed at one year following release compared to 63.1 percent of the comparison group. In addition, the evaluation documented a 24 percent reduction in recidivism among male participants (but no impact on females).[49]

The Prison Industry Enhancement Certification Program (PIECP) established by Congress in 1979 is perhaps the most widely implemented prison industries program in the country, operational in thirty-seven state prison systems and four counties.[50] To be eligible for the program, which places people exiting from prison in private-sector jobs in the community, one must have a GED or high school diploma and have no disciplinary reports for the six months prior to program enrollment.[51] PIECP participants were slower to reoffend than comparators participating in traditional prison industries programs,[52] and effects on recidivism were more pronounced for participants of color.[53]

In as much as the aforementioned research evidence provides justification for the delivery of educational and employment readiness opportunities behind bars, the flaws and limitations of the knowledge base on these topics are considerable. They can be divided into two general categories: flaws in program design and delivery, and flaws in program evaluation. These two intersect in ways that can mask the true nature of research findings, undercut the theoretical validity of the program under study, and compromise the degree to which it is impactful.

PROGRAM DESIGN AND DELIVERY CHALLENGES

This section describes the limitations of evaluation that may mislead program developers to design interventions that are not as impactful as possible.

"Single Tool" Programs

There's an old saying that when the only tool you have is a hammer, everything looks like a nail to you. This phenomenon features prominently in the field, where reentry program delivery is often specialized—you have housing providers, substance use treatment providers, employment placement services, and so on—and is reinforced in the literature when researchers categorize and bundle evaluations by one specific program type. Indeed, a critical shortcoming of the above summary of research findings is that they compartmentalize reentry challenges and needs as if just one type of intervention is necessary to reduce recidivism.

This runs counter to a growing body of evidence that the most successful reentry programs are both holistic and tailored to each program participant. Comprehensively addressing all needs, while also building on oft-overlooked assets, appears to be particularly promising. For example, a recent evaluation of the Allegheny County reentry program designed to comport with this holistic approach employed a QED using propensity score matching and found that program participants had a 10 percent chance of rearrest, compared with a 34 percent chance for the comparison group.[54]

Similarly, a study of the ComALERT program, designed to offer a suite of program, treatment, and housing services to people paroled to Brooklyn, New York, detected a 26 percent lower likelihood of rearrest and re-incarceration among participants, along with higher rates of employment and higher average earnings.[55]

Risk and Gender Neutral

Research syntheses and summaries rarely attend to the risk level of the participant. While meta-analyses are useful in compiling findings across studies in a way that can yield statistically significant impacts, they treat all programs as if they are equal. In reality, the programs that make up the meta-analysis have different characteristics and serve different populations. This is particularly true with regard to the risk level and gender of program participants.

Research finds that people are differentially responsive to program impacts based on their level of risk, and nature and degree of need. The risk-needs-responsivity model advocates for focusing on those at higher risk of reoffending, addressing their underlying criminogenic needs, and providing treatment tailored to the individual's learning style and strengths.[56] Focusing program delivery on risk level is also smart public policy; it stands to reason that targeting scarce resources on those most likely to benefit from them is in the interests of both taxpayers and public safety.

Evaluations that combine findings among programs that serve both men and women are equally problematic. Separate from meta-analyses and research syntheses, a strong body of evidence exists that gender-responsive programming is necessary to achieve desired outcomes. Programs designed for men do not work well for women; this is underscored in WWRC, which finds that therapeutic substance abuse treatment programs tailored to women are much more likely to be impactful for them.[57]

Absence of Context

Program evaluations of all types often overlook the importance of the setting and mode of program delivery. This includes whether the program provides a continuum of care in program delivery from the prison to the community, a practice that is considered to be evidence based.[58] However, research compilations, whether meta-analyses or systematic reviews, do not distinguish between programs that are solely offered behind bars versus those that continue after the participant's release.

Another example of a program context that is rarely documented in evaluation compilations is the way in which practice of caseworkers, treatment providers, and supervision officers interact with criminal justice populations. For instance, recent research suggests that employing strengths-based delivery models that highlight participants' assets—family, skills, talents—hold considerable promise. Often termed "motivational interviewing" in the context of community supervision, this delivery mode has been found to yield better compliance with conditions of supervision and lower recidivism rates.[59]

Limited Outcomes

As a body of knowledge, program evaluations that focus on reentry populations are heavily biased toward studies that examine a single type of outcome: recidivism. This is true across a wide array of program and treatment types and can best be explained by researchers resort-

recidivism to easy to track

ing to the outcome data that is most easily accessible—namely, documentation of a return to prison or jail confinement.

By way of example, of the twenty-eight studies on employment programs featured in the WWRC, all but one examined recidivism outcomes. Only nineteen examined employment outcomes, such as the share of participants who found jobs, the length of time they were employed following release, their wages, and their earnings.[60] Similarly, only half of educational program evaluations examine employment outcomes despite the clear linkage between education and employment.[61]

Confining evaluation of reentry programs to a sole focus on recidivism outcomes creates a tremendous gap in understanding the mechanisms of what works in program delivery. Meaning, if we only know whether an employment program reduces recidivism and not whether it helped people obtain and retain jobs, it is impossible to know what led to the recidivism reduction and casts doubt about the degree to which the program is responsible for that reduction.

Worse yet, measures of recidivism are exceedingly uneven. Some studies measure recidivism as rearrest, regardless of whether that rearrest resulted in a conviction. Return to custody is another commonly used measure of recidivism, but it is imprecise in cases for which that return is the result of a failure of conditions of supervision (a "technical violation") rather than the commission of a new crime. Other studies examine reconviction, arguably the most precise metric among administrative data sources. Finally, very few studies define recidivism based on self-reported reoffending. Collecting such data is resource intensive, and respondents may not be entirely forthcoming.

EVALUATION DESIGN AND DELIVERY FLAWS

The above-referenced limitations of research findings and their implications for practice are often caused or exacerbated by flaws in the manner in which program evaluations are executed. These flaws are not inconsequential. Of the 917 program evaluations reviewed by the WWRC, only 164—or 18 percent—were found to be sufficiently rigorous enough to merit inclusion.[62] As illustrated in figure 4.1, among those studies that were excluded, the reasons varied from insufficient sample size, to lack of a credible comparison group, to inadequate statistical controls.[63]

Not only do the majority of program evaluations fail to comport with basic standards of methodological rigor (and yet are embraced and replicated in the field), but specific challenges exist even among those studies that pass muster. These include poor compliance with random assignment procedures and the troubling dearth of implementation evaluations. Both flaws render program evaluation results difficult to interpret absent the context of program delivery. Indeed, fewer than one in three evaluations featured in the WWRC provide any documentation of quality of implementation whatsoever.[64] These various flaws in evaluation design are described individually below.

The Absence of a Comparison Group

Despite the best intent of those who aspire to measure the impact of programs, a rookie mistake, often made by program developers aspiring to evaluate their own programs, is to compare program participants to themselves. This seems logical on its face: If a person joins a weight loss program and after six months is twenty pounds lighter, doesn't that mean the pro-

Primary Reason for Exclusion

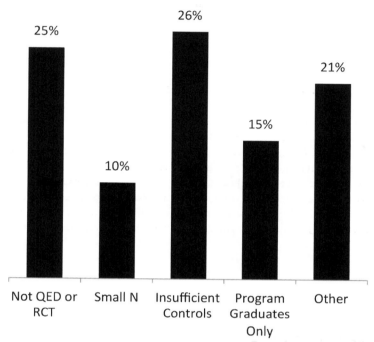

Figure 4.1. Reasons for Excluding Evaluation Studies from the What Works in Reentry Clearinghouse
Source: Mathew Lynch and Nancy La Vigne, "What Works in Reentry: Methods and Findings from the What Works in Reentry Clearinghouse," presentation at the 72nd Annual Meeting of the American Society of Criminology, New Orleans, Louisiana, November 15, 2016.

gram works? Yes, the program works for that individual. However, in the context of program evaluation, it is crucial to have a persuasive counterfactual—someone just like the program participant who is not subject to the program. Program evaluations absolutely must have a convincing comparison group; yet, as depicted in figure 4.1, 26 percent of evaluation studies identified by the WWRC were rejected for lacking one.

Evaluating Only Program Completers

A related and all-too common error among those who are not specifically trained in evaluation methodology is the exclusion of program dropouts (attrition) from impact analyses. This practice is far too common: in its review of the research on effectiveness of correctional education, WWRC researchers found the primary reason that a study was excluded from review was that it removed program dropouts from the analysis, comparing only individuals who successfully completed a correctional program with a comparison group consisting of individuals who did not participate in the program. This approach introduces selection bias,

*imp
to get
true, BAD
results
to learn/
to improve...*

since individuals who completed a program may have characteristics, such as motivation to succeed, that differ from those of the comparison group.

By contrast, the "intent to treat" approach includes program dropouts in outcome analyses. Doing so removes the bias in outcomes that would result when participants who are at greater risk of failure drop out of the study. The intent to treat approach is a pragmatic evaluation method when one aspires to learn the effect of a policy or program as it is implemented on the ground, rather than the best case (yet unlikely) scenario of all program participants completing the program from beginning to end. This is particularly relevant for criminal justice populations, for whom program attrition rates are particularly high.

Low Sample Size/Insufficient Statistical Power

Many evaluators fail to acknowledge that programs designed to reduce recidivism have relatively small impacts or "effect sizes." While evaluations of high-quality reentry programs have an impact on recidivism ranging between 20 and 30 percent, programs identified as "typical" deliver just 5–10 percent reductions.[65] While this appears small, the impact on public safety may be considerable depending on the extent and type of reoffending that is prevented.

Nonetheless, evaluation designs often do not account for anticipated low effect sizes, which need to be balanced with a larger sample size. If statistical power is insufficient, the most rigorous of evaluation designs will not detect an impact even if one exists. That means that a countless number of programs have likely been rejected as ineffective based on evaluation design alone.

Limited Follow-Up

Rare is the case that an evaluation of a reentry program tracks outcomes for more than a year. Yet some research finds that positive impacts may wane with time,[66] while other research suggests that programs take time to mature, with more nascent programs less likely to have an impact than ones that have been in place for a while. For example, an evaluation of the Serious Violent Offender Reentry Initiative (SVORI) identified the following results: no outcomes in an early assessment;[67] modest outcomes in increased employment and housing; and reduced substance use with a longer follow-up period, although it found no statistically significant impact on recidivism.[68]

This stands to reason, since ideally program fidelity should improve as implementers become more skilled at delivery. Conversely, sustaining program fidelity over time may be a challenge. Both scenarios suggest that evaluations should include longer follow-up periods and be designed to measure impacts as program implementation matures and perhaps becomes more consistent with program goals.

Insufficient Dosage

Another important and often overlooked consideration in the evaluation of reentry programs concerns issues of both dosage and what the counterfactual consists of. The field of reentry has evolved dramatically since the 1980s and 1990s, during which prisons were viewed by the public as places to punish people and by corrections officials as places to house people securely. By contrast, today the notion that correctional systems have a stake in helping ensure that people have access to programs and treatment during incarceration, and are supported in their return from prison or jail, is widely accepted.

As such, the baseline of reentry programs and service delivery overall has likely risen, raising the question of how much programs subject to evaluation go above and beyond that base level of service provision and support. This makes it critical for a program to be not only evaluable from a technical perspective—based on the size of the intended program participant pool and ability to measure outcomes—but also based on the program's ability to deliver enough dosage—sufficient "added value," so to speak—to yield a measurably different impact on those outcomes.

Overemphasis on RCTs

It may come as a surprise to readers that a subheading under a section titled "substandard evaluation methodologies" is none other than the "gold standard" RCT. Nonetheless, given the increasing emphasis on random assignment, it is important to acknowledge the often overlooked limitations of this methodology in the context of its real-world application.

First, RCTs are not always feasible due to insufficient sample sizes, particularly in the context of evaluating pilot programs and those that serve hard-to-reach populations. And, as underscored earlier, if the program to be evaluated serves a specific and narrow population—say, women exiting jail who are chronically homeless—random assignment will reduce the number of program participants by half. RCTs with insufficient sample sizes, and thus insufficient statistical power, will not, by definition, yield useful findings.

RCTs may also come with ethical challenges associated with the decision to withhold treatment from those who could benefit from it. It is very difficult to persuade program deliverers to withhold treatment that could help improve people's lives and outcomes simply for the sake of an evaluation. This is particularly germane in the context of potentially life-saving medications. Those ethical concerns are somewhat mitigated if resources are not sufficient to serve all those in the target population, in which case a lottery system—random assignment—is often justifiable.[69]

Apart from methodological concerns, a sole focus on RCTs may minimize opportunities for experimentation and innovation in that pilot programs are unlikely to have enough program capacity to support randomization with sufficient sample sizes. This practice runs counter to social impact financing models such as Pay for Success (PFS), which leverage private capital to support funding innovative programs that the government might not otherwise be in a position to support, with the impact savings—in this case, averted costs to the criminal justice system due to reduced recidivism—returned to the investors.

Given their rigor, RCTs are best suited to quantify the recidivism reduction results of a PFS-funded program with credibility. But adhering to RCTs requires PFS implementers to guide prospective investors toward programs of sufficient size to support random assignment. This renders smaller pilot programs off the table and could have the unintended impact of inhibiting innovation, as most innovative programs start small.

Finally, RCTs have been held up by some academics as being relatively inexpensive.[70] This is rarely the case with regard to randomizing program delivery to correctional populations. Ensuring that randomization is conducted properly in the field requires close attention and intensive coordination with corrections agencies and programmatic staff. This requires an investment. Moreover, the cost of conducting RCTs can be underestimated because far too often they are conducted without an accompanying implementation evaluation.

Lack of Replication

Meta-analyses might be considered a form of "statistical replication" in that multiple studies on the same types of interventions are combined. But true replication tests out the impact of the same program in a different place or with different populations. Replication in the area of reentry programs is exceedingly rare, likely due to the dearth of funding in support of evaluation. Lack of replication leads to what Muhlhausen[71] terms the "single-instance fallacy" whereby wholesale extrapolations are made based on the evaluation results of a single program. Doing so can lead to wasted investment of scarce resources, particularly when the program's study lacks details on why and exactly how the program works.

Inattention to Fidelity

Perhaps the most serious flaw among program evaluations that meet methodological rigor is the absence of any effort to document how the program was implemented and whether that implementation was commensurate with the program's intent. This lack of attention to the quality of program delivery, known as "implementation fidelity," is the Achilles heel of program evaluation. Implementation evaluations, also known as process evaluations, measure the fidelity of program delivery to discern whether the intended population receives the intended treatment.[72]

Implementation evaluation is a crucial component of a comprehensive impact evaluation. It measures the following: what the intended target population is; whether that population was served; what the envisioned nature of program delivery and content was; the degree to which that vision was met; whether program delivery fidelity varied for different types of program participants; and perceptions of program quality of content and delivery from the perspective of both program deliverers and recipients.

In the absence of this information, findings from an impact evaluation are lacking in details that can enhance program delivery, impact, and replication, at best. At worst, they can be outright detrimental to the field, the knowledge base, and program participants who stand to benefit. For example, if an impact evaluation finds a significant effect on intended outcomes of interest but lacks an implementation evaluation, program implementers and the field writ large will have little context with which to understand the mechanism behind how the program worked, for whom, and why.

Worse yet is the result of an impact evaluation that finds no effect on outcomes. Absent an implementation evaluation, it is impossible to know whether the failure of the program to achieve its intended outcomes was because the intervention itself or its implementation was flawed. Why is this problematic? Because intervention types that are theoretically and conceptually sound may nonetheless be disbanded based on impact evaluations that yield inconclusive findings, rather than pointing to ways in which the program could be more impactful.

For instance, it could be that program delivery was sound, but the intended target population—people at medium to high risk of recidivism—did not receive the program due to disinterest, with those at low risk of recidivism participating instead. It is entirely conceivable that the program, when delivered to the correct population, might well be impactful. Similarly, implementation evaluation may shed light on ways in which the program intensity, or "dosage," wasn't as strong as intended.

Perhaps program participants were supposed to have three months of employment readiness training but a significant share transferred to other facilities, and, thus, the average number of participation days was half that. An impact evaluation will unearth those details and yield constructive context that can enable program implementers to refine and enhance program content and delivery in a manner that can increase the odds that it will have an impact.

TOWARD A PLATINUM STANDARD EVALUATION MODEL

The above discussion points to several flaws in the current state of reentry program evaluation methodology that might lead one to question the value of continuing to invest resources in such evaluations moving forward. Rather than throwing the baby out with the bathwater, the time is ripe to embrace a new model of reentry evaluation that does the following:

- draws from the lessons learned from both flawed methodology and flawed implementation;
- integrates interim evaluation results along the way;
- solicits input from program developers as well as program participants; and
- allows researchers and practitioners to engage in authentic partnerships by which both learn from each other.

A platinum standard evaluation model does all of this.

Elements of a Platinum Standard Evaluation

Evaluations must have both sufficient rigor and sufficient data to be useful. But something that is often overlooked by people tasked with assessing the impact of programs is whether they are evaluable in the first place. Rigor is characterized by having a sufficient sample size, a persuasive and comparable comparison group, credible data that accurately measures outcomes of interest, and an accompanying implementation evaluation to document program fidelity.

Consider the simple 2 × 2 table depicted below, which examines whether a program evaluation is sufficiently rigorous to detect a statistically significant impact and whether it includes an implementation evaluation. Drawing from reference to the RCT as the "gold standard" of evaluation methodologies, each cell is classified in accordance to its value. It is clear studies that are rigorous and include an evaluation of implementation fidelity are the best possible evaluations, or those that could be termed "platinum" evaluations. But what comes next in the hierarchy?

Based on the earlier discussion of the importance of attending to program implementation, one could argue that rigorous evaluations alone, including those employing RCTs, are not

Table 4.1. Classifying Studies by Rigor and Attention to Fidelity

		Rigorous Design	
		Yes	No
Includes Implementation Evaluation	Yes	Platinum	Gold
	No	Silver	Scrap Metal

Source: Nancy La Vigne.

gold standard but, perhaps, silver. That's because impact alone without knowledge of implementation yields very little in the way of useful information. This is a problem.

By contrast, a study of low rigor that includes a thorough process evaluation still yields constructive information, generating knowledge on problems encountered in program delivery and ways in which they can be improved. The final cell in the table, representing evaluations with both low rigor and an absence of implementation evaluation, could best be described as scrap metal. Perhaps some nuggets of use can be salvaged from the study, but its value pales by comparison.

Participatory Action Research

In addition to ensuring that evaluations include robust implementation evaluation, much can be learned by documenting fidelity in an ongoing manner. The action research model is one such approach, which contends that research conducted in the traditional academic approach is not informed by the context and implementation nuances that are a reality in the field. The concept is generally credited to Kurt Lewin, who famously said, "Research that produces nothing but books will not suffice."[73]

Lewin not only argued for research in which evaluators play an important role in the subject of evaluation—collecting data and documenting context—but also advocated for the all-important "feedback loop," whereby researchers share information as they gather it in order to guide the intervention in improving and becoming more impactful. This approach ran counter to the thinking of the time, which continues to prevail today: that evaluators should keep the subject of their evaluation at arm's length in order to maintain objectivity. Years later, the popularity of action research waned, but it waxed again upon introduction of the participatory action research model (PAR) that embraces an equal partnership between researcher and practitioner in the evaluation process.[74]

Building Evaluation Capacity

Many assume knowledge of the field equals knowledge of evaluation; this is not always a safe assumption. People well schooled in criminal justice research, for example, may have only had cursory exposure to the intricacies of sound program evaluation. Much can, and should, be done to train local, on-the-ground evaluators and to support research-practitioner partnerships established while programs are being developed. This will enable program developers to conceive of and plan for programs that researchers advise are "evaluable"—programs that are large enough and differ enough from the counterfactual that they are suitable for rigorous evaluation.

One means of developing a deeper bench of program evaluators is to establish a hub of evaluation resources, training, and knowledge, and to deliver that information to locally based researchers to enhance their ability to partner with practitioners on the ground. This training hub would be staffed with faculty who are schooled in both rigorous evaluation methodologies and implementation science. This "teach them to fish" model would build an entire army of local researchers well equipped to team up with program developers and build in evaluability at the outset.

Because local evaluators are geographically proximate to the program implementers, the likelihood of ongoing research-practitioner partnerships is high, making it more feasible to conduct evaluations with longer follow-up periods and supporting replication evaluations. If successfully implemented, this evaluation hub model would yield more evaluations and promote more rigorous ones. Indeed, supporting the evaluation hub could be far more impactful than funding large research firms to conduct so-called national evaluations of federal initiatives consisting of programs that differ considerably from each other on content.

CONCLUSION

The field of reentry research has come a long way since the "nothing works" philosophy of the 1970s. Today, with the benefit of meta-analyses and research syntheses, a compelling body of evidence exists on the promise of educational and employment programs in promoting successful reentry. That said, the devil is in the details, and many of these details are overlooked by studies that fail to examine all relevant outcomes, do not follow participants over a sufficient period of time, and omit that all-important documentation of implementation fidelity. Moreover, the level of rigor of studies that are accepted as "evidence" is generally quite poor, with the vast majority of published studies not meeting basic levels of rigor.

To improve how researchers evaluate reentry programs to inform policy makers, correctional leaders, and employers about "what works," this chapter presents a new model of evaluation—a "platinum grade" approach—that embodies the best of what is known from both high-level program evaluation and implementation science. This approach could be bolstered by a participatory action research model that acknowledges the expertise, experience, and field wisdom of practitioners, and includes the perspectives of the most important experts of all: the program participants.

The platinum evaluation may sound like a pipe dream. It is not. With proper support from key stakeholders, it could be quickly disseminated through a national reentry evaluation hub and a "train the trainers" approach. Doing so will instruct local researchers in evaluation methodology and incentivize them to partner with practitioners to build new and more credible evidence for the field.

NOTES

1. National Research Council, *The Growth of Incarceration in the United States: Exploring Causes and Consequences* (Washington, DC: National Academies Press, 2014).

2. Danielle Kaeble and Lauren Glaze, *Correctional Populations in the United States, 2015*, Bureau of Justice Statistics, December 2016, https://www.bjs.gov/content/pub/pdf/cpus15.pdf.

3. Jeremy Travis, *But They All Come Back: Facing the Challenges of Prisoner Reentry* (Washington, DC: Urban Institute Press, 2005).

4. Kaeble and Glaze, *Correctional Populations in the United States, 2015.*

5. Ram Subramanian et al., *Incarceration's Front Door: The Misuse of Jails in America*, Vera Institute of Justice, February 2015, http://www.safetyandjusticechallenge.org/wp-content/uploads/2015/01/incarcerations-front-door-report.pdf.

6. Patrick A. Langan and David J. Levin, *Recidivism of Prisoners Released in 1994*, Bureau of Justice Statistics Special Report, June 2002, https://www.bjs.gov/content/pub/pdf/rpr94.pdf.

7. William Rhodes et al., "Following Incarceration, Most Released Offenders Never Return to Prison," *Crime & Delinquency* 62, no. 8 (September 29, 2014): 1003–102.

8. E. G. Thomas et al., "Health-Related Factors Predict Return to Custody in a Large Cohort of Ex-Prisoners: New Approaches to Predicting Re-Incarceration," *Health and Justice* 3, no. 1 (2015): 10.

9. Jocelyn Fontaine, *Examining Housing as a Pathway to Successful Reentry: A Demonstration Design Process*, Urban Institute, November 2013, https://www.urban.org/sites/default/files/publica tion/24206/412957-Examining-Housing-as-a-Pathway-to-Successful-Reentry-A-Demonstration-De sign-Process.PDF.

10. Douglas McDonald, Christina Dyous, and Kenneth Carlson, *The Effectiveness of Prisoner Reentry Services as Crime Control*, Abt Associates, November 20, 2008, https://www.ncjrs.gov/pdffiles1/nij/grants/225369.pdf.

11. Joan Petersilia, "What Works in Prisoner Reentry? Reviewing and Questioning the Evidence," *Federal Probation* 68 (2004): 4–8.

12. Charlotte Gill and David B. Wilson, "Improving the Success of Reentry Programs: Identifying the Impact of Service–Need Fit on Recidivism," *Criminal Justice and Behavior* 44, no. 3 (2016): 336–59; and Francis T. Cullen and Paul Gendreau, "Assessing Correctional Rehabilitation: Policy, Practice, and Prospects," *Criminal Justice* 3, no. 1 (2000): 299–370.

13. Pamela K. Lattimore and Christy A. Visher, *The Multi-Site Evaluation of SVORI: Summary and Synthesis*, RTI International, December 2009, https://www.ncjrs.gov/pdffiles1/nij/grants/230421.pdf.

14. Sesha Kethineni and David N. Falcone, "Employment and Ex-Offenders in the United States: Effects of Legal and Extra Legal Factors," *Probation Journal* 54, no. 1 (2007): 36–51.

15. Torbjorn Skardhamar and Kjetil Telle, "Post-Release Employment and Recidivism in Norway," *Journal of Quantitative Criminology* 28, no. 4 (2012): 629–49.

16. Caroline W. Harlow, *Education and Correctional Populations*, Bureau of Justice Statistics Special Report, January 2003, https://www.bjs.gov/content/pub/pdf/ecp.pdf.

17. Samantha Harvell et al., *Reforming Sentencing and Corrections Policy: The Experience of Justice Reinvestment Initiative States*, Urban Institute, December 2016, https://www.urban.org/sites/default/files/publication/86691/reforming_sentencing_and_corrections_policy_2.pdf. Alabama, Arkansas, Delaware, Georgia, Kentucky, Nebraska, Ohio, Pennsylvania, South Dakota, and Utah expanded or mandated the use of evidence-based programs and practices as a part of reform legislation or related administrative changes.

18. Harvell et al., *Reforming Sentencing and Corrections Policy.*

19. Random assignment alone, however, does not guarantee equivalence in characteristics related to the outcome of interest, in that sometimes one group is unequal to the other on some share of these factors. Thus, any differences between the two groups should be identified and controlled for statistically.

20. Jillian Berk, "Does Work Release Work?" (PhD diss., Brown University, November 2007).

21. William D. Bales and Daniel P. Mears, "Inmate Social Ties and the Transition to Society: Does Visitation Reduce Recidivism?" *Journal of Research in Crime & Delinquency* 45, no. 3 (2008): 287–321.

22. C. R. Bleick and A. I. Abrams, "The Transcendental Meditation Program and Criminal Recidivism in California," *Journal of Criminal Justice* 15, no. 3 (1987): 211–30; and M. V. Rainforth, C. N. Alexander, and K. L. Cavanaugh, "Effects of the Transcendental Meditation Program on Recidivism among Former Inmates of Folsom Prison: Survival Analysis of 15-Year Follow-Up Data," *Journal of Offender Rehabilitation* 36, no. 1 (2003): 181–203.

23. R. Martinson, "What Works? Questions and Answers about Prison Reform," *The Public Interest* 35 (1974): 22–54; and D. Lipton, R. Martinson, and J. Wilks, *The Effectiveness of Correctional Treatment: A Survey of Treatment Evaluation Studies* (New York: Praeger, 1975).

24. M. R. Gottfredson, "Treatment Destruction Techniques," *Journal of Research in Crime and Delinquency* 16, no. 1 (1979): 39–54.

25. Frank Cullen and P. Gendreau, "From Nothing Works to What Works: Changing Professional Ideology in the 21st Century," *Prison Journal* 81, no. 3 (2001): 313–38.

26. Cullen and Gendreau, "From Nothing Works to What Works."

27. David B. Wilson, Catherine A. Gallagher, and Doris L. MacKenzie, "A Meta-Analysis of Corrections-Based Education, Vocation, and Work Programs for Adult Offenders," *Journal of Research in Crime and Delinquency* 37, no. 4 (2000): 347–68.

28. Wilson, Gallagher, and MacKenzie, "A Meta-Analysis of Corrections-Based Education."

29. Steve Aos, Marna Miller, and Elizabeth Drake, *Evidence-Based Adult Corrections Programs: What Works and What Does Not*, Washington State Institute for Public Policy, January 2006, http://www .wsipp.wa.gov/ReportFile/924/Wsipp_Evidence-Based-Adult-Corrections-Programs-What-Works-and -What-Does-Not_Preliminary-Report.pdf.

30. Christy A. Visher, Laura Winterfield, and Mark Coggeshall, "Ex-Offender Employment Programs and Recidivism: A Meta-Analysis," *Journal of Experimental Criminology* 1, no. 3 (2005): 295–315.

31. Lois M. Davis et al., *Evaluating the Effectiveness of Correctional Education: A Meta-Analysis of Programs That Provide Education to Incarcerated Adults* (Santa Monica, CA: RAND Corporation, 2013).

32. What Works in Reentry Clearinghouse, https://whatworks.csgjusticecenter.org/.

33. What Works in Reentry Clearinghouse, "Focus Area: Education," n.d., https://whatworks.csgjus ticecenter.org/focus-area/education.

34. Laura Winterfield, Mark Coggeshall, Michelle Burke-Storer, Vanessa Correa, and Simon Tidd, *The Effects of Postsecondary Correctional Education: Final Report*, Urban Institute, May 2009, https://www.urban.org/sites/default/files/publication/30626/411954-The-Effects-of-Postsecondary -Correctional-Education.PDF.

35. F. S. Blackburn, "The Relationship between Recidivism and Participation in a Community College Associate of Arts Degree Program for Incarcerated Offenders," *Journal of Correctional Education* 32, no. 3 (1981): 23–25.

36. V. Callan and J. Gardner, *Vocational Education and Training Provision and Recidivism in Queensland Correctional Institutions* (Adelaide, Australia: National Centre for Vocational Education Research, 2005); and V. Callan and J. Gardner, "The Role of VET in Recidivism in Australia," in *Vocational Education and Training for Adult Prisoners and Offenders in Australia: Research Readings*, ed. S. Dawe (Adelaide, Australia: National Centre for Vocational Education Research, 2007), 34–46.

37. William Sabol, "Local Labor-Market Conditions and Post-Prison Employment Experiences of Offenders Released from Ohio State Prisons," in *Barriers to Reentry? The Labor Market for Released Prisoners in Post-Industrial America*, ed. Sean Bushway, Michael Stoll, and David Weiman (New York: Russell Sage Foundation, 2007), 257–303.

38. Kristen M. Zgoba, Sabrina Haugebrook, and Kevin Jenkins, "The Influence of GED Obtainment on Inmate Release Outcome," *Criminal Justice and Behavior* 35, no. 3 (2008): 375–87.

39. John H. Tyler and Jeffrey R. Kling, "Prison-Based Education and Reentry into the Mainstream Labor Market," in *Barriers to Reentry? The Labor Market for Released Prisoners in Post-Industrialized America*, ed. Sean Bushway, Michael Stoll, and David Weiman (New York: Russell Sage Foundation, 2007), 227–56.

40. Grant Duwe and V. Clark, "The Effects of Prison-Based Educational Programming on Recidivism and Employment," *Prison Journal* 94, no. 4 (2014): 454–78.

41. Richard Cho and John H. Tyler, "Prison-Based Adult Basic Education (ABE) and Post-Release Labor Market Outcomes," Reentry Roundtable on Education, Urban Institute, April 1, 2008, http:// citeseerx.ist.psu.edu/viewdoc/download?doi=10.1.1.571.4207&rep=rep1&type=pdf.

42. What Works in Reentry Clearinghouse, "Focus Area: Education."

43. What Works in Reentry Clearinghouse, "Focus Area: Education."

44. B. M. Crouch, Craig H. Blakely, and David M. Carmichael, *The Reintegration of Ex-Offenders: A Process Study of Project Rio*, Public Policy Resources Laboratory, 1989; Craig Blakely, David M. Carmichael, and Julian Eltinge, *An Evaluation of Project Rio Outcomes: A Preliminary Report*, Public Policy Resources Laboratory, 1991; Ramdas Menon, Craig Blakely, Dottie Carmichael, and Laurie Silver, *An Evaluation of Project RIO Outcomes: An Evaluative Report*, Public Policy Resources Laboratory, 1992; and Peter Finn, *Texas' Project RIO (Re-Integration of Offenders)*, National Institute of Justice, 1998, https:// www.ncjrs.gov/txtfiles/168637.txt.

45. Grant Duwe, "The Benefits of Keeping Idle Hands Busy: An Outcome Evaluation of a Prisoner Reentry Employment Program," *Crime & Delinquency* 61, no. 4 (November 6, 2012): 559–86.

46. Dan Bloom, *Transitional Jobs Reentry Demonstration: Testing Strategies to Help Former Prisoners Find and Keep Jobs and Stay out of Prison*, MDRC, July 2009, https://www.mdrc.org/sites/default/files/policybrief_36.pdf; Cynthia Redcross et al., *Work after Prison: One-Year Findings from the Transitional Jobs Reentry Demonstration*, MDRC, October 2010, https://www.mdrc.org/sites/default/files/full_615.pdf; and Erin Jacobs Valentine, *Returning to Work after Prison: Final Results from the Transitional Jobs Reentry Demonstration*, MDRC, 2012, https://www.mdrc.org/publication/returning-work-after-prison.

47. Berk, "Does Work Release Work?"

48. Grant Duwe, "An Outcome Evaluation of a Prison Work Release Program: Estimating Its Effects on Recidivism, Employment and Cost Avoidance," *Criminal Justice Policy Review* 26, no. 6 (March 11, 2014): 1–24.

49. William G. Saylor and Gerald G. Gaes, "The Post-Release Employment Project: Prison Work Has Measurable Effects on Post-Release Success," *Federal Prisons Journal* 2, no. 4 (1992): 33–36; William G. Saylor and Gerald G. Gaes, "PREP: Training Inmates through Industrial Work Participation, and Vocational and Apprenticeship Training," *Corrections Management Quarterly* 1, no. 2 (1996): 32–43, https://www.ncjrs.gov/pdffiles1/Digitization/150221NCJRS.pdf; William G. Saylor and Gerald G. Gaes, *The Differential Effect of Industries and Vocational Training on Post-Release Outcome for Ethnic and Racial Groups*, US Department of Justice, 1999, https://www.bop.gov/resources/research_projects/published_reports/equity_diversity/oreprprep_s1.pdf; and William G. Saylor and Gerald G. Gaes, *PREP Study Links UNICOR Work Experience with Successful Post-Release Outcomes*, US Department of Justice, 1992.

50. US Department of Justice, "Prison Industry Enhancement Certification Program (PIECP)," n.d., https://www.bja.gov/ProgramDetails.aspx?Program_ID=73.

51. US Department of Justice, "Prison Industry Enhancement Certification Program (PIECP)."

52. Robynn J. A. Cox, "An Economic Analysis of Prison Labor" (PhD diss., Georgia State University, 2009).

53. Cindy J. Smith et al., *Correctional Industries Preparing Inmates for Re-Entry: Recidivism and Post-Release Employment*, National Institute of Justice, June 2006, https://www.ncjrs.gov/pdffiles1/nij/grants/214608.pdf.

54. Janeen Buck Willison, Samuel G. Bieler, and KiDeuk Kim, *Evaluation of the Allegheny County Jail Collaborative Reentry Program*, Urban Institute, October 6, 2014, https://www.urban.org/research/publication/evaluation-allegheny-county-jail-collaborative-reentry-programs.

55. Erin Jacobs and Bruce Western, *Report on the Evaluation of the ComALERT Prisoner Reentry Program* (October 2007), https://scholar.harvard.edu/files/brucewestern/files/report_1009071.pdf.

56. James Bonta and D. A. Andrews, *Risk-Need-Responsivity Model for Offender Assessment and Treatment* (User Report No. 2007-06), Public Safety Canada, 2007, https://www.publicsafety.gc.ca/cnt/rsrcs/pblctns/rsk-nd-rspnsvty/index-en.aspx.

57. Mathew Lynch and Nancy La Vigne, "What Works in Reentry: Methods and Findings from the What Works in Reentry Clearinghouse," presentation at the 72nd Annual Meeting of the American Society of Criminology, New Orleans, Louisiana, November 15, 2016.

58. Gerald G. Gaes et al., "Adult Correctional Education," in *Crime and Justice*, vol. 26, *Prisons*, ed. Michael Tonry and Joan Petersilia (Chicago: University of Chicago Press, 1999), 361–426.

59. James Bonta et al., "An Experimental Demonstration of Training Probation Officers in Evidence-Based Community Supervision," *Criminal Justice and Behavior* 38, no. 11 (2011): 1127–48.

60. Lynch and La Vigne, "What Works in Reentry."

61. Lynch and La Vigne, "What Works in Reentry."

62. Lynch and La Vigne, "What Works in Reentry."

63. Lynch and La Vigne, "What Works in Reentry."

64. Lynch and La Vigne, "What Works in Reentry."

65. Steve Aos et al., *The Comparative Costs and Benefits of Programs to Reduce Crime, Version 4.0,* Washington State Institute for Public Policy, May 2001, http://www.wsipp.wa.gov/ReportFile/756/Wsipp_The-Comparative-Costs-and-Benefits-of-Programs-to-Reduce-Crime-v-4-0_Full-Report.pdf.

66. Cindy Redcross, Bret Barden, and Dan Bloom, *Implementation and Early Impacts of the Next Generation of Subsidized Employment Programs: The Enhanced Transitional Jobs Demonstration,* MDRC, November 2016, https://www.mdrc.org/publication/implementation-and-early-impacts-next-generation-subsidized-employment-programs.

67. Pamela K. Lattimore and Christy Visher, *The Multi-Site Evaluation of SVORI: Summary and Synthesis,* RTI International, December 2009, https://www.ncjrs.gov/pdffiles1/nij/grants/230421.pdf.

68. Pamela K. Lattimore et al., *Prisoner Reentry Services: What Worked for SVORI Evaluation Participants?,* RTI International, April 2012, https://www.ncjrs.gov/pdffiles1/nij/grants/238214.pdf.

69. Robert Boruch et al., "Resolving Ethical Issues in Randomised Controlled Trials," in *Perspectives on Evaluating Criminal Justice and Corrections: Advances in Program Evaluation,* ed. Erica Bowen and Sarah Brown (Bingley, UK: Emerald Group Publishing, 2012), 95–128.

70. Melissa Parker, Asmaa Manan, and Mark Duffett, "Rapid, Easy, and Cheap Randomization: Prospective Evaluation in a Study Cohort," *Trials* 13, no. 1 (2012): 90.

71. David G. Muhlhausen, *Studies Cast Doubt on Effectiveness of Prisoner Reentry Programs,* Heritage Foundation, December 15, 2015, https://www.heritage.org/crime-and-justice/report/studies-cast-doubt-effectiveness-prisoner-reentry-programs.

72. Linda Dusenbury et al., "A Review of Research on Fidelity of Implementation: Implications for Drug Abuse Prevention in School Settings," *Health Education Research* 18, no. 2 (2003): 237–56.

73. Kurt Lewin, "Action Research and Minority Problems," in *Resolving Social Conflicts,* ed. G. W. Lewin (New York: Harper & Row, 1948), 202–3.

74. Robin McTaggart, "Participatory Action Research: Issues in Theory and Practice," *Educational Action Research* 2, no. 3 (1994): 313–37.

5

The Legal Case for Education in Prison

Ames C. Grawert

Education can be a source of great pride and opportunity. For those most in need of both—the 2.3 million men and women in our jails and prisons—education can be even more vital, presenting a chance to build a new future.[1] With unemployment and underemployment pervasive among the 3 percent of American adults who have been to prison, expanding prison education may even be an economic imperative: a way to put our fellow citizens back to work and recoup the tens of billions of dollars lost to families, communities, and the broader economy.[2]

Unfortunately, inmates have not always had easy access to education while incarcerated. Instead, they have had to fight for that chance in and out of court. Some legal efforts succeeded, building on a string of civil-rights-era legal victories, or capitalizing on backlash to the worst abuses of the prison system. Others have fallen short, exposing the limits of the state and federal judiciary's ability to mandate a right to an education inside prison walls. Ultimately, these cases show that the fight for expanded prison education can be an uphill battle.

While prisoners have often served as their own best advocates, they have just as frequently depended on legislators and activists to fuse their courtroom strategy with a legislative one. If we hope to expand correctional education to help people returning from incarceration, eager for a second chance, we will have to think creatively about how to use the law—or pair our legal strategy with advocacy.

EDUCATION AND REHABILITATION: EARLY DEMANDS FROM BOTH REFORMERS AND PRISONERS

Broad-ranging education programs have been part of American prisons for more than a century but often suffered from poor funding, restrictive eligibility requirements, and other shortcomings.[3] By the mid-1960s, prison administrators and the advocacy community generally recognized correctional education could improve prison life and help returning citizens reintegrate at home.

In *The Challenge of Crime in a Free Society*, President Lyndon Johnson's Commission on Law Enforcement and the Administration of Justice proposed a wholesale reinvention of the nation's

LBJ Reform Period / commission recommend.

prisons to help "shift the focus of correctional efforts from temporary banishment of offenders to a carefully devised combination of control and treatment."[4] The commission recommended that prisons adopt broad educational programs, "extending them to all inmates who can profit from them," and more than double the number of teachers employed in the nation's prisons.[5]

This expansion never occurred. Less than a decade later, in 1974, sociologist Robert Martinson published a seminal study of prison rehabilitative services, concluding that there is "very little reason to hope that we have in fact found a sure way of reducing recidivism through rehabilitation."[6] Martinson's paper struck a chord with a new generation of "tough on crime" legislators and prison administrators, providing casus belli to slash funding for certain prison education programs.[7] Recast as the "nothing works" doctrine—a nihilistic view that Martinson cautiously rejected—this paper helped undermine efforts to expand correctional education.[8]

Martinson "Nothing works"

Just as the public soured on correctional education, prisoners began to demand it. In November 1970, men incarcerated in California's Folsom State Prison staged a strike, attracting national attention and sparking a broader movement for prisoners' rights.[9] The strike's leaders documented their views in an "anti-oppression platform" praising "man's right to knowledge and the free use thereof," and demanded, among other things, unionized vocational education.[10]

Folsom

A year later, in September 1971, inmates in New York State's Attica Correctional Facility seized control of their facility. The uprising capped months of peaceful protests and efforts to draw attention to the prison's poor living conditions.[11] Among other abuses, Attica's men were fed on a budget of 72 cents per day, based not on any nutritional guidelines but on how much, or how little, New York State was willing to pay.[12] Prison labor paid too little for them to supplement that meager diet, or even to buy additional toilet paper. Medical care was poor to nonexistent.[13]

Attica

On the very first day of the uprising, Attica's inmates formulated a list of demands, seeking redress for each of these basic denials. They also asked the state to "modernize the inmate educational system"—a demand state prison authorities were prepared to accept.[14]

Notably, Attica *had* an education program at the time, including popular classes in English and sociology.[15] Its high school equivalency program was limited but "relatively successful."[16] Even so, these classes and the prison's five teachers were inadequate to serve the 80 percent of inmates, roughly eighteen hundred men in total, who had not completed high school.[17] Inmates were also given only 25 cents a day for attending class. This amount was not enough to pay for the daily necessities the state skimped on, depressing attendance. Worse, administrators viewed Attica's school as a "'dumping ground,' since the number of inmates in a class could be increased without an appreciable threat to security."[18] According to one of Attica's correctional teachers, prison education staff "were laboring under so many frustrations that there was no way it could be termed adequate."[19]

What Attica's men demanded was an *adequate* education. Particularly important to them was the addition of a Spanish-language library to meet the demands of Attica's growing Hispanic population.[20] The experiences of prisoners in Attica and Folsom exemplify a broader trend: by 1970, American prisons were poor and deteriorating. Where education programs existed, they were often inadequate. Hoping for some chance to improve their lives, prisoners around the country began to turn to the courts to enforce and expand their rights.

A BRIEF HISTORY OF PRISONERS' LEGAL RIGHTS

From unapologetic racial discrimination to the denial of basic medical care, the conditions of America's prisons in the 1960s seem shocking to modern readers.[21] How could such abuses persist? Regrettably, the law is one reason. Until the 1960s, courts viewed incarcerated people as utterly without rights. Describing the legal status of prisoners in 1871, the Virginia Supreme Court wrote in *Ruffin v. Commonwealth*:

> He has, as a consequence of his crime, not only forfeited his liberty, but all his personal rights except those which the law in its humanity accords to him. He is for the time being the slave of the State. He is *civiliter mortuus* ["dead to civil life"]; and his estate, if he has any, is administered like that of a dead man.[22]

While the *Ruffin* Court was blunter than most, this view was widely shared by circuit judges after Reconstruction and during the Jim Crow era. "[T]he United States is not concerned with, nor has it power to control or regulate the internal discipline of the penal institutions of its constituent states," wrote the US Court of Appeals for the Seventh Circuit in 1957. In a one-word opinion ("Denied"), the Supreme Court declined to review the case, letting the judgment stand.[23]

This approach came to be known as the "hands-off doctrine," a judge-made limitation that functionally barred courts from reviewing any complaint about prison life, on the assumption that prison administration was too technical for courts to comprehend.[24] The doctrine did have its detractors. As early as 1944, the Sixth Circuit wrote that "[a] prisoner retains all the rights of an ordinary citizen except those . . . taken from him by law."[25] But "hands-off" remained the majority view until the 1960s, when it was swept aside by two products of the civil rights era: mobilized, well-funded attorneys, and new judicial interest in how states treated their citizens.[26]

One of the most significant victories of this period may seem trivial at first glance. In 1962, the Supreme Court implied that the Eighth Amendment's ban on cruel and unusual punishment applied to the states—and state prisons.[27] This was revolutionary for the time. As originally understood, the Bill of Rights applied only to the *federal* government. While the Fourteenth Amendment nominally changed that, it took decades for the courts to work through the ramifications.[28]

The Eighth Amendment's sudden "incorporation" against the states meant citizens could protest "cruel and unusual punishment" at state *and* federal hands, significantly expanding the types of rights prisoners could win in court. Unique among other guarantees, the Eighth Amendment's prohibition on "cruel and unusual punishments" was meant to change with the times, and grow to incorporate those "evolving standards of decency that mark the progress of a maturing society."[29] This broad understanding means that courts handling Eighth Amendment claims could think creatively about prison conditions—within limits.

Perhaps unsurprisingly, such creativity allowed inmates to successfully use the courts to expand their education opportunities. Arkansas is where an Eighth Amendment claim, decades of litigation, and years of close judicial supervision finally led to the creation of the state's first prison education program.

HOLT V. SARVER: REFORM IN ARKANSAS

Arkansas's prisons in 1960 were some of the worst in the nation. After the Civil War, the state privatized their correctional system by "leasing" inmates to companies. Called "convict leasing," this system absolved the state of the need to pay for its prisoners' care. But "leased" inmates were treated little better than slaves.[30] Thankfully, Arkansas and the rest of the South gradually shifted away from convict leasing.[31]

But harsh conditions persisted. In 1960, most inmates were housed in one of two "farms"—Cummins Farm and Tucker Farm—where they lacked access to medical care and "were required to work in the fields six days per week, ten hours each day, planting, weeding, and harvesting the[ir] crops by hand."[32] They were not paid, and some were forced to sell their own blood to obtain necessities. Rape, drugs, and violence ran rampant.[33] Opportunities for education were "sporadic," unfunded, or nonexistent.[34] But they were sorely needed. One survey estimated that around three-quarters of Arkansas's prisoners had never finished high school.[35]

Progress began in 1965, when Arkansas inmates filed a pro se petition in federal court, arguing that such inhumane conditions entitled them to release. Rather than dismiss the claim out of hand, as most would have done in prior years, Judge J. Smith Henley of the Eastern District of Arkansas appointed two lawyers to represent the inmates. Dropping their clients' demand for release, the attorneys argued instead that Arkansas's prison conditions were so harsh as to deprive inmates of their Eighth Amendment rights.

After a token victory, more inmates filed petitions of their own, and the state began to take notice. A police report on Cummins Farm "documented institutionalized torture, near starvation diets, rampant violence, and widespread corruption."[36] Corrections officers held press conferences highlighting poor conditions in their own facilities, calling for funding to fix them. With the political consensus beginning to crystalize around reform, Judge Henley certified a group of inmate complaints as a class action.[37]

After a week-long trial, Judge Henley issued a decision in *Holt v. Sarver* ordering the state to correct unconstitutional disciplinary practices and overcrowding.[38] Addressing corrections officials *and* the legislature, which would need to provide additional funding, Judge Henley kept jurisdiction over the case so he could monitor compliance.[39] When the state failed to meet his expectations, the result was *Holt II*, a sweeping critique of Arkansas's prisons.

Rather than analyzing individual claims, such as the denial of dental or medical care, Judge Henley interpreted inmate complaints as a broadside attack on the entire state prison system—an assertion that "conditions and practices within the system are such that confinement there amounts to a cruel and unusual punishment"—and worked through each contributing factor.[40]

Significantly, *Holt II* dedicated an entire section to Arkansas's failure to provide inmates with education. First, Judge Henley applauded the goals of prison education and rehabilitation: "If a man who is ignorant and unskilled when he goes into prison can come out with some education and some usable skill, he has an improved chance of staying out of prison in the future." Otherwise, he wrote, "recidivism on his part is almost inevitable."[41] That did not necessarily mean that prisoners were legally entitled to an education. At least not in an ordinary prison system:

> This Court knows that a sociological theory or idea may ripen into constitutional law; many such theories and ideas have done so. But, this Court is not prepared to say that such a ripening has occurred as yet as far as rehabilitation of convicts is concerned. Given an otherwise unexceptional penal institution, the Court is not willing to hold that confinement in it is unconstitutional simply because the institution does not operate a school, or provide vocational training, or other rehabilitative facilities and services.[42]

But Arkansas's prisons were not, Judge Henley found, "otherwise unexceptional penal institution[s]." Instead, he concluded that "[t]he absence of an affirmative program of training and rehabilitation may have constitutional significance where[,] in the absence of such a program[,] conditions and practices exist which actually militate against reform and rehabilitation."[43]

[handwritten: lack of edu not dispositive, but a factor]

In other words, a prison's failure to provide schooling or training opportunities to its inmates "remains a factor in the overall constitutional equation," can "aggravate the more serious prison defects and deficiencies," and *contribute* to a finding that conditions violate the Eighth Amendment's ban on cruel and unusual punishment.[44]

Judge Henley went on to find that Arkansas operated its prison system in a way that violated the Eighth Amendment rights of its inmates, in part because it demonstrated no interest in inmates' rehabilitation. "It is one thing for the State to send a man to the Penitentiary as a punishment for crime. It is another thing for the State . . . to do nothing meaningful for his safety, well-being, and possible rehabilitation."[45]

At first blush, Judge Henley's finding seems like judicial opining, unconnected to the actual case outcome (what lawyers call "dicta"), and unlikely to prove enforceable even if pronounced as a rule of law. But the judgment was affirmed on appeal to the Eighth Circuit, which warned that "a federal court should be reluctant to interfere with the operation and discipline of a state prison" but wholeheartedly approved of the trial court's critical assessment of Arkansas's prison conditions.[46]

Judge Henley's decision to single out Arkansas's failure to provide an education to its inmates even drew a sympathetic concurrence. Judge Donald P. Lay noted that "[a]s far back as 1870 the American Prison Association recognized rehabilitation and moral regeneration, rather than vindictive retribution, to be the fundamental aims of correction." He would have held that "until immediate and continued emphasis is given to an affirmative program of rehabilitation the district court should retain jurisdiction" and supervise the prison's improvement.[47]

[handwritten: 1973 Arkansas Edu!]

The Eighth Circuit's decision vindicated Judge Henley's focus on rehabilitation. Better yet, it produced results. In 1973, Arkansas established a school district for prison inmates, something only recently attempted at the federal level, "for the purpose of providing elementary, secondary, and vocational technical education to all persons incarcerated in the Department who are not high school graduates, irrespective of age."[48]

Continuing adult education programs were also available, and students were expected to attend "four hours [of class] in the morning and four hours in the afternoon one day a week."[49] In 1976, Judge Henley commended the state for offering "extensive vocational training," as well as classes in automotive repair and even ceramics. "The educational program offered by [the prison system] is comparable," Judge Henley wrote, "to the program available in the public schools of the State. If a trustworthy inmate completes his high school education while an inmate of the Department, he can arrange to pursue his education at the college level if he desires to do so."[50]

[handwritten: Judge Henley]

This progress was not achieved overnight. It was the result of years of work, new funding, and outright lobbying by Judge Henley, who took an increasingly personal interest in reforming Arkansas's prisons. He spoke from the bench "directly to the legislature and governor" to demand new correctional funding.[51] He even toured Arkansas's prisons.

Other judges have done so in comparable cases,[52] though doing so technically breaks with the rule that judges should consider only facts placed before them in court.[53] Nonetheless, the higher courts encouraged this involvement. In 1973, Judge Henley tried to close his role in the case, but the Eighth Circuit ordered him to continue, applauding his efforts to correct the "sub-human environment" in Arkansas's prisons.[54]

After ten years of litigation, judicial supervision had remade Arkansas's prisons and helped enshrine prison education in state law.[55] By 1979, people in Arkansas's prisons read, on average, one grade level higher than inmates in other states.[56] Today, Arkansas retains an independent school district for its prisoners, funded from the state's general education budget, and requires all inmates with less than a high school education to attend.[57]

As of 2016, the most recent year with data available, the correctional school district had awarded around 23,000 GEDs.[58] Arkansas is currently funding the first comprehensive review of its correctional education program, evaluating its effects on both recidivism and post-release employment. Results are due in 2019.[59] Even if Arkansas's program proves merely average, it could show significant benefits and inspire further innovation.[60]

PUGH V. LOCKE: DIRECT INTERVENTION IN ALABAMA

Other courts soon learned from Judge Henley's example and used the Eighth Amendment to back expansive orders directing states to create or expand prison education. *Pugh v. Locke* in Alabama is another case in point. There, inmates across the state brought a class action challenging the conditions of their confinement. After surveying the grim state of Alabama prisons, from overcrowding to unsanitary food, the court found that Alabama prisoners were "denied any meaningful opportunity to participate in vocational, educational or work activities."[61] Instead, "most inmates must spend substantially all of their time crowded in dormitories in absolute idleness."[62]

While the average reading level of newly admitted prisoners was "below the sixth-grade level," and 59 percent were "unskilled," according to Chief Judge Frank M. Johnson, "[b]asic education classes [were] available to only a small number of inmates," and heavily restricted based on disciplinary record. One prison, "with more than 750 inmates, offer[ed] Adult Basic Education for only 40 inmates at any one time."[63]

At another, "an inmate conducts [the] only basic education class." Citing *Holt*, the court tied these failures back to the prisons' generally "inhumane" conditions: "even if rehabilitation programs, adequate in number and quality, were available, whatever benefit might be derived from them could be undone quickly by this inhumane environment."[64] A mandate to improve prison education was part and parcel of remedying the "massive constitutional infirmities which plague Alabama's prisons."[65]

To address it, the court directed Alabama to provide each inmate with "a meaningful job on the basis of the inmate's abilities and interests," "a vocational training program designed to teach a marketable skill," and "the opportunity to participate in basic educational programs."[66] As in *Holt*, this remedy seems far beyond the traditionally limited role of courts in resolving disputes. "It is with great reluctance that federal courts intervene in the day-to-day operation of state penal systems," the court acknowledged. But it is "a function they are increasingly required to perform."[67] Here, too, the appellate courts upheld *Pugh*'s far-reaching order. The Supreme Court even intervened but only to correct a minor matter of civil procedure. The order remained intact.[68]

LAAMAN V. HELGEMOE: REFORM IN NEW HAMPSHIRE

Moving beyond the South, a 1978 New Hampshire case, *Laaman v. Helgemoe*, exemplifies *Holt*'s effect on the legal landscape. In a lengthy opinion reviewing conditions at New Hampshire State Prison, the court claimed a duty to ensure that chances for rehabilitation through education (or otherwise) were available to every prisoner:

Thus far, no court has recognized a federal constitutional right to rehabilitation in the sense that an individual has a positive right to leave a penitentiary equipped to function as a law abiding member of society. However, there is a growing recognition that convicts have a right to be incarcerated in conditions that: [f]irst, do not threaten their sanity or mental well-being; [s]econd, are not counterproductive to the inmates' efforts to rehabilitate themselves; [t]hird, do not increase the probability of the inmates' future incarceration. This emergent right is based on the dual interests of society and the individual. It plainly defeats society's interests to cultivate recidivism.[69]

A decade after *Holt*, this idea was now on firm legal footing, as the federal district court's heavily cited opinion made clear. Applying that framework, the court dove deep into the education needs at New Hampshire prisons and concluded that state officials had failed to meet them. "In approximate figures," the court wrote, "70 [percent] of the inmates do not have a high school diploma or its equivalent; 35% have less than a ninth grade education; and only 2% have finished college."[70]

Higher and vocational education opportunities were also lacking. Although the prison had an auto repair trade school and an education department "responsive to" the needs of "60 percent of the inmate population," high school equivalency classes were "at capacity," and "[n]o college level courses currently exist at NHSP."[71]

Summarizing testimony, the court found that inmates had "expressed a desire to further their education but testified that the opportunities offered to them generally did not fit their needs."[72] Further, this deficit was within the court's power to correct. "Courts have not been hesitant to order prison administrations to institute and/or expand educational, vocational training, and work study and/or work release opportunities," the court surmised, again citing a long string of post-*Holt* cases.[73]

It went on to order a far-reaching reinvention of the state's correctional education program, including the creation of "[p]re-college and college level courses or, in the alternative, state funded college level correspondence courses."[74] Nor was this a fleeting victory: the state prison remained under court supervision through 2001.[75]

These are representative cases. More could be cited to show how far courts were willing to go in the 1970s and 1980s to strengthen prison education. Some, for example, applied the *Holt* analysis to jails. In Duval County, Florida, and Lucas County, Ohio, courts noted the lack of rehabilitative programs—for sentenced inmates and those awaiting trial alike—and ordered the creation of "basic and remedial education programs."[76] The need for education was, if anything, *stronger* in jails, the court wrote, since jails house people still entitled to a presumption of innocence.[77]

But not every court felt compelled to wade into the finer points of state correctional education.[78] In 1982, the Eighth Circuit affirmed a Nebraska federal court's conclusion that the absence of job opportunities for inmates, on its own, did not violate the Eighth Amendment. "It may well be good penology for state prisons to provide rehabilitative programs, including jobs, for inmates," the court held. "But no violation of the Constitution was made out on this record."[79]

Taken together, these cases show that in the wake of *Holt*, many federal courts were willing to use the Eighth Amendment as a tool to scrutinize prison conditions closely and, once enmeshed in the details of correctional administration, were prepared to order the creation of prison education programs to give those behind bars a shot at a better life. They show that courts can recognize the value of correctional education and have even helped expand it. Significantly, though, the Supreme Court was not a leader in this field. It took until 1974 for the Court to declare that "[t]here is no iron curtain drawn between the Constitution and the prisons of this country."[80]

That case, Wolff v. McDonnell, implicitly blessed a string of cases like *Holt*, where judges used the Eighth Amendment to order far-reaching evaluations of conditions in predominantly Southern prisons.[81] But for the most part, the Court was content to let the law of prisons evolve on its own. That meant victories like *Holt* and *Laaman* rested on a weak foundation, making them difficult to expand and unlikely to survive a changing political climate.

THE LIMITS OF FEDERAL CONSTITUTIONAL LAW

So far, we have seen only cases where courts ordered the creation or modernization of prison education programs to correct for other, more severe deficiencies. Can these cases be generalized? Are there tools prisoners can use, today, to argue in court for more and better education funding?

Regrettably, federal courts have resisted almost all attempts to constitutionalize a right to an education for prisoners. They have even pared back some rights. At a big-picture level, legislative backlash and judicial retrenchment have at times worked hand-in-hand.

Judicial backlash to prison reform started with a concern for cases that, like *Holt*, placed prisons under judicial supervision for years at a time. In 1979, then justice William Rehnquist sounded the first note of resistance, reversing an order against a federal jail and criticizing courts for "becom[ing] increasingly enmeshed in the minutiae of prison operations." He continued: "The inquiry of federal courts into prison management must be limited to the issue of whether a particular system violates any prohibition of the Constitution or, in the case of a federal prison, a statute."[82]

In 1981, the Supreme Court concluded in *Rhodes v. Chapman* that the denial of an education behind bars does not *on its own* violate the Eighth Amendment. While technically consistent with *Holt* and similar cases, *Rhodes* showed that courts would not go any further than they already had to expand prison education.[83]

Over the next decade, the Court pared back other rights extended to prisoners, too.[84] Then Congress joined in, passing the Anti-Terrorism and Effective Death Penalty Act and Prison Litigation Reform Act (PLRA). The former substantially curtails a defendant's ability to challenge the constitutionality of his conviction;[85] the latter makes complaints about prison conditions harder to file and easier to dismiss,[86] immediately impacting ongoing cases.[87]

Courts have ordered broad-sweeping prison reform at least once since the PLRA passed. One example is *Brown v. Plata*, where California was forced to remedy unconstitutional overcrowding by freeing nearly fifty thousand inmates. But that was a close case (decided 5–4) and addressed a relatively narrow issue: the denial of adequate medical care.[88] It also drew a withering dissent from Justice Scalia, who criticized judicial "factfinding-as-policymaking" and other "nonjudicial features of institutional reform litigation."[89]

Modern courts are now more careful about when and how to involve themselves in the conditions of state and federal prisons. That makes it questionable that a sweeping institutional reform case like *Holt* could succeed today. The days of years-long cases surveying every piece of prison life, and ending in broad remedial orders, may have passed.

DUE PROCESS AND STATE-BASED
CLAIMS TO EDUCATION IN PRISON

While the Eighth Amendment falls short, there are other legal guarantees to consider. What about the Due Process Clause, the most natural home for freestanding constitutional rights?

Regrettably, there is no constitutional right to an education, even outside prison. "Education is not among the rights afforded explicit protection under our Federal Constitution. Nor do we find any basis for saying it is implicitly so protected," the Supreme Court held in 1973.[90]

While inmates lack any *general* right to education, prisoners' rights advocates have been hard-pressed to argue that any *specific* right to education for inmates exists under the Due Process Clause. "So long as treatment, rehabilitation, and reformation services and facilities may not be demanded of the state as of [*sic*] right by her free citizens," one Alabama court concluded in 1974, "this Court is unpersuaded that such services may be demanded by convicted felons."[91] Claims premised on a *federal* right to correctional education seem doomed.[92]

That's not necessarily the end of the matter. Some states recognize a fundamental right to education.[93] And *Wolff v. McDonnell*, the Supreme Court case whose ringing language signaled the final death of the "hands-off" era, allowed prisoners to use the federal Due Process Clause to enforce rights created by state law, such as a right to early release through good behavior.[94]

Theoretically, *Wolff* (modified by *Hewitt v. Helms*, which refined its constitutional framework) could be used to stretch a state-created education right to benefit prisoners.[95] By citing a state right to education, inmates could theoretically challenge the adequacy of classes at their facility, as well as the arbitrary denials or closures that have prevented so many incarcerated students from finishing their education.[96]

In New York, this theory nearly worked. There, young people at Rikers Island, the city's infamous jail, sued based on the city's "failure to provide them with adequate general and special educational services" during their incarceration. State law provided for free public education; the argument was that this guarantee applied to all New Yorkers, incarcerated or not.[97] The district court agreed: "New York law grants class members a property right to a free and appropriate education. Under any reasonable interpretation of the relevant laws, defendants have prevented [young people incarcerated at Rikers] from enjoying this property right."[98]

In an inspiring defense of the value of education, the court actually ordered the city to provide schooling to Rikers inmates:

> This court cannot overstate the importance of education for youngsters in general but especially for youth whose encounters with the legal system have gained them membership in the plaintiff class. . . . The court has ordered defendants to devise a plan to ensure that the City defendants provide adequate educational services to inmates on Rikers Island in years to come. The better the educational services provided the greater the chance that the seeds of learning may bloom in prison air so that someday only ignorance will waste and wither there.[99]

Had this verdict stood, it would have offered a replicable model to advocates across the country: leverage state education law to force prisons and jails nationwide to extend schooling to, at a minimum, young people in the criminal justice system.

The Second Circuit disagreed. Focusing on a separate part of state law, one that provided an education specifically to incarcerated young people, the appellate court concluded that New York "treats youths who are incarcerated differently than those who are not," and that this distinction was constitutionally permissible.[100] (The reasons why are briefly explored later in this chapter.)

While New York's corrections law required that "each inmate shall be given a program of education which . . . seems most likely to further the process of socialization and rehabilitation," there was no constitutional entitlement to more extensive education while behind bars.[101] Simply put, absent a clear statement, the court would not assume that New York's general education law created a broad right to correctional education. Nor would it police the adequacy of existing education in an otherwise functioning jail system.

Similar results have played out across the country. As in New York, the absence of clear statutory language doomed a claim that incarcerated Arizonans were entitled to an education.[102] In California, federal courts have dismissed claims seeking access to prison education programs in perfunctory opinions.[103] A few cases have taken a closer look but, ultimately, reached the same conclusion, citing state law guarantees that were too vague to be stretched to cover prisoners.[104]

Changing Supreme Court law threatens to make these claims even more daunting. In 1995, the Court decided *Sandin v. Conner,* which questioned the very idea that prisoners could use the Due Process Clause to enforce rights "created" by state law. *Sandin* held that, instead, the Due Process Clause protects prisoners from the denial of a "liberty interest" only if its loss represents an "atypical and significant hardship on the inmate in relation to the ordinary incidents of prison life."[105]   *Relative to "ordinary prison life"*

Sandin also brought back some of the language originally used to justify the hands-off doctrine, criticizing "the involvement of federal courts in the day-to-day management of prisons" and opining that "federal courts ought to afford appropriate deference and flexibility to state officials trying to manage a volatile environment."[106]

It remains unclear how *Sandin* will affect prisoners hoping to use the courts to expand or enforce their rights to an education behind bars. *Sandin* by its terms applies only to prisoners' "liberty interests": more ephemeral, constitutionally based guarantees such as the right to be free from unreasonable disciplinary segregation.[107] It might not apply to "property interests"— the term for legal entitlements created directly by the government.[108] Even under *Sandin* prisoners may be able to *advocate* for state legislatures to expand prison education, creating a legal "property interest" in correctional education, and then *enforce* that interest in court.[109]

In fact, this is a promising option. Thanks to its clear statutory basis, if Arkansas's correctional education program were to arbitrarily shut down tomorrow, inmates could block such a capricious, unlawful closure in court.[110] Armed with similarly clear statutory entitlements to education, prisoners in other states could do the same. But this is a tacit acknowledgment that the law cannot on its own expand correctional education programs; a legal strategy must start with advocacy.

[margin note: have to first create prop. interest]

EQUAL PROTECTION AND THE PELL GRANT PROGRAM

Other constitutional guarantees have also fallen short, failing even to keep prison education programs running where they once existed. That was the lesson of the 1990s when determined litigants failed to stop Congress from cutting prisoners out of the Pell Grant program, shuttering prison classrooms nationwide.

By the 1960s, many states had established at least fledgling postsecondary schooling options for prisoners.[111] In 1965, another major funding stream opened up as prisoners became eligible for federal higher education grants (Pell Grants) if they met generally applicable, need-based criteria. Many prisoners did. And even though inmates received around 1 percent of total Pell Grant funding, by 1982, around 8 percent of state prison inmates were enrolled in a course of higher education, an expansion partially driven by grant eligibility.[112]

That changed when Congress passed the bipartisan Violent Crime Control and Law Enforcement Act of 1994, known as the "1994 crime bill."[113] Maligned for its contribution to the growth of mass incarceration, the 1994 crime bill also quietly changed life inside prisons, making "any individual who is incarcerated in any Federal or State penal institution" ineligible for a Pell Grant.[114] Like so many other theoretically "tough on crime" policies, this change

[margin note: 1994 crime bill]

was premised on fear and moral panic. "Some convicts have figured out that Pell [G]rants are a great scam," said Senator Kay Bailey Hutchison (R-TX), introducing the provision as an amendment in 1993. "Rob a store, go to jail, and get your degree." Senator Hutchison also claimed, falsely, that "Pell [G]rants claimed by convicts deprived about 100,000 law abiding kids of federal assistance."[115]

In the House, Representative Bart Gordon (D-TN) agreed: "Just because one blind hog may occasionally find an acorn does not mean many other blind hogs will. The same principle applies to giving Federal Pell grants to prisoners." He also offered the same false choice as Senator Hutchison, saying that "law-abiding students have every right to be outraged when a Pell [G]rant for a policeman's child is cut but a criminal that the officer sends to prison can still get a big check."[116]

Some attacked the amendment as an assault on prisoners' rights dressed up as a budgetary measure. "Denying Pell [G]rants [to] prisoners," said Representative Vic Fazio (D-CA), "may satisfy the public's demand to be tough on criminals, but is shortsighted and misguided."[117] But on September 13, 1994, the prohibition on correctional Pell Grants became law. Overnight, school and training programs had become unaffordable to many behind bars. "One academic year after the passage of the 1994 Crime Bill, the number of college-level programs in prisons decreased by 40 percent and the number of prisoners utilizing such programs, by 44 percent."[118] *A huge decrease in post-secondary edu*

Students moved quickly to block this threat to their futures, but two key court cases went nowhere. In the first, *Nicholas v. Riley,* a New York inmate, Jason B. Nicholas, sued the Federal Department of Education directly. Nicholas had been "enrolled in and attending college programs offered inside the prison by private colleges since 1992" and relied on Pell Grants.[119] He argued that blocking inmates from receiving critical federal help was an unnecessary attack on an already vulnerable group. As such, it violated the Equal Protection Clause.

Nicholas v Riley, EPC Rational Basis

From a moral standpoint, this is a compelling argument. As Senator Hutchison's remarks make clear, the motivation for stripping prisoners of Pell Grants had much to do with trumped-up claims of fraud and little to do with sober, even-handed budgeting.[120] This, Nicholas argued, is the kind of mean-spirited lawmaking the Constitution ought not permit. But the law was not on his side. While the Equal Protection Clause prevents "discrete and insular minorities" from being singled out for persecution, it does little to prevent the government from legislating the rights of non-"protected" groups based on their status.[121]

In legal terms, laws based on immutable traits like race or religion warrant "strict scrutiny," an exacting standard that few classifications survive.[122] Laws based on some other, more transient status, such as incarceration, need only be "rationally related to a legitimate state purpose."[123] This is not a searching inquiry because in applying a "rational basis" review, courts seek only *some* legal justification. If one is found, courts are forbidden to judge "the wisdom, fairness, or logic of legislative choices" of the justification—it is enough that one exists.[124]

Applying this well-settled framework, Washington, DC's federal district court rejected Nicholas's claim in a summary opinion. First, the court found that every judge to consider the matter has declined to treat incarcerated people as a "suspect" or a "protected class" insulated from government power.[125] Lacking that protection, the decision to strip prisoners of Pell Grant eligibility could be upheld "if any state of facts reasonably may be conceived to justify it."[126]

The court found that justification easily: "Whether because of budgetary constraints, the desire to increase the funding available to law-abiding students . . . [or] the notion that prisoners and non-prisoners are not similarly situated," Congress could lawfully end Pell Grants for state and federal prisoners.[127] Nicholas's remaining claims could not save his complaint, which was dismissed without ever going to trial.

Tremblay, ex post facto law! (handwritten)

A later claim met a similar end. Stephen Tremblay, another New York prisoner who would "no longer be able to take college courses" and "not be able to accumulate the 120 credit hours that he needs to receive a Bachelor's degree" without Pell Grants, took a more creative approach. He argued that stripping education funding from prisoners amounted to an ex post facto law: an unconstitutional punishment for past conduct.[128] As Tremblay saw it, blocking him from finishing college amounted to a new punishment for an old crime. This unconventional claim turned upon a simple question: Was the 1994 crime bill's rescission of Pell Grants "punishment" in the constitutional sense?[129] *Interesting* (handwritten)

New York's western federal court held that it was not. Finding that restricting Pell Grants was "motivated in part by concerns about the allocation of limited resources for higher education" and "temporary," since funding was restored upon release, the court disclaimed any need to further investigate Congress's motivations.[130] "I am not oblivious to the fact that this amendment was enacted as part of a crime bill, not an education bill. It may be that some members of Congress did see it as a punitive, 'tough on crime' measure."

But "'[j]udicial inquiries into Congressional motives are at best a hazardous matter, and when that inquiry seeks to go behind objective manifestations it becomes a dubious affair indeed.'"[131] Relying heavily on the *Nicholas* decision, the court went on to dismiss Tremblay's Equal Protection and Due Process claims and held that the denial of Pell Grants could not count as an Eighth Amendment violation either, since "the denial of Pell Grant funds is not punishment at all, much less cruel and unusual punishment."[132]

That was it. *Tremblay* would become another brick in a wall separating people behind bars from any legal entitlement to an education. It was cited in 1998 for the proposition that prisoners have no right to special education while behind bars.[133] Simply put, the Equal Protection Clause generally allows states to treat incarcerated students differently from others, and states have responded by outright exempting prisons from the state school system.[134]

To be sure, some of the assumptions of these cases could reasonably be questioned today. The Supreme Court increasingly second guesses the *true* motivations of laws that single out vulnerable groups.[135] "A law declaring that in general it shall be more difficult for one group of citizens than for all others to seek aid from the government is itself a denial of equal protection of the laws in the most literal sense," the Court wrote in 1996, striking down a law that would have exposed gay men and women to almost any form of discrimination.[136]

But this principle lies at the frontier of constitutional law, and it has its limits. It has only been applied to groups facing discrimination based on immutable traits, such as sexual orientation or mental illness, or political beliefs.[137] It seems unlikely that courts will extend the same scrutiny to a status like incarceration, which is temporary and bears some relationship to an orderly criminal justice system.

Since the 1980s, it seems no legal strategy, standing on its own, has successfully advanced the cause of prison education. "Once the very worse practices [of the prison system] were successfully attacked," summarize scholars Malcolm Feeley and Roger Hanson, "court-based action in other areas was more problematic."[138] Where does that leave advocates seeking to create or improve options for correctional education? What lessons can be learned from these cases?

CONCLUSION

Phrases such as "what works, and what doesn't" influence the legal landscape when it comes to criminal justice reform. Institutional reform cases like *Holt v. Sarver* changed the landscape of

American corrections, sweeping in lasting advances in prison education. But they also tested the limits of the federal judiciary and depended on a unique (and hard to replicate) set of circumstances. Worse, for our purposes, they left little trace on the law. When the Supreme Court intervened, it largely looked the other way, allowing advocates to win through "salutary neglect" what they might not have been able to win through strict application of legal doctrine. To continue expanding correctional education through the courts, then, we may have to look elsewhere.

One option is to play within the traditional rules of the courts. Traditionally, judges strive to avoid embroiling themselves in bold, sweeping cases that (like *Holt v. Sarver*) threaten to entangle them in the day-to-day work of governing or veer into policy making. Instead, judges limit themselves to adjudicating discrete, isolated issues through the application of clearly established rules.[139]

As we have seen, those clearly established rules tend to work *against* efforts to expand correctional education. Neither the Equal Protection Clause nor the Due Process Clause are enough to support a right to prison education on their own. But the law could be used to support a broader strategy, one focused on *establishing* prison education programs in the legislatures, and then *enforcing* a right to those programs, or ensuring their adequacy, in the courts. This approach has the advantage of avoiding the 1990s-era backlash to prisoners' rights litigation, though it envisions courts as just one part of a broader advocacy strategy.

Alternately, advocates can work to change the way the law views correctional education. Today, the Eighth Amendment does not require states to give inmates a chance for education or self-improvement during their incarceration.[140] But the Eighth Amendment was also designed to change with the times: to incorporate the "evolving standards of decency that mark the progress of a maturing society."[141] With broad support from advocates, inmates, and the culture as a whole, the value and importance of correctional education could, as Judge Henley wrote in *Holt v. Sarver*, "ripen into constitutional law" and become a constitutional imperative.[142]

This would take time; expanding the Eighth Amendment to incorporate some legal right to rehabilitation generally, and education specifically, would require an almost complete rethinking of the way the law relates to American prisons. And judges aren't the best moralists.[143] With data showing the value of correctional education to inmates, to public safety, and to society as a whole, though, some incremental progress might be made. Courts once understood the value of not giving up on those confined in our nation's prisons. In time, they can be made to understand again.

NOTES

1. Danielle Kaeble and Lauren Glaze, *Correctional Populations in the United States, 2015*, Bureau of Justice Statistics, 2016, https://www.bjs.gov/content/pub/pdf/cpus15.pdf; and E. Ann Carson, *Prisoners in 2016*, Bureau of Justice Statistics, 2018, https://www.bjs.gov/index.cfm?ty=pbdetail&iid=6187.

2. For recent estimates of the number of people who have been to prison or affected by the criminal justice system, see Sarah Shannon, Christopher Uggen, Jason Schnittker, Michael Massoglia, Melissa Thompson, and Sara Wakefield, "The Growth, Scope, and Spatial Distribution of People with Felony Records in the United States, 1948–2010," *Demography* 54 (2017): 1796–97, http://users.soc.umn.edu/~uggen/Shannon_Uggen_DEM_2017.pdf. For analysis of the economic cost of incarceration, see Cherri Bucknor and Alan Barber, *The Price We Pay: Economic Costs of Barriers to Employment for Former Prisoners and People Convicted of Felonies*, Center for Economic and Policy Research, 2016,

1, http://cepr.net/publications/reports/the-price-we-pay-economic-costs-of-barriers-to-employment-for -former-prisoners-and-people-convicted-of-felonies. For a government perspective on the same issue, see President's Council of Economic Advisers, *Economic Perspectives on Incarceration and the Criminal Justice System*, April 23, 2016, 41–47, https://obamawhitehouse.archives.gov/sites/default/files/page/ files/20160423_cea_incarceration_criminal_justice.pdf.

3. See, for example, Edgardo Rotman, "The Failure of Reform: United States, 1865–1965," in *The Oxford History of the Prison: The Practice of Punishment in Western Society*, edited by Norval Morris and David J. Rothman (New York: Oxford University Press, 1998), 174–76, 184. See also Lois M. Davis et al., *Evaluating the Effectiveness of Correctional Education: A Meta-Analysis of Programs That Provide Education to Incarcerated Adults* (Santa Monica, CA: RAND Corporation, 2013), 4, https://www.rand. org/pubs/research_reports/RR266.html.

4. President's Commission on Law Enforcement and the Administration of Justice, *The Challenge of Crime in a Free Society* (Washington, DC: Government Printing Office, 1967), 173.

5. President's Commission on Law Enforcement and the Administration of Justice, *The Challenge of Crime in a Free Society*, 175.

6. Robert Martinson, "What Works? Questions and Answers about Prison Reform," *Public Interest* 35 (1974): 48–50.

7. Rachel E. Barkow, "The Court of Life and Death: The Two Tracks of Constitutional Sentencing Law and the Case for Uniformity," *Michigan Law Review* 107 (2009): 1145.

8. Robert Martinson, "New Findings, New Views: A Note of Caution regarding Sentencing Reform," *Hofstra Law Review* 7 (1979): 252–54; and Francis T. Cullen, "The Twelve People Who Saved Rehabilitation: How the Science of Criminology Made a Difference," *Criminology* 43, no. 1 (2005): 1–10.

9. Donald F. Tibbs, *From Black Power to Prison Power: The Making of* Jones v. North Carolina Prisoners' Labor Union (New York: Palgrave Macmillan, 2012), 107–12.

10. Eric Cummins, *The Rise and Fall of California's Radical Prison Movement* (Stanford, CA: Stanford University Press, 1994), 201. See also *The Folsom Prisoners Manifesto of Demands and Anti-Oppression Platform*, accessed September 8, 2017, https://www.freedomarchives.org/Documents/Finder/DOC510_ scans/Folsom_Manifesto/510.folsom.manifesto.11.3.1970.pdf.

11. Heather Ann Thompson, *Blood in the Water: The Attica Prison Uprising of 1971 and Its Legacy* (New York: Penguin Random House, 2017), 31–37.

12. Herman Badillo and Milton Haynes, *A Bill of No Rights: Attica and the American Prison System* (New York: Outerbridge & Lazard, 1972), 65.

13. Thompson, *Blood in the Water*, 7–17.

14. Thompson, *Blood in the Water*, 79–80, 111–26.

15. Thompson, *Blood in the Water*, 28–29.

16. Robert B. McKay et al., *Attica: The Official Report of the New York State Special Commission on Attica* (New York: Bantam Books, 1972), 29, 40–42.

17. McKay et al., *Attica*, 28–29, 41.

18. McKay et al., *Attica*, 41.

19. McKay et al., *Attica*, 21, 33, 40–42.

20. Badillo and Haynes, *A Bill of No Rights*, 60, 67. By 1971, nearly 9 percent of Attica's inmates were Spanish speaking; and McKay et al., *Attica*, 3.

21. Thompson, *Blood in the Water*, 7–17.

22. *Ruffin v. Commonwealth*, 62 Va. 790, 796 (1871).

23. *Atterbury v. Ragen*, 237 F.2d 953, 955 (7th Cir. 1956), *cert. denied*, 353 U.S. 964 (1957); *accord Banning v. Looney*, 213 F.2d 771, 771 (10th Cir. 1954) ("Courts are without power to supervise prison administration or to interfere with the ordinary prison rules or regulations"), *cert. denied*, 348 U.S. 859 (1954).

24. "Beyond the Ken of the Courts: A Critique of Judicial Refusal to Review the Complaints of Convicts," *Yale Law Journal* 72 (1963): 506–9, 515–16.

25. *Coffin v. Reichard*, 143 F.2d 443, 445 (6th Cir. 1944).

26. Michael B. Mushlin, 1 Rights of Prisoners § 1:4 (West 2016); and Malcolm M. Feeley and Edward L. Rubin, *Judicial Policy Making and the Modern State: How the Courts Reformed America's Prisons* (Cambridge: Cambridge University Press, 1998), 36–39.

27. *Robinson v. California*, 370 U.S. 660, 675 (1962) (Douglas, J., concurring).

28. See, generally, Akhil Reed Amar, *America's Constitution: A Biography* (New York: Random House, 2005).

29. *Trop v. Dulles*, 356 U.S. 86, 101 (1958). See also *Estelle v. Gamble*, 429 U.S. 97, 99–103 (1976) ("Our more recent cases, however, have held that the Amendment proscribes more than physically barbarous punishments"). Of course, whether other constitutional provisions should also evolve along with our society is one of the longest-running questions in constitutional law, one that animates debates about everything from abortion to civil procedure. See, for example, *Burnham v. Superior Court of California*, 495 U.S. 604, 622–28 (1990) (Scalia, J.) (asking "whether changes are to be adopted as progressive by the American people or decreed as progressive by the Justices of this Court") and id. at 628–40 (Brennan, J., concurring). I do not mean to take a side in this debate—only to note the Eighth Amendment's unique place in the constitutional structure, as an amendment explicitly tied to subjective notions of "cruelty" and morality.

30. Calvin R. Ledbetter Jr., "The Long Struggle to End Convict Leasing in Arkansas," *Arkansas Historical Quarterly* 52, no. 1 (1993): 1–9.

31. Ledbetter, "The Long Struggle to End Convict Leasing in Arkansas," 3, 20; and Malcolm M. Feeley, "The Significance of Prison Conditions Cases: Budgets and Regions," *Law & Society Review* 23, no. 2 (1989): 278–79.

32. Feeley and Rubin, *Judicial Policy Making*, 53.

33. Feeley and Rubin, *Judicial Policy Making*, 51–55.

34. William V. Glover III, "Successfully Implementing a Full Mandatory Attendance Policy in the Arkansas Department of Correction School District," *Journal of Correctional Education* 53, no. 3 (2002): 102.

35. The earliest such survey dates to 1974, the year after broad educational programing came to Arkansas's prisons. Accordingly, this figure likely *overestimates* educational attainment among Arkansas inmates. See National Archive of Criminal Justice Data, Survey of Inmates of State Correctional Facilities and Census of State Adult Correctional Facilities, 1974 (ICPSR 7811), last accessed October 24, 2017, https://www.icpsr.umich.edu/icpsrweb/NACJD/studies/7811. Variables examined were VAR274 and VAR275, signifying pre-incarceration high school and college educational attainment.

36. Feeley and Rubin, *Judicial Policy Making*, 58.

37. Feeley and Rubin, *Judicial Policy Making*, 55–59.

38. See *Holt v. Sarver* ("*Holt II*"), 309 F. Supp. 362, 367–69 (E.D. Ark. 1970) (summarizing prior case history).

39. Feeley and Rubin, *Judicial Policy Making*, 59–61.

40. *Holt II*, 309 F. Supp. at 364.

41. *Holt II*, 309 F. Supp. at 379.

42. *Holt II*, 309 F. Supp. at 379.

43. *Holt II*, 309 F. Supp. at 379.

44. *Holt II*, 309 F. Supp. at 379–80.

45. *Holt II*, 309 F. Supp. at 381.

46. *Holt v. Sarver* ("*Holt III*"), 442 F.2d 304, 307, 309 (8th Cir. 1971).

47. *Holt III*, 442 F.2d at 310 & n.2 (Lay, J., concurring).

48. Act of March 9, 1973, No. 279, 1973–74 Ark. Acts 882–83 (1974). For the modern federal attempt at a similar reform, see "Justice Department Announces Reforms at Bureau of Prisons to Reduce Recidivism and Promote Inmate Rehabilitation," US Department of Justice, November 30, 2016, https://www.justice.gov/opa/pr/justice-department-announces-reforms-bureau-prisons-reduce-recidivism-and-promote-inmate.

49. *Rutherford v. Hutto*, 377 F. Supp. 268, 270–72 (E.D. Ark. 1974).

50. *Finney v. Hutto*, 410 F. Supp. 251, 262 (E.D. Ark. 1976).

51. Feeley and Rubin, *Judicial Policy Making*, 68–74.

52. Bradley S. Chilton and Susette M. Talarico, "Politics and Constitutional Interpretation in Prison Reform Litigation: The Case of *Guthrie v. Evans*," in *Courts, Corrections, and the Constitution: The Impact of Judicial Intervention on Prisons and Jails*, ed. John DiIulio (New York: Oxford University Press, 1990), 120–21.

53. Chilton and Talarico, "Politics and Constitutional Interpretation," 120–21. For the general rule about when, and how rarely, judges can consider facts not presented by the parties before them, see *Federal Rules of Evidence* 201 (governing when a judge may take "judicial notice of adjudicative facts").

54. *Finney v. Arkansas Bd. of Correction*, 505 F.2d 194, 215 (8th Cir. 1974). See also Feeley and Rubin, *Judicial Policy Making*, 69.

55. Ark. Code. 12-29-301 *et sequens* (2017).

56. Hurshell Qualls, "Arkansas Department of Correction School District Tutorial Reading Program," *Journal of Correctional Education* 30, no. 1 (1979): 15–16.

57. Ark. Code. 12-29-301 *et sequens* (2017); and Glover, "Successfully Implementing a Full Mandatory Attendance Policy," 101–5. For services continuing through today, see "Re-Entry Events," Arkansas Department of Corrections, accessed October 17, 2017, http://adc.arkansas.gov/facilities/facilities5.html.

58. "ADM/GED Stats," Arkansas Correctional School, accessed October 22, 2017, https://www.arkcs.arkansas.gov/aboutus/ged_stats.html.

59. Dr. Kevin M. Roessger, PhD, discussion with the author, October 20, 2017.

60. Davis et al., *Evaluating the Effectiveness of Correctional Education*, 33, 39–40, 47.

61. *Pugh v. Locke*, 406 F. Supp. 318, 322–23 (M.D. Ala. 1976).

62. *Pugh*, 406 F. Supp. at 326.

63. *Pugh*, 406 F. Supp. at 326.

64. *Pugh*, 406 F. Supp. at 325–27.

65. *Pugh*, 406 F. Supp. at 328.

66. *Pugh*, 406 F. Supp. at 335.

67. *Pugh*, 406 F. Supp. at 328 & n.12.

68. *Alabama v. Pugh*, 438 U.S. 781, 782–83 (1978) (Stevens, J., dissenting).

69. *Laaman v. Helgemoe*, 437 F. Supp. 269, 295–96 (D. N.H. 1977) (emphasis added, internal citations omitted).

70. *Laaman*, 437 F. Supp. at 295.

71. *Laaman*, 437 F. Supp. at 275–76, 295–96.

72. *Laaman*, 437 F. Supp. at 295–96.

73. *Laaman*, 437 F. Supp. at 318.

74. *Laaman*, 437 F. Supp. at 330.

75. See *Laaman v. New Hampshire State Prison*, 238 F.3d 14 (1st Cir. 2001) (vacating and remanding a trial court order that would have terminated a 1990s consent decree).

76. *Jones v. Wittenberg*, 330 F. Supp. 707, 717 (N.D. Ohio 1977); and *Miller v. Carson*, 330 F. Supp. 707, 899–901 (M.D. Fla. 1975).

77. *Miller*, 330 F. Supp. at 900.

78. See, for example, *Laaman*, 437 F. Supp. at 315–19 (collecting authorities).

79. *Byrd v. Vitek*, 689 F.2d 770, 711 (8th Cir. 1982).

80. *Wolff v. McDonnell*, 418 U.S. 539, 555–56 (1974).

81. Feeley and Rubin, *Judicial Policy Making*, 38–44.

82. *Bell v. Wolfish*, 441 U.S. 520, 562 (1979).

83. See *Rhodes v. Chapman*, 452 U.S. 337, 348 (1981).

84. Feeley and Rubin, *Judicial Policy Making*, 48–50.

85. See, for example, 28 U.S.C. § 2254(d)(1) (requiring the denial of federal post-conviction relief to state defendants unless a state court decision "resulted in a decision that was contrary to, or involved

an unreasonable application of, clearly established Federal law, as determined by the Supreme Court of the United States").

86. See 42 U.S. Code § 1997e(a) (requiring prisoners to "exhaust" administrative remedies before filing a federal claim).

87. Stacey Heather O'Bryan, "Note: Closing the Courthouse Door: The Impact of the Prison Litigation Reform Act's Physical Injury Requirement on the Constitutional Rights of Prisoners," *Virginia Law Review* 83 (1997): 1189–93.

88. See *Brown v. Plata*, 563 U.S. 493, 499–509 (2011) (providing background to the case and underlying constitutional violations).

89. See *Brown v. Plata*, 563 U.S. 493, 555–56, 562–63 (2011) (Scalia, J., dissenting).

90. *San Antonio Indep. Sch. Dist. v. Rodriguez*, 411 U.S. 1, 35 (1973). Significantly, Justice Brennan took issue with this holding, viewing education as "inextricably linked to the right to participate in the electoral process and to the rights of free speech and association guaranteed by the First Amendment," and therefore of constitutional significance. Id. at 63 (Brennan, J., dissenting). See, generally, Charles J. Ogletree Jr. and Kimberly Jenkins Robinson, eds., *The Enduring Legacy of Rodriquez: Creating New Pathways to Equal Educational Opportunity* (Cambridge, MA: Harvard Education Press, 2015).

91. *James v. Wallace*, 382 F. Supp. 1177, 1180 (M.D. Ala. 1974).

92. See Christine D. Ely, "A Criminal Education: Arguing for Adequacy in Adult Correctional Facilities," *Columbia Human Rights Law Review* 39 (2008): 811–15.

93. See, generally, Allen W. Hubsch, "The Emerging Right to Education under State Constitutional Law," *Temple Law Review* 65 (1992): 1325.

94. *Wolff*, 418 U.S. at 556–58.

95. *Hewitt v. Helms*, 459 U.S. 460, 468–69 (1983).

96. See, for example, Susan Burton and Cari Lynn, *Becoming Ms. Burton: From Prison to Recovery to Leading the Fight for Incarcerated Women* (New York: New Press 2017).

97. *Handberry v. Thompson* ("*Handberry I*"), 92 F. Supp.2d 244, 245–48 (S.D.N.Y. 2000) (citing N.Y. Educ. Law 3205).

98. *Handberry I*, 92 F. Supp.2d at 249.

99. *Handberry I*, 92 F. Supp.2d at 249.

100. *Handberry v. Thompson* ("*Handberry II*"), 446 F.3d 335, 354 (2006) (citing N.Y. Educ. L. § 3202[7]).

101. *Handberry II*, 446 F.3d at 354.

102. *Mayer v. Bishop*, 972 F.2d 1340, 1340 (1992) ("Here, it does not appear that Arizona has created a liberty interest in employment or education programs for prisoners").

103. *Gilbert v. Alameda County of California Sheriff*, 2011 WL 2183166, at *1 (N.D. Cal. June 2, 2011); *Brucs v. Ducart*, 2010 WL 4314727, at *1–2 (N.D. Cal. October 25, 2010).

104. *Wimbley v. Borg*, 972 F.2d 1348, 1348 & n.1 (9th Cir. 1992); and *Estrada v. Gomez*, 1995 WL 581148, at *3–4 (N.D. Cal. September 13, 1995).

105. *Sandin v. Conner*, 515 U.S. 472, 483–84 (1995) (Rehnquist, C. J.).

106. *Sandin*, 515 U.S. at 482–83.

107. See, generally, Kaitlin Cassel, "Note: Due Process in Prison: Protecting Inmates' Property after *Sandin v. Conner*," *Columbia Law Review* 112 (2012): 2110–24.

108. Charles A. Reich, "The New Property," *Yale Law Journal* 73 (1964): 734–37.

109. See, generally, Cassel, "Due Process in Prison," 2110–24, 2144–48.

110. Ark. Code. 12-29-301 *et sequens* (2017).

111. Thom Gehring, "Post-Secondary Education for Inmates: An Historical Inquiry," *Journal of Correctional Education* 48, no. 2 (1997): 49.

112. Mary C. Wright, "Pell Grants, Politics and the Penitentiary: Connections between the Development of U.S. Higher Education and Prisoner Post-Secondary Programs," *Journal of Correctional Education* 52, no. 1 (2001): 14; and Gehring, "Post-Secondary Education for Inmates," 48, 53.

113. Violent Crime Control and Law Enforcement Act of 1994, Pub. L. No. 103-322, 108 Stat. 196 (codified as amended in scattered sections of 42 U.S.C.).

114. Violent Crime Control and Law Enforcement Act of 1994, Pub. L. No. 103-322, § 20411, 108 Stat. 1796, 1828 (current version at 20 U.S.C. § 1070a[b][6]). For the bill's legacy, see Lauren-Brooke Eisen and Inimai M. Chettiar, "Analysis: The Complex History of the Controversial 1994 Crime Bill," MSNBC, April 14, 2016, http://www.msnbc.com/msnbc/analysis-the-complex-history-the-controversial-1994-crime-bill.

115. 139 Cong. Rec. 28,449 (1993) (statement of Sen. Hutchison). Hutchinson's statement is disputed in SpearIt, "The Return of Pell Grants for Prisoners," *American Bar Association Criminal Justice Magazine* 31 (2016): 10 (citing research by the General Accounting Office that "If incarcerated students received no Pell grants, no student currently denied a Pell award would have received one").

116. 140 Cong. Rec. H2,544 (daily ed. April 20, 1994) (statement of Rep. Gordon).

117. 140 Cong. Rec. H8,989 (daily ed. August 21, 1994) (statement of Rep. Fazio).

118. Wright, "Pell Grants, Politics and the Penitentiary," 14.

119. *Nicholas v. Riley*, 874 F. Supp. 10 (D.D.C. 1995), *aff'd* 1995 WL 686227 (DC Cir. October 10, 1995).

120. Wright, "Pell Grants, Politics and the Penitentiary," 14.

121. *United States v. Carolene Products Co.*, 304 U.S. 144, 152n4 (1938). The *Carolene* Court was the first to propose a distinction between invidious racial discrimination and the ordinary government business of classifying and regulating (for example) different types of businesses or products. See William D. Araiza, "Deference to Congressional Fact-Finding in Rights-Enforcing and Rights-Limiting Legislation," *NYU Law Review* 88 (2013): 911.

122. *Fullilove v. Klutznick*, 448 U.S. 448, 507 (1980) (Powell, J., concurring) ("Indeed, the failure of legislative action to survive strict scrutiny has led some to wonder whether our review of racial classifications has been strict in theory, but fatal in fact"), overruled by *Adarand Constructors, Inc. v. Pena*, 515 U.S. 200 (1995).

123. *Nicholas*, 874 F. Supp. at 12–13.

124. *FCC v. Beach Communications*, 508 U.S. 307, 313 (1993).

125. *Nicholas*, 874 F. Supp. at 12–13 (citing *Jones v. Grundewarld*, 644 F. Supp. 256, 259 (S.D.N.Y. 1986). This remains true today. See *Saunders v. Vinton*, 554 F. App'x 36, 38 (2d Cir. 2014); and *Boivin v. Black*, 225 F.3d 36, 42 (1st Cir. 2000) (collecting cases).

126. *Nicholas*, 874 F. Supp. at 12–13.

127. *Nicholas*, 874 F. Supp. at 13.

128. U.S. Const., Art. I., § 9, cl. 3.

129. *Tremblay v. Riley*, 917 F. Supp. 195, 196 (W.D.N.Y. 1996).

130. *Tremblay*, 917 F. Supp. at 198–99.

131. *Tremblay*, 917 F. Supp. at 199 (quoting *Flemming v. Nestor*, 363 U.S. 603, 617 [1960]).

132. *Tremblay*, 917 F. Supp. at 198–202.

133. *Giano v. Cuomo*, No. 94-CV-809, 1998 WL 760262, at *5–6 (N.D.N.Y. October 28, 1998).

134. See Ely, "A Criminal Education," 819 and n120, 826–28 (citing *Tunstall ex rel. Tunstall v. Bergeson*, 5 P.3d 691 [Wash. 2000]).

135. See, generally, Austin Raynor, "Note: Economic Liberty and the Second-Order Rational Basis Test," *Virginia Law Review* 99 (2013): 1065–1102.

136. *Romer v. Evans*, 517 U.S. 620, 633 (1996).

137. Raynor, "Note: Economic Liberty and the Second-Order Rational Basis Test," 1081–82, supra note 129 (interpreting *U.S. Dep't of Agric. v. Moreno*, 413 U.S. 528, 533–38 [1973], and *City of Cleburne, Tex. v. Cleburne Living Ctr.*, 473 U.S. 432, 447–48 [1985], as applying heightened rational basis to, respectively, a public benefit restriction allegedly designed to burden "hippie" communes, and a zoning restriction burdening a home for the mentally ill).

138. Malcolm M. Feeley and Roger A. Hanson, "The Impact of Judicial Intervention on Prisons and Jails: A Framework for Analysis and a Review of the Literature," in *Courts, Corrections, and the*

Constitution: The Impact of Judicial Intervention on Prisons and Jails, ed. John DiIulio (New York: Oxford University Press, 1990), 28.

139. See Burt Neuborne, "Judicial Review and the Separation of Powers in France and the United States," *NYU Law Review* 57 (1982): 370 (describing the American judicial function as "the particularization of rules to specific fact situations in the context of resolving disputes between parties"); and Herbert Wechsler, "Toward Neutral Principles of Constitutional Law," *Harvard Law Review* 73 (1959): 6 ("Only when the standing law, decisional or statutory, provides a remedy to vindicate the interest that demands protection against an infringement of the kind that is alleged, a law of remedies that ordinarily at least is framed in reference to rights and wrongs in general, do courts have any business asking what the Constitution may require or forbid, and only then when it is necessary for decision of the case that is at hand").

140. See *Rhodes v. Chapman,* 452 U.S. 337, 348 (1981).

141. *Trop v. Dulles,* 356 U.S. 86, 101 (1958).

142. *Holt II,* 309 F. Supp. at 379.

143. Consider, for example, Jeremy Waldron's critique of judicial review and its tendency to avoid, rather than enhance, the moral dimensions of a policy debate. Jeremy Waldron, "The Core of the Case against Judicial Review," *Yale Law Journal* 115 (2006): 1382–86. See also Richard H. Fallon Jr., "The Core of an Uneasy Case for Judicial Review," *Harvard Law Review* 121 (2008): 1697–98 (conceding Waldron's point) ("As Waldron points out, courts have an understandable tendency to confront issues that are fundamentally moral in legalistic, logic-chopping terms in which head-on engagement with the contending moral considerations often is almost wholly washed out").

6

Young Men's Initiative

Nine Lessons for Elected Officials, Investors, and Criminal Justice Advocates

Linda Gibbs

As Michael Bloomberg started his last term as mayor of New York City in January 2010, he challenged his leadership team to make the most of the opportunity to lead the city for the upcoming four years. The worst threat of the Great Recession of 2008 had passed; yet the city was still struggling to reboot the economy and assist those hardest hit by the job losses. Our city needed a solution.

As the city's deputy mayor for health and human services (HHS), I managed a multibillion-dollar portfolio that oversaw public assistance, mental health, and homeless service, as well as the departments of corrections, probation, and juvenile justice. A major focus of HHS was on programs that would positively impact our most challenged communities—poor youth in New York City, particularly young men of color.

Citywide unemployment had doubled from 4.3 percent to 8.8 percent in early 2010. For young men of color, unemployment skyrocketed from 14.8 percent to 24.6 percent.[1] These economically challenging times exacerbated the barriers faced by youth in city neighborhoods and impacted their education and social lives. In a State of the City speech delivered that January, Mayor Bloomberg laid out the facts:

> Just think about this: Across the five boroughs, black and Latino young men have a poverty rate that is 50 percent higher than white and Asian young men. Their rate of unemployment is 60 percent higher. They are two times more likely not to graduate from high school, far more likely to become a teen father and—most troubling of all—more than 90 percent of all young murder victims and perpetrators are black and Latino.[2]

Mayor Bloomberg then asked of his leadership team and city residents:

> How can we help those who've been hit hardest by these hard times[?] . . . How can we connect Black and Hispanic young people—especially young men—to the opportunities and support that can lead them to success and allow them to participate in our recovery?[3]

With this goal in mind, the Young Men's Initiative (YMI) was born.

Officially launched in August 2011, YMI was a cross-agency project charged with the responsibility to look across all sectors—education, health, employment, and criminal justice—

97

PURPOSE:

to understand the nature of disparities between black and Latino young men and their white peers, and to develop promising public-private strategies to alleviate those disparities. Within the YMI, which invested $127 million over four years in forty separate initiatives, HHS and its partners pioneered the nation's first Social Impact Bond (SIB) to test a justice reform initiative targeted to one of society's most challenging populations—incarcerated youth.

Like the entire nation, New York City exhibits some of the deepest disparities in outcomes for young men of color in the justice system. In 2014, 22.5 percent of young black men ages sixteen to twenty-four had a misdemeanor arrest, compared to less than 5 percent of their white peers. Young black men were thirty-five times more likely to go to juvenile detention, and ten times more likely to go jail, than their white peers.[4] A significant part of the YMI was committed to addressing the needs of justice-involved youth through prevention, rehabilitation, and support upon their return to the community.

Reforms ranged from a fundamental redesign of the entire juvenile justice system, a repurposing of probation from a monitoring approach into a youth-centered resource coordination and support, to reentry employment investments. And in true Bloomberg fashion, the initiative was accompanied by a demand for clear and measurable outcomes to understand what works and what does not, a commitment to expand efforts showing success, and a call to discontinue those that did not.

Many of the YMI's justice efforts focused on community supports for young people after incarceration. At the same time, the team also believed it had an opportunity to work more effectively with young people while they were still in jail to reduce the chances they would reoffend upon release. In particular, YMI wanted to make a special effort to improve the experience of young men ages sixteen to eighteen who were housed in the adolescent wing of the New York City adult correctional facility named Rikers Island.[5]

 Rikers Island sits in the mouth of the Long Island Sound between the boroughs of Queens and the mainland of the Bronx, just north of La Guardia Airport. It is a complex of multiple jail facilities managed by the New York City Department of Corrections (DOC). It houses around eight thousand of the total ten thousand inmates in the New York City jail system—including adolescents—who in other states would be housed in developmentally appropriate juvenile justice facilities instead of an adult correctional facility. Eight-five percent of inmates on the island are being held pending resolution of charges against them. The remainder are serving sentences of one year or less.

Outcomes for young men of color who spend time at Rikers are shockingly bad. Nearly half of the young men at Rikers in 2013 returned to jail within one year.[6] Nationally, an incarceration during adolescence decreases lifetime earnings by as much as 30 percent.[7] The purpose of this YMI initiative was to determine whether a different approach could change these poor outcomes and disrupt the pattern of rearrest and re-incarceration for those who served time at Rikers. As Mayor Bloomberg asked, how do we put the *corrections* back into "Corrections"?

With this question in mind, our team set out to create a new psycho-therapeutic approach to improve the social and emotional decision making of young men during their school days at Rikers.

USING THE EVIDENCE TO CREATE THE INTERVENTION

At the time YMI was starting at Rikers, DOC already incorporated many innovative approaches to assist young men during their incarceration. These included the introduction of

Rikers interventions

an on-island, credit-bearing school; skill training and employment preparation; and discharge planning and coordination integrated into the daily activities of those at Rikers.

We decided to take a hard look at these interventions and determine what was working and whether there were opportunities for improvement. This assessment included a literature review of evidence-based practices that were proven to reduce recidivism for young adults, particularly men of color.

CBT :

Through the research, we were drawn to the successful use of Cognitive Behavioral Therapy (CBT) for justice-involved youth because of the strong evidence that complemented the traditional skills and education that many prison reformers had already adopted. CBT started more than fifty years ago as an intervention to help with depression. It has since expanded to cover eating disorders, smoking cessation, and anxiety, in addition to other mental health disorders. At the time, many jurisdictions were documenting success with the use of CBT for justice-involved youth, and we were taking note.

CBT is a form of psychotherapy that emphasizes the importance of how people think in influencing how they feel and what they do. CBT therapists believe that clients can learn how to think differently and act on that thinking to reverse negative behaviors.[8] Because there were a full range of education, training, and discharge services already in effect at Rikers, layering on a new approach to complement and strengthen the impact of these other services was appealing. Across a number of applications of CBT, research has demonstrated that participants exhibit a significantly lower likelihood of being re-incarcerated after a stay in jail or prison.

PROS : As the assessment was made, there were several attractive features of this intervention. First, it could be done in a group (rather than one on one), and the group did not have to have the same membership over time. This lowered costs for implementation, and allowing the entire adolescent population on Rikers Island to be served meant it could do so at scale. The programming was also short term and modular, which made it appealing.

Typical CBT counseling could run from six to eighteen individual sessions lasting an hour each, over a series of days and weeks, leaving time for "homework" in between sessions. The series of interventions could be interrupted without losing effect. A student could drop out and drop back in—an important feature for young people who might not be in the same setting for long.

Don't have to finish for pos. results

Some CBT also shows effects at intermittent stages along the process, with results for some but not all of the sessions. This was valuable for our setting, where young people would be discharged from jail according to their court schedules before they completed all stages of the program. Additionally, facilitators could be easily trained and did not require a specific professional degree. Apart from these aspects of the intervention, there was abundant evidence that it worked. Dozens of randomized controlled trials (RCTs) have documented its many benefits and successes.

Vanderbilt study

Several comprehensive reviews of the literature—meta-analyses—have also been performed. One in particular caught our attention. A research team at the Vanderbilt Institute for Public Policy Studies had conducted a comprehensive review of CBTs done in the area of reducing recidivism and outlined lessons of what made CBT work and not work.[9] They found the average CBT reduced recidivism by 25 percent, with the most successful programs achieving more than a 50 percent reduction.

The characteristics among the fifty-eight individual programs studied that produced the greatest impact were programs that (1) treated higher risk participants; (2) were well implemented (primarily through well-trained and skilled counselors); and (3) focused on a certain programmatic component (including anger control and interpersonal problem solving).

MRT

With this as our roadmap, further research into what we believed best suited our circumstances at YMI led us to Moral Reconation Therapy (MRT) as the preferred intervention model. MRT is a form of CBT that seeks to increase moral reasoning and has been used extensively to decrease recidivism with juvenile and adult criminal offenders. It takes the form of education, plus group and individual counseling, to foster moral development.

The full complement of sessions could be completed in three to six months, based on the individual progress or graduation of the participant through the twelve self-directed stages. Importantly, it has been found to be particularly successful with populations who may not be willingly participating in the program. As this was to be implemented as a mandatory program for all adolescents at Rikers, this attribute was valuable.

Overall, MRT was an attractive complement to the many existing services at Rikers to help young men better cope with their environment and the circumstances they faced. Through a series of group interactions and individual homework, CBT progressively helps participants reflect on their actions and think through their motivations and their implications. Importantly, it takes them through a process of acknowledging how their actions have harmed themselves and harmed people around them.

This process gradually replaces negative thinking with positive thinking and drives positive action for the future, involving contemplation of those they love the most.[10] In the justice domain, particularly for adolescents, this is a critical life skill that prevents hasty actions without regard to consequences, including continued risky behaviors that can lead to arrest and incarceration. With a clear implementation model in mind, it was time to fund it.

USE OF SOCIAL IMPACT BONDS TO FUND JUSTICE INTERVENTIONS

While HHS was having ambitious discussions about how to improve young men's life chances, New York City was still facing a multiyear budget deficit of more than $2 billion, and the budget director was sending out notices on the need to cut agency spending. Struggling to bridge the gap between our visionary goals for YMI to change the life trajectories for justice-involved black and Latino young men and our ability to pay for it, the team came upon an emerging financing mechanism—social impact bonds (SIBs)—to bring private investment into promising social programs.[11]

According to Goldman Sachs, a pioneer in the public-private social impact marketplace and an investor in the Rikers project, an SIB is designed to address the following challenges:

 City, state and federal budgets may be declining, but the social challenges those governments face aren't going away. To fill the gap, policy-makers are turning to a new financing mechanism called a social impact bond. It's a public-private partnership designed to deliver ambitious social programs to underserved communities.[12]

Britain introduced the first SIB in 2010 when the United Kingdom's Ministry of Justice contracted with nonprofit Social Finance UK to reduce recidivism rates for three thousand former Peterborough Prison inmates over a five-year period. Results showed an 8 percent reduction in reconviction for the first thousand prisoners in the program relative to a comparable baseline in 2014.[13] Since the launch of the first SIB in Britain more than a decade ago, Austria, Canada, Germany, and Sweden, among others, have invested in SIBs.[14]

As of June 2016, at least ten states and the District of Columbia have enacted SIB legislation and programs in states ranging from Colorado (general services) and Idaho (education) to Massachusetts (general services and workforce development) and Texas (government contracts).[15] New York City's was the first social impact bond in the nation.

The funding partnership was critical, as SIBs were untested in the United States. Goldman Sachs Urban Investment Group developed a strong interest in the SIB financing mechanism as a potential vehicle through which Goldman could bring socially minded investments to their portfolio. Bloomberg Philanthropies, our partner on the YMI work overall and representative of the mayor's strong philanthropic interest in providing second chances to young people caught up in the justice system, shared an interest in the SIB model and were enthusiastic leaders in structuring the deal.

Vera Institute, a New York City–based action research organization, had a long track record of working with many city agencies and fit in naturally as the evaluation partner. The key players in an SIB deal must share a strong alignment of interests and commitment to reform. Any one of them—investor, agency, intermediary, or evaluator—might undermine the goals of the project and chances for success. A foundation of shared values and trust, driven by a true commitment to improve social outcomes, is vital.

The proposition of an SIB is simple: government dollars are often tied up in producing ineffective results, and because these dollars are tied up in existing programs, government has less ability to pay for preventive interventions that could produce better outcomes and reduce costs. In our program's context, these costs are well documented and can first and foremost be seen in the money the government spends on the "prison industrial complex." This problem is very harmful to urban communities and, most significantly, tremendously hurts the population HHS was most trying to help.[16]

For instance, a jail bed could cost as much as $250,000 a year, while a preventive intervention that would keep a youth out of jail would cost just a fraction of that. Across the spectrum, society pays high costs to ameliorate the negative consequences of poverty and the lack of access to services. Responding to a crisis is a government imperative. Preventing the crisis is smarter, strategic, often cheaper, and more effective, but it is not as urgent and, therefore, seen as a luxury. HHS was trying to change that thinking by implementing an SIB that would prevent youth from going to jail and help create positive, lifelong change.

The investment proposition of an SIB is that the intervention's success is a risk borne by the investor. If it works, the investor is repaid their loan, with an agreed-upon return of capital. If it fails, government has no obligation to repay the debt. Thus, while the public dollars remain tied up dealing with negative outcomes, new private investments frontload the intervention to reduce the negative outcome, thus reducing government cost in the future. Savings are reallocated to repay the investor and sustain the successful intervention.[17] The team became a quick convert to the cause of SIBs. So did others on the YMI team who saw the potential and decided to proceed.

Having established that YMI had a programmatic initiative with a strong chance of reducing recidivism for a population desperately in need of service, and believing the program would be able to generate fiscal savings to the jail system as a result, the time was ripe to put that evidence together to the satisfaction of the investors and our budget office. To the YMI team, CBT looked good on paper, but it had to answer the tough question: Can it work in our setting?

Needless to say, our structure was complicated. Most simply put, the YMI team needed to reduce returns to Rikers—less arrests, thus less detentions; less convictions, thus less incarcerations. This would be measured by the number of days ("recidivism bed days") any program participant was committed to Rikers after the time of his initial discharge.

Beyond the straightforward calculations of reductions in bed days came the complication of monetizing savings. Our proposition had to be that length of stay reductions would actually translate into reduced costs. Another great strength New York City had in evaluating SIBs was that DOC had a great deal of knowledge about the costs of running facilities, and the analytic capacity to provide estimates for different scenarios, complete with refined staffing models and detailed administrative cost data.

Carrying costs for a residential facility are not very flexible. You have to keep the lights on whether there are ten people in the facility or fifty. The marginal cost per person doesn't produce much. Those fixed costs of running, heating, staffing, and maintaining the entire facility would not translate into savings unless the magnitude of impact from the intervention was enough to close *entire* jail buildings.

Translating length of stay reductions into savings was made more complicated because there was only one residential facility for sixteen- to eighteen-year-old adolescents at Rikers. The adolescent facility is composed of a number of separate one-hundred-bed housing units, and the savings potential was found in the possibility to close individual units. The question became whether there were any scalable savings to be achieved, and what magnitude of change had to occur to generate savings of sufficient size to pay for the cost of the program and repay any investor interest.

We calculated that it would save just $4,600 per jail bed for closing any one bed. That number jumped to $28,000 per jail bed if at a one-hundred-bed increment. (The bulk of these savings came in the form of reducing staffing of each independently secured unit.) It was determined that a 10 percent reduction in bed days would be enough to close a housing unit and pay for the intervention. An 11.5 percent reduction would be enough to pay the investor a return. A tiered repayment schedule that repaid the investor based on these graduated moments, and capped the return should recidivism decline by 20.0 percent, was established (see table 6.1).

At the same time, the SIB repayment model did not allow for the potential of return on investment in excess of that 20.0 percent or $11.7 million (i.e., a gain of $2.1 million), even though the potential for savings to the city might greatly exceed that. To do so, the team believed, would be an inappropriate rewarding of the investor's risk, at a cost too high to the taxpayer. It was unseemly and could have compromised the SIB concept as a whole given the skepticism that existed around the perception that Wall Street was involved in deciding the fates of social programs.

Table 6.1.   New York City Social Impact Bond

Recidivism Reduction Rate (%)	Department of Correction Success Payment ($)	Net Projected Taxpayer Savings ($)
≥20.0	11,712,000	20,500,000
≥16.0	10,944,000	11,700,000
≥13.0	10,368,000	7,200,000
≥12.5	10,272,000	6,400,000
≥12.0	10,176,000	5,600,000
≥11.0	10,080,000	1,700,000
≥10.0	9,600,000	<1,000,000
>8.5	4,800,000	<1,000,000

Source: Timothy Rudd, Elisa Nicoletti, Kristin Misner, and Janae Bonsue, *Financing Promising Evidence-Based Programs*, MDRC, December 2013, https://www.mdrc.org/publication/financing-promising-evidence-based-programs.

Having set clear goals, a rigorous evaluation to know whether the program worked was necessary to discount any influences of policy and practice changes in the justice field in New York City as the initiative was being implemented. From the investor perspective, we would need to answer whether a change in crime or punishment was driving up arrests and incarcerations despite the success of the program for individuals served. From the budget office's perspective, they would want to know the opposite—that drops in crime in general were not driving the reduction in bed days.

This became our evaluation question—and the standard by which to assess the impact of the program. The most rigorous approach to answer this would be through an RCT. A three-month pilot phase was planned in 2012, separating the new adolescent entrants onto Rikers Island into *ethical 2* a program group that would receive the service and a separate control group that would not. Populations were adjusted to ensure the assignments created groups with similar characteristics.

This proved to be a considerable challenge. Managing the population at Rikers is complex. Young people had to be segregated into housing assignments based on status (i.e., those pending trial versus the sentenced population), and each assignment also needed to consider factors related to risk, crime severity, and understanding of the bonds and rivalries individuals bring with them to Rikers. *crews*

Complicating this formula was the need to be constantly attuned to relationships that develop during confinement given the highly volatile redefinition of allegiances and fast-forming crews (less disciplined and porous "mini-gangs") that defied traditional gang affiliation and discipline. Putting rival crewmembers in the same housing unit was a recipe for chaos. This required staff to continually reassign young people to reduce the chances of fights and injuries.

Not possible It was not long before the team found that the program and control groups quickly intermingled in the service setting, making separation for treatment purposes impossible. While it was possible to make the initial designations, it was not possible to manage the population to keep them separate. At one point, it was determined that more than 40 percent of the program group was housed together with control group members. Because the investors had early on articulated the desire for a random control environment to demonstrate impact, it was believed the team would be unable to proceed.

But the team members persevered, and an alternative approach was conceived and accepted: propensity score matching. *Alt. Approach*

The idea was this: compare the recidivism of the population receiving the service now to the recidivism of a matched group of young people who were at Rikers in the years preceding the intervention. Historic jail population data showed that they followed a common recidivism trajectory; thus, the program group of all sixteen- to eighteen-year-olds at Rikers received the service, and their outcomes were compared to the outcomes of sixteen- to eighteen-year-olds who were at Rikers in prior years.

They were also compared to outcomes of nineteen-year-olds at Rikers at the same time, knowing that both age cohorts follow a similar recidivism trajectory. All parties embraced the evaluation approach, and the program was launched.

RESULTS

With agreement on the rigor of the newly developed research design, the partners were able to move forward on finalizing the terms of the deal. We structured the costs of the program and determined the implementation strategy. The Urban Investors Group of Goldman Sachs made a $9.6 million loan for the cost to operate the program over three years. Bloomberg

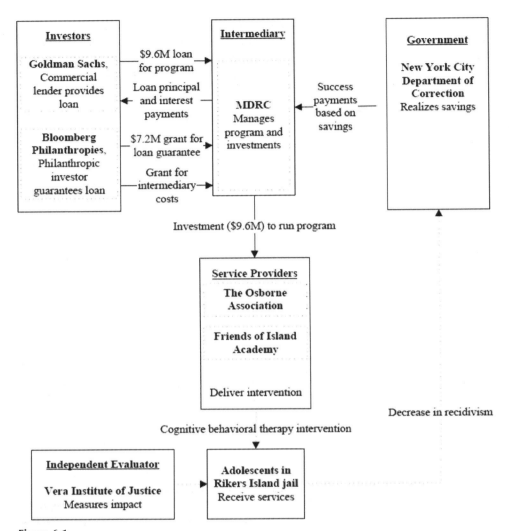

Figure 6.1.

Source: Timothy Rudd, Elisa Nicoletti, Kristin Misner, and Janae Bonsue, *Financing Promising Evidence-Based Programs*, MDRC, December 2013, https://www.mdrc.org/publication/financing-promising-evidence-based-programs.

Philanthropies provided a $7.2 million grant to in part guarantee the Goldman loan. The grant was made to MDRC, a New York City–based research organization, as the intermediary. MDRC paid and managed the nonprofit partners and worked with the evaluators to estimate impact (see figure 6.1). *2013, Begins!*

The program started for every adolescent entering Rikers from January through December 2013. Progress was measured by whether participants completed a stage of the intervention to the satisfaction of the trained instructor, allowing them to advance to the next stage. To evaluate the impact on recidivism, a period of time was needed to allow the majority of the population to be discharged, and then to have time for those participants in the community to demonstrate success without rearrest or re-incarceration. Thus, the impact would not be understood until more than two years' time from the start of the intervention.

result :

At the end of the day, YMI showed no impact on reducing recidivism.[18] The majority of inmates at Rikers participated in the program (85 percent of those stayed more than seven days), and a large population received services (1,470 youth overall). They completed a median number of twelve sessions, and a sufficient number of participants completed enough milestones of the program to expect to see changes in recidivism (52 percent advanced through stage 3 of 12, which research showed could produce a modest recidivism reduction).[19]

Yet participants' chances of rearrest and re-incarceration did not improve as hoped. The program group spent 37.2 days incarcerated after rearrest compared to 32.8 days for the comparison cohort in the 2006–2010 period, a 13.4 percent increase. In a parallel fashion, nineteen-year-olds in the intervention spent 28.9 days re-incarcerated compared to 26.8 days in the prior period, an 8 percent increase. The program group could be discounted by that 8 percent to reflect the impact of system-level changes outside of Rikers. Thus, there was a change of a 5.1 percent growth in re-incarceration. This was not a statistically significant change, and therefore, equivalent to no impact.

Based on these early findings, according to the terms of the agreement, the program ended a year early. The final payment to MDRC for that year was not made and the program was suspended. Goldman was paid $6 million from the guarantee fund against $7.2 million spent to date.

LESSONS LEARNED

Upon reflection of YMI five years later, the team learned a great deal about SIBs, the process of implementing one, and the successes and barriers associated with this type of enterprise within a government sector. As Jim Anderson from Bloomberg Philanthropies and Andrea Phillips from Goldman Sachs noted in their *Huffington Post* article, while the program was discontinued because it did not achieve its recidivism goal, the SIB worked as a *financing mechanism.*[20]

SIB did work

In other words, the value proposition of the SIB to government was that the city could try out a promising new approach at no cost to taxpayers if it did not work. Although we were deeply disappointed that the intervention didn't produce the results hoped for, the experiment provided an opportunity to test a promising intervention with a great deal of knowledge generated through rigorous analysis demanded in the SIB environment. The rigor of the design, the well-honed theory of change, and the careful data metrics and evaluation brought discipline to program operation in a way that should be the standard, not the exception, in government.

Knowing what I do today, here are nine lessons for city and state leaders, private investors, service providers, and corrections professionals who are contemplating the adoption of an SIB in criminal justice reforms.

Lesson 1: Acknowledge the Culture of Survival versus Vulnerability

Several observations are worth noting about the challenges of offering restorative services in a jail setting. A jail facility is a difficult place. It is a chaotic, constantly churning environment. Part of survival as a young person in jail is to demonstrate strength for survival. This is more so for short-term jail stays than in prison, where individuals know they will be there for the long term and measure relationships accordingly.

In contrast to survival through demonstrating strength, success of the MRT intervention depends on a young person showing vulnerability and acknowledging to peers the need to

req. vulnera. in place that req. strength

be more compassionate and thoughtful about the welfare of others. That kind of behavior could put a young person at risk when they are establishing themselves in a jail setting. This observation alone points to a need for broader jail reform. Meanwhile, it is a reality incarcerated young people face. *asserting innocence*

Another dynamic to consider is that the overwhelming majority of the population participating in the program had been charged with a crime but had not yet had their innocence or guilt established. Not only are inmates in a period of unpredictable and demanding scheduling, with attorneys and the court constantly disrupting their engagement in the classroom and counseling, but they are also in a mental state of asserting their innocence.

While the MRT intervention was not structured to engage the alleged crime that brought them to Rikers, it did ask them to address the consequences of their actions on people in their lives. There might have been some cognitive dissonance there that impeded program effectiveness. Working with trainers to ensure that they are not limited to engaging the youth in reflecting on the events that precipitated the arrest, but about any behaviors that may have caused harm to their relationships at home and in the community, would help to address that.

Stakeholders must carefully consider how the jail environment can be structured to offer a safe space to create openness in communications between the youth and the staff. Consideration might be given to inviting community members, peers, and victims into the jail environment consistent with the design of the intervention, as well as avoiding presentations in front of hostile peers. Continuing follow-up sessions when young people are discharged to their communities would allow increased opportunity for more complete, useful results.

Lesson 2: Get Buy-In from Corrections Officers

Corrections officers must demonstrate strength in managing the inmate population. At the time of program implementation, violence at Rikers was on the rise, and the culture among the officers was to reinforce their strength to maintain order. When the program began, there had not yet been any identified solutions to the growing violence. Thus, bringing about a restorative service on the island was challenging because it was a point in time when there was a particularly hostile environment, and corrections officers had not sufficiently bought into our intervention.

Having nonprofit providers deliver the service, and offering the service in the school setting rather than in housing units managed by the officers, addressed this challenge in part. These were decisions intended to increase the probability of success.

 give officers a role

It may have been wiser to incorporate the MRT into an approach in which corrections officers engaged in a jointly managed program. Doing so may have engaged correctional officers to buy into a culture of openness with inmates that might have improved the chance for success. Although placing a program in areas controlled by corrections officers is not a guarantee of success, it might force facility leadership to work more directly with officers in managing a successful program.

Lesson 3: System Dynamics in One Program Are Not Always Transferrable

It was believed the CBT intervention would save money by reducing the number of inmates returning to Rikers, which meant fewer arrests, convictions, and time spent in jail. At first glance, the team believed this would come simply in the form of a reduced number of detentions after arrest that brought young people to Rikers in the first place. There was a potential

potential [handwritten]

for another form of savings as well—that the young people who did return would stay for fewer days. This was very similar in concept to an unexpected finding discovered through an evaluation of our homeless prevention program in New York City: HomeBase.

HomeBase was created by Mayor Bloomberg in 2004 on the belief that community-based prevention could avert the disruption of homelessness for families with children in New York City. An RCT identified that HomeBase produced a significant reduction in homelessness, which was a great win. What was also learned for those who received HomeBase, yet nonetheless became homeless, was that the average duration of their stay in shelter was 50 percent less than the sheltered population who never participated in the services.[21] Somehow, the supports they received helped them not only avoid the disruption of a shelter but also overcome homelessness more quickly if they did need shelter.

Despite the success of HomeBase and the model it employed, a similar dynamic did not play out for YMI. Once confined, an inmate has limited ability to reduce jail time, while there are strategies a client can adopt to more quickly overcome homelessness. There might have been reductions in jail time had judges exercised their discretion to sentence young people to more probation or "split bids"—part jail, part probation—on the judgment that their CBT experience made them better candidates for probation supervision than incarceration. The fact that they were not first-time offenders may have dissuaded judges from exercising such leniency.

would it though? [handwritten]

A parallel effort to inform judges about the program's design and effect, and equip them with decision-making tools to better inform their sentencing rulings, would increase the chances of reduced time in a subsequent detention. Through examination of other justice reform efforts, it has been determined that a well-orchestrated education campaign directed at members of the justice system deepens and reinforces the restorative benefits of both programming investments and decision-making supports and, ultimately, produces "knock-on" benefits down the road.

Lesson 4: Be Willing to Provide Flexibility in Evaluation Standards

The criminal justice arena is particularly challenging for measuring the impact of any one intervention, making an SIB evaluation challenging. The work does not occur in a vacuum. Quite the opposite, multiple institutional players and broad policy agendas have the potential to influence outcomes. Changes in policing, court reform, correctional policy, and parole supervision can all impact outcomes. The challenge for the SIB was to determine whether our program was producing results, not only to attribute positive impact to the intervention but also to discount external influences if a change in crime or punishment was driving up arrests and incarcerations despite the success of the program for individuals served.

An RCT was adopted to address this issue because it is the most rigorous approach. When the RCT approach did not work, the team almost abandoned the effort. Moving to a propensity score matching design solved that, but there was resistance to let go of the RCT as the evaluation standard. Even with that settled, the reality of implementation taught us a lot. For example, only those who remained at Rikers for at least seven days, due to the high level and unpredictable nature of who would stay and who would not, should have been counted as program participants. It can take a while to hone a program to make it work effectively.

Some programs can go through several iterations before kinks are worked out and the program is effectively operating to show impact. "A deal's a deal" mentality resisted this alteration. It would be ideal for a program to be given adequate lead time to get its bearings and work out the operational protocols before the evaluation period begins.

Adopting very rigorous evaluation standards is strongly advised—not just to satisfy investors and budget officials but also to establish knowledge. Reformed-oriented stakeholders desperate for solutions that work for justice-involved youth must demand strong evidence. That being said, programs operate in real time, with real people, and under unpredictable circumstances. Being open to adjust and modify along the way—be it in program design, evaluation, or both—respects the value to learn and strengthens service design that cannot be placed second to purity in evaluation models.

Lesson 5: Access to Historic and Ongoing Administrative Data Is Crucial

One of the great advantages for the team was the ability to calculate accurate estimates from the rich administrative data available from DOC. It had automated data on every stay at Rikers going back for years. This included information about the inmates (race, age, gender), the nature of their offense (misdemeanor or felony, including specific charges), their home borough, and their prior record, including duration of prior stays at Rikers. This information allowed us to calculate the length of stay on the island by year, broken down by any one of these independent factors (blacks versus Latinos, misdemeanor versus felony charges, sixteen-year-olds versus seventeen-year-olds, etc.).

For instance, in the years preceding the intervention, the average length of stay for the population as a whole was 32.8 days. This historic data set allowed us to generate scenarios about the possible reductions the MRT might produce and gave us the ability to adjust assumptions should the population on the island change in composition (e.g., become more overwhelmingly felony-charged individuals).

Clear outcomes for every government program should be established, and data should be routinely collected to measure progress. Sadly, this remains the exception rather than the rule. Without these data in the SIB, it would have been difficult to shape our evaluation framework or measure the impact of the intervention. Well beyond the SIB environment, knowing whether programs have impact is impossible without carefully collecting and analyzing data and embracing the use of data to manage programs.

Lesson 6: Calculating Costs and Savings Is Not Easy

Beyond the straightforward calculations of reductions in bed days came the complication of monetizing savings. Our proposition had to be that length of stay reductions would actually translate into reduced costs. The budget office resistance was strong, and they jealously guarded their veto authority over fiscal liabilities. Therefore, strong alliance in structuring deals with agency budget officials and executive budget staff was essential.

This was a comparatively easy deal—the savings were generated in the agency undertaking the initiative. Often savings are generated elsewhere—often referred to as the "wrong pocket problem." Executive budget staff can help broker efforts where one agency's actions produce another's cost savings.

Additionally, agency budget officials are intimately familiar with how pressure exerted within programs generates impact in other places and across multiple organizations. A collaborative partnership among agencies with the executive budget office can open up SIBs to a wider range of potential scenarios and cost-sharing agreements.

Stakeholders must also be open to undertake SIBs that don't produce cost savings in the near term necessary to reimburse investment capital. As savings are lagged (e.g., an initiative to improve higher graduation rates would also produce higher employment for many years down the road, generating savings as a result of lower costs in public welfare benefits and higher individual income tax payments), investors seeking quick returns lose the incentive to participate, taking innovation opportunities off the table. A creative and flexible SIB arrangement could acknowledge intermediate outcome improvements that are not immediately capable of being monetized are nonetheless a good investment and merit consideration.

Even further than that, SIBs might be considered when there are no savings. Why should innovative investment dollars be limited to cost savings scenarios? Government should be willing to pay for risk taking that improves quality of life and decreases disparities, even if that does not translate into taxpayer savings. A saving-less SIB would allow innovation dollars to be infused across a much broader range of experiments, with government paying only when success against a predetermined social outcome is proven.

Government would pay a premium on those investments for the experimentation phase and adopt the proven programs as taxpayer funds align with desired outcomes. The public benefit of opening up an innovation pipeline in this manner could be well worth the premium paid on such experiments.

Finally, the exercise of participating in an SIB strengthens and reinforces the skills of public agency managers to outcome-based management and infuses rigor and accountability in programming. These are valuable tools that can be imported across programs. Skeptics of SIBs argue that public administrators do not have the skill and sophistication to stand up to the wiles of private investors. This is a caution but not a prohibitive barrier. The act of structuring an SIB can generate and reinforce these necessary capabilities in public administration.

Lesson 7: Choose Wisely between Evaluation- and Management-Based SIBs

SIBs can be structured as either evidence-building interventions or management-based incentives, and one must be clear as to which one they are selecting. At the point of the initial undertaking of this SIB, the primary rationale advanced by investors was that the SIB was a vehicle to explore what works to produce improved outcomes for justice-involved youth. The rigor of the approach was intended to produce strong evidence of programmatic impact.

Participating in a more rigorous outcome evaluation also involves cost in design, program group assignment, tracking, and analysis. Measuring these kinds of outcomes requires time, adding delay to determining measurable impacts during and post-program involvement. These are the consequences of leveraging the capital of the investment community to help build the field of evidence for innovative social programming.

Evaluation-based SIBs are structured to pay for outcomes—not for inputs or outputs but for measurable social change. It can primarily favor knowledge production for researchers and policy makers and not focus as great a priority to feeding information to the front line managers about what is going on day to day to support them with operational improvement. Because a controlled evaluation environment does not allow for a great deal of iteration during the intervention, one has to see it through and cannot make significant adjustments that supposedly might improve implementation.

Management-based SIBs argue that an alternative way of infusing capital into performance-based settings is to structure the SIB as a tool to increase integrity, efficiency, and effectiveness of implementation. By intermingling performance milestones (enrollment, attendance, completion) into the outcome-based payment structure, programs are incentivized to meet performance standards that can be critical building blocks to longer-term program success.

It also means crucial stages of work will be more carefully delineated, and performance data will be fed to the front line to apprise them of their status and assist them with corrective actions to improve milestone achievements. Careful attention to this distinction is essential. It may be that these are not contradictory approaches; instead, they may exist in a complementary and parallel manner, or even through a blended approach.

The challenge will be to keep a focus on building real evidence for what works to improve the long-term outcomes for the populations being served, not just the skills of those serving them. The price is that an evaluation-based approach will demand stronger parameters around fidelity to program design for stronger evaluation integrity, sacrificing learning and adjustment along the way to strengthen program learning and delivery.

Lesson 8: Effective Partnerships Make a Difference

The foundation of YMI included many partners who were engaged in improving youth outcomes. Several of these became the backbone of the Rikers SIB. Each had unique skills, and all were bound together in a commitment to serve the population and experiment with SIB financing as a promising new tool.

The leadership from the city on this project came primarily from City Hall, with my chief of staff coordinating all public and private partners. Programmatically, DOC was the sponsoring agency, and it had a long history of collaborating with nonprofit partners conducting programs at Rikers Island. The Osborne Society and the Friends of Island Academy, nonprofits with on-the-ground experience working with justice-involved youth, formed a partnership to provide services on the island. Another partner, Correctional Counseling, trained the Rikers teams in the form of CBT selected for the program—Moral Reconation Therapy.

The intermediary organization that held all the partners together in operation was MDRC, a New York City–based research organization. MDRC had long been partners with city government in identifying and creating evidence-based programs for young people in need. So it made sense to partner with MDRC as the coordinating intermediary to structure and document the initiative.

Lesson 9: SIBs Are Appropriate for the Criminal Justice Field

The justice field is ripe for program reforms to improve outcomes for inmates, to save money for taxpayers, and which can be successfully implemented without compromising public safety. What our experience taught us is that this work is challenging, and if interventions are structured with a clear understanding of the culture prevailing in the service setting where the intervention is being employed—and with appreciation to the motivations driving the participants—the task is not impossible to accomplish.

Despite the outcome at Rikers Island, I still support private investment as an effective source of capital for government innovation. This work can be done with the investors carrying the risk of failure. The taxpayers gain the benefit of the potential for savings and improved outcomes through a private capital investment. The fact that our intervention did not work cost the taxpayers nothing.

The opposite is true of failed government program innovations funded through taxpayer dollars. Indeed, much remains unclear about how best to measure or know the effect of programs using large swaths of government spending. In the case of this SIB, the investment capital opened up the potential for a service that would not have occurred otherwise and demanded a level of evidence and public-sector accountability that advanced our knowledge of what works—and what does not—in serving justice-involved youth.

CONCLUSION

Across the forty initiatives of the YMI, many worked to improve outcomes for an extremely vulnerable population of youth who are disconnected from work and education. These initiatives saw large impacts in graduation rates at the high school and community college level through education investments, decreases in juvenile incarceration and recidivism from parallel justice initiatives, and increases in employment and civic commitment in work engagement strategies. At the same time, the Rikers initiative for justice-involved youth did not meet our success metrics.

Lessons on why the Rikers Island CBT did not work are valuable contributions to the field and build our knowledge as the practices of correctional education and reentry move forward. While our program did not reduce recidivism for the target population, the undertaking was not a wasteful engagement. For example, the SIB financing mechanism allowed an innovative program to be tested at no cost to the taxpayers and held all parties accountable to the SIB terms.

In the end, we gained insights to inform future program designs for a mayor, county executive, or governor who decides to tackle criminal justice reform through an SIB. In fact, MRT is again being offered now at Rikers with several programmatic changes learned from our SIB experience. This includes expanding it to include up to twenty-one-year-olds, increasing occupational training and therapeutic supports, and providing post-discharge follow-up in the community. The providers operate under a performance-based contract that rewards their achievements in client program attendance, post-discharge employment placements, educational engagement, and housing stability.

Our success overall was in knowing the difference between those initiatives that failed and those that succeeded by investing in rigorous evaluation—expanding what worked and discontinuing what did not. The SIB was a particularly successful tool in this effort.

NOTES

1. New York City Office of the Mayor, *Disparity Report*, New York City Center for Innovation through Data Intelligence, 2016, 40, www1.nyc.gov/assets/ymi/downloads/pdf/Disparity_Report.pdf.

2. David Banks and Anna Oliveira, *Young Men's Initiative: Report to the Mayor from the Chairs*, New York City Mayor's Office, August 2011, www.nyc.gov/html/om/pdf/2011/young_mens_initiative_re port.pdf.

3. Official Website of the Office of New York, "Mayor Bloomberg Delivers 2010 State of the City Address Detailing His Plans for the Recovery Ahead and the Strategy behind It," news release, January 20, 2010, www1.nyc.gov/office-of-the-mayor/news/029-10/mayor-bloomberg-delivers-2010-state-the-city-address-detailing-his-plans-the-recovery-ahead.

4. NYC Office of the Mayor, *Disparity Report*, 60–70.

5. Thankfully, that law was amended in the adoption of the New York State budget in spring 2017 to treat most adolescents under eighteen as juveniles such that they will no longer be held in the adult jail and prison system. 2017 Laws of New York State, Chapter 59, Part WWW.

6. NYC Office of the Mayor, *Disparity Report*, 72.

7. Bruce Western, "The Impact of Incarceration on Wage Mobility and Inequality," *American Sociological Review* 67, no. 4 (August 2002): 526–46.

8. J. S. Beck, *Cognitive Behavior Therapy: Basics and Beyond*, 2nd ed. (New York: Guilford Press, 2011).

9. Nana A. Landenberger and Mark W. Lipsey, "The Positive Effects of Cognitive-Behavioral Programs for Offenders: A Meta-Analysis of Factors Associated with Effective Treatment," *Journal of Experimental Criminology* 1, no. 4 (December 2005): 451–76.

10. Landenberger and Lipsey, "The Positive Effects of Cognitive-Behavioral Programs for Offenders."

11. Lisa Barclay and Diane Mak, *A Technical Guide to Developing a Social Impact Bond: Vulnerable Children and Young People*, Social Finance, March 2011, www.socialfinance.org.uk/resources/publications/technical-guide-developing-social-impact-bond-vulnerable-children-and-young.

12. Goldman Sachs, "What Is a Social Impact Bond?" October 2014, www.goldmansachs.com/our-thinking/pages/social-impact-bonds.html.

13. Emma Disley et al., *The Payment by Results Social Impact Bond Pilot at HMP Peterborough: Final Process Evaluation Report* (Santa Monica, CA: RAND Corporation, 2015), www.rand.org/pubs/research_reports/RR1212.html.

14. Annie Dear et al., *Social Impact Bonds: The Early Years*, Social Finance, July 5, 2016, https://thegiin.org/research/publication/social-impact-bonds-the-early-years.

15. National Council of State Legislatures, "Social Impact Bonds," SIB Review, July 2016, http://www.ncsl.org/research/labor-and-employment/social-impact-bonds.aspx.

16. Children's Defense Fund, *America's Cradle to Prison Pipeline*, October 2007, www.childrensdefense.org/library/data/cradle-prison-pipeline-report-2007-full-lowres.pdf.

17. Jeffrey Liebman and Alina Sellman, "Social Impact Bonds: A Guide for State and Local Governments," Harvard Kennedy School Social Impact Bond Technical Assistance Lab, June 2013, http://siblab.hks.harvard.edu/files/siblab/files/social-impact-bonds-a-guide-for-state-and-local-governments.pdf?m=1419347623.

18. Jim Parsons, Chris Weiss, and Qing Wei, *Impact Evaluation of the Adolescent Behavioral Learning Experience (ABLE) Program*, Vera Institute of Justice, September 2016, https://storage.googleapis.com/vera-web-assets/downloads/Publications/rikers-adolescent-behavioral-learning-experience-evaluation/legacy_downloads/rikers-adolescent-behavioral-learning-experience-evaluation.pdf.

19. Parsons, Weiss, and Wei, *Impact Evaluation of the Adolescent Behavioral Learning Experience (ABLE) Program*, 17.

20. James Anderson and Andrea Phillips, "What We Learned from the Nation's First Social Impact Bond," *Huffington Post*, July 2, 2016, http://m.huffpost.com/us/entry/7710272.

21. Howard Rolston, Judy Greyer, and Gretchen Locke, *Final Report: Evaluation of the HomeBase Community Prevention Program*, Abt Associates, June 6, 2013, www.abtassociates.com/AbtAssociates/files/cf/cf819ade-6613-4664-9ac1-2344225c24d7.pdf.

7

Collateral Damage

The War on Drugs and the Impact on Women, Children, and Families

Renita L. Seabrook

As the world's ranking leader in incarceration, the United States has witnessed an unprecedented increase of men and women imprisoned in its penal institutions over the past forty years. Recent estimates have indicated there are around 6.9 million people under some form of correctional supervision, with 2.2 million people currently in federal and state prisons or in local jail systems.[1] *700% increase!*

Although women only account for 7 percent of the prison population, their rate of incarceration has increased by 700 percent between 1980 and 2014.[2] To put this into perspective, the number of female prisoners rose from 26,378 in 1980 to 215,332 in 2014.[3] In light of the significant increase of imprisoned women, many of whom are mothers, further research and reforms are warranted.

The purpose of this chapter is to promote public discourse to help explain women's involvement in the criminal justice system in a context that examines the following: the rise of their incarceration; adverse effects of their imprisonment on the familial bond; challenges in maintaining parental relationships during incarceration; and evidence-based programs that are deemed best practices for female offenders. This chapter will also focus on a reentry program named Helping Others 2 Win (HO2W), which seeks to reduce those collateral consequences for incarcerated women and support their transition back into their communities.

THE RISE OF FEMALE INCARCERATION

During the 1980s, the "war on drugs" and "get tough on crime" movements incited politicians to create laws that resulted in a significant increase of men and women being charged and sentenced for drug-related offenses.[4] Researchers and practitioners have acknowledged that the link between drugs and crime has led to the escalation of female offenders.[5] Even though property and drug-related offenses have had a major impact on female crime trends, more punitive sentencing of drug-related crimes have significantly contributed to the increase of incarcerated women in both jail and prison facilities.[6]

WOMEN IN JAIL AND PRISONS

Let's begin with women in jails, an overlooked topic in criminal justice reform today. The estimated number of women in local jails is almost as large as the number of women in state prisons nationwide, 96,000 and 99,000, respectively.[7] Between 1970 and 2014, the number of women confined in America's jail facilities increased fourteen times more than any other correctional population.[8] This increase is vastly due to most women being charged with nonviolent crimes that include property, drug, and public order offenses and, in some cases, violating a condition of their parole or probation supervision.[9]

Women's involvement in the criminal justice system, and the unique challenges and systemic issues they face once they are incarcerated in jail, is strikingly different in comparison to their male counterparts. For women, social and economic needs that contribute to incarceration are significant, and their challenges often include a lack of essential basic education and life skills, poor medical health, unemployment, poverty, lack of housing, histories of mental illness, trauma, and alcohol/drug addiction.

 Women in jail tend to have higher rates of mental health disorders, including serious psychological distress, than either women in prisons or men in jail or prison.[10] On top of that, demographically, they are increasingly women of color, single mothers with children under the age of eighteen, and women who reside in poverty and high-crime communities.

Although the collateral damages incarceration has on the mother and child will be discussed later in this chapter, it is important to note that, for incarcerated mothers in jail, even a brief stay can have unfavorable effects on the family dynamic. Some 60 percent of women in jail are awaiting trial and have not been convicted of any crime.[11] A mother's stay in jail can wreak havoc on a child's overall well-being, which can lead to her or his placement in foster care or the mother's parental rights being terminated.

Turning to women in prison, it is important to note that, in 2014, women in state prisons were more likely than men to be imprisoned for drug or property crimes—24 percent to 15 percent (drugs) and 28 percent to 19 percent (property), respectively.[12] In addition, women have outpaced men in federal prisons, serving time for drug-related crimes: 59 percent to 50 percent.[13] Even though drug dependency increases the number of crimes committed by both men and women in their effort to generate income to buy drugs, this goal more often motivates women than men.[14]

The increase in female incarceration is noteworthy because women have faced, traditionally, greater constraints related to deviant behavior.[15] In other words, societal norms may be more likely to expect and forgive deviant and criminal behavior perpetuated by a man than such behavior committed by a woman.

THE RELATIONSHIP BETWEEN GENDER
AND WOMEN'S CRIMINAL OFFENSES

For the past several decades, significant attention has been given to issues related to women's involvement in the criminal justice system. The work of Kathleen Daly is pertinent to any discussion about pathways to female criminality. A commended scholar, Daly has championed her research agenda to examine apposite issues such as gender, race, crime, restorative justice, and her most recent work on sexual and violent victimization.

Daly's work is still relevant today as researchers view property and drug offenses as "crimes of survival."[16] She created five categories to place gender and other influences at the forefront of explanations for female offending: *street women*; *harmed and harming women*; *battered and entrapped women*; *drug-connected women*; and *economically motivated women*.[17] These categories place gender and other influences at the forefront of explanations for female offending.[18] In brief, each pathway is defined as follows:

> *Street women* are viewed as having been severely abused throughout their childhood—many were homeless, and they have been continuously in court because of a drug addiction, prostitution, and/or stealing.
>
> *Harmed and harming women* were abused as children and respond to situations in their life with anger that leads to violent behavior if exacerbated by drugs and alcohol use.
>
> *Battered and entrapped women* typically have no criminal record but fall into criminality by either harming or killing men who abused or threatened to harm them.
>
> *Drug-connected women* have a limited criminal record but have either used or sold drugs as a result of being involved in an intimate relationship with someone involved in drug dealing.
>
> *Economically motivated women* commit crimes out of poverty or pure greed.[19]

The common thread among these pathways to female offending is poverty, substance abuse, and survival of abuse.

COLLATERAL DAMAGE FOR THE CHILDREN OF INCARCERATED MOTHERS

As the number of women behind bars continues to rise, it stands to reason that the penal system has also seen a massive increase in the number of imprisoned mothers. Among individuals engaged in drug offenses, women are more likely to be the sole caretaker for their children. Consequently, the increase of incarcerated mothers can be detrimental to their family unit, specifically their children.

Maternal incarceration may result in more adverse consequences for children than paternal incarceration. When a female head of household becomes incarcerated, her children no longer have their sole primary caretaker available. This change disrupts not only the relationship between mother and child but also the overall continuity of care for the child.[20] Maternal incarceration also leads to increased foster care placement. This may also be harmful for the child as studies have shown that youth in foster care are more likely to have emotional and behavioral problems, including delinquency, which renders them more vulnerable to engaging in criminal activities compared to other children and adolescents.[21]

For the most part, incarcerated parents whose children are placed in the foster care system are susceptible to having their parental rights terminated. This is especially true of mothers since the enactment of the federal Adoption and Safe Families Act of 1997.[22] This federal law is significant, as it has a strict time line that terminates parental rights if a child has been in the foster care system for at least fifteen months.[23]

It is also important to acknowledge that incarcerated women have limited access to social service programs and assistance benefits (e.g., public housing, Temporary Assistance for

Needy Families), and, in some cases, unnecessary burden is placed on other immediate or extended familial relationships.[24]

To date, there are an estimated 2.5 to 2.7 million children in the United States that have a parent behind bars, which is approximately one out of every twenty-eight children, a substantial increase from 2007.[25] Unfortunately, black, Native American, and Hispanic children are more likely to have an incarcerated mother than white children.[26] In 2010, approximately one in nine black children, one in twenty-eight Hispanic children, and one in fifty-seven white children had an incarcerated parent.[27]

More important, the impact of maternal incarceration is heightened significantly for black children due to their overall prevalence and representation in the child welfare system, in which black children are four times more likely than white children to be placed in foster care.[28]

Given that most studies have examined the adverse effects of parental or paternal incarceration generally rather than maternal incarceration specifically, there is a growing body of research that has examined the negative consequences associated with incarcerated mothers and the negative impact their incarceration has on their children.[29] These include poor mental health outcomes, insecure attachment, depression, low academic performance and behavioral problems, and increased likelihood of adult criminality.[30]

Policies and reform must be put in place to decrease the negative impact of maternal incarceration. For example, the Dignity for Incarcerated Women Act of 2017 (i.e., the Dignity Act), cosponsored by US senators Cory Booker (D-NJ), Elizabeth Warren (D-MA), Richard Durbin (D-IL), Kamala Harris (D-CA), and Tammy Duckworth (D-IL), is a landmark bill that intends to extend several important protections to female inmates in federal prisons.[31]

The Dignity Act would help address the challenges and barriers women housed in prisons face.[32] For instance, the bill seeks to establish reforms to include the provision of adequate feminine hygiene products, banning of shackles for pregnant women, expansion of visitation policies, geographic location of the prison to make it much easier for children to visit their mothers, and protection of women from sexual abuse from male correctional officers.[33]

In essence, the Dignity Act focuses on how the federal prison system should treat incarcerated women in order to curtail the negative impact maternal incarceration has on children and other family members and, additionally, would better prepare incarcerated women for reunification with their families and communities.[34] Although this bill is a representation of a larger policy movement toward caring more about the female incarcerated population, much more needs to be done at every level of the criminal justice system.

BEST PRACTICES FOR FEMALE OFFENDERS

Evidence-based programs such as trauma-informed modalities, gender-responsive approaches, and cognitive-behavioral treatment have been considered effective best practices for female offenders.

Trauma is an essential element to understand in developing rehabilitation programs for women offenders.[35] Many female offenders have been physically and/or sexually abused one or more times as children and/or as adults. Therefore, they are survivors of trauma before entering the criminal justice system and are traumatized further while in the system due to the conditions of incarceration that include body searches and isolation.[36] Trauma hinders psychological development, so many women use drugs and alcohol all too frequently to medicate the pain of their traumatic experiences.[37]

The implementation of integrated trauma-informed services for female offenders can facilitate recovery and rehabilitation, as well as provide the needed treatment to be productive citizens in the community.[38] More important, these programs are uniquely designed to combat the effects of trauma- and substance-abuse-related problems in a supportive and proactive environment.

The basic tenets of gender-responsive approaches involve creating a milieu that attempts to reverse the painful effects on a variety of large-scale issues such as poverty, race, abuse, gender disparities, and personal factors that women face while in the criminal justice system.[39]

The core foundation of this type of programming lies in the integration of theoretical formulations: women's psychological development/relational theory (recurring themes of relationship and family as seen in the life of women offenders); addiction theory (viewing addiction as a type of relationship to maintain relational connections); and trauma theory (considering disconnection of relationships to be a result of trauma).[40]

Overall gender-responsive programs can improve outcomes for female offenders by considering histories, behaviors, and life circumstances. For the past two decades, numerous criminal justice programs and agencies have implemented gender-responsive models.

Cognitive Behavioral Therapy (CBT) is another example of a program aimed to reduce offender recidivism. Over the past thirty years, research results have strongly indicated that CBT is one of the most widely practiced psychological interventions in the world and is effective within a variety of offender populations, including females and substance abusers.[41] CBT programs focus on changing negative thoughts and behaviors into prosocial thoughts and behaviors by implementing various role-playing and skill-building scenarios, activities, and exercises.[42]

Based on my work with formerly incarcerated women, CBT has incorporated a focus on resolving problems such as victimization, unemployment, lack of legitimate income, addiction, and physical and psychological trauma. One such initiative that combines CBT with elements of gender-responsive programming for women in transition from prison is Helping Others 2 Win (HO2W).

A NEW APPROACH TO FEMALE INCARCERATION: HO2W

For more than twenty years, I have researched and worked extensively with various offender populations for several state governmental and nonprofit agencies in Maryland, Georgia, and Virginia. The goal of this work is to provide women (and men) returning to their homes with transferable skills (i.e., life skills, job readiness, financial literacy, and cognitive skills) that will afford them greater opportunities for long-term gainful employment, resulting in a better life for themselves and their families.

More important, as an African American female criminologist and program developer dedicated to curbing the plight and social injustices that confront women in general, particularly women of color, I understand the pathways to female criminality. HO2W is designed with this in mind. For instance, even though research has indicated that men and women offenders share many of the same risk factors, circumstances, and reentry obstacles (e.g., lack of education, unemployment, etc.), women more often experience specific challenges associated with being a mother and often serve as the sole caretaker of children.[43]

Individual and social challenges present a systemic issue germane not only to the successful reentry for men and women in transition from prison but also to their families and the overall community. With such a heavy concentration of former prisoners returning to impoverished neighborhoods, these challenges are exacerbated in the absence of effective reentry services.[44]

Research indicates that, as a whole, successful community reintegration requires individuals to undergo several forms of social, behavioral, and cognitive changes. This includes development of prosocial relationships, employable skills, and abstinence from drugs and alcohol. This approach can help a person become a productive member in their community.[45] Regarding women, reentry efforts can be more successful when their unique needs and risk factors are addressed. For instance, more emphasis should be placed on the reunification of the mother and child, public benefits and support, job opportunities, counseling, drug treatment, and education.[46]

Based on the need to provide an effective reentry program specifically designed for women in transition from prison, I formed Helping Others 2 Win (HO2W) in 2014 through a fellowship from the Open Society Institute–Baltimore (OSI-Baltimore) and a collaborative partnership with Alternative Directions Inc. (ADI), a Baltimore-based reentry nonprofit organization. HO2W uses five evidence-based programmatic domains to achieve this goal:

Level 1: *Cognitive Behavioral Therapy*: Reasoning & Rehabilitation 2: For Girls and Young Women (R&R2: FGYW) curriculum is designed to improve decision-making skills.[47]

Level 2: *Education*: designed to improve developmental math skills and college placement score. This level also includes a GED component.

Level 3: *Employment*: workforce development designed to provide job readiness skills, résumé writing, mock interviewing, and computer literacy.

Level 4: *Financial Literacy*: designed to improve their financial future through investment education and a review and refinement of basic financial principles.

Level 5: *Civic Engagement, Relationship Building, Advocacy, and Mentoring*: involvement in events that build respectable relationships and afford the women an opportunity to be part of conversations and solutions that can assist with the plight of their immediate community and their family.

PRELIMINARY EVALUATION FINDINGS OF HO2W

To date, thirty-one women have participated in the HO2W program, with seven new women starting the program in late 2018. Of the thirty-one women, seventeen (55 percent) graduated from the program; nine (29 percent) did not complete the program for various reasons; and five (16 percent) are currently participating in various levels of the program. Most of the women are black, single, and between twenty-six and fifty-five years of age; most have a high school diploma or GED equivalent educational level. Reasons for participant attrition included loss of interest in the program (the most frequently cited reason), apprehension for a new crime, a technical violation for not reporting to a parole officer, and parole revocation.

The women have also achieved several goals through participation in HO2W. For example, all seventeen have obtained affordable housing; twelve have gainful employment; six completed a university preparatory college math course; five are receiving disability benefits; and one completed an AA degree from a local community college. In addition, some participants have been presenters in college classrooms and at a national criminal justice conference, and most have reunited with their children and grandchildren and refrained from drug and alcohol use.

Of the seventeen women who graduated from the program, HO2W celebrated the women's success with a highly publicized gala attended by family members, friends, supporters (including various Maryland and Baltimore city lawmakers), community/grassroots organizations, and college educators.

The basis for the development of each phase was to create new knowledge in helping to test the effectiveness of the R&R2: FGYW curriculum in level 1 for program participants and the ADI administrative staff. It is important to note that ADI's staff members help men and women transition from prison to become independent, responsible citizens.

Additionally, ADI staff provide legal pro se services to those in prison as well as comprehensive case management to those returning to their communities. Program participants and ADI administrative staff were given qualitative and quantitative instruments to assess their skill levels.

HO2W's phase 1 focused on ADI staff's knowledge and coaching behaviors of the R&R2: FGYW curriculum implemented in level 1. A focus group session was conducted with four ADI staff members—the executive director, the director of civil legal services, a case manager, and a board member—which targeted the following areas:

1. the overall impact of R&R2: FGYW on facilitator training;
2. the impact the R&R2: FGYW curriculum has on the participant;
3. the participant's overall expectations of the R&R2: FGYW curriculum;
4. the participant's capacity to effectively facilitate the R&R2: FGYW curriculum; and
5. the level of knowledge and coaching behaviors the client received from the facilitator training as well as staff's knowledge of the curriculum program.

Based on the focus group report, there were several key findings concerning program fidelity, cultural understanding between the facilitator and participant, and the impact of observing program delivery.

Program Fidelity (?) → what does this mean

By adhering to the program as designed, there is a much greater chance that negative behaviors will be more directly addressed. Fidelity ensures that participants will attain greater awareness that participants' behaviors have been a problem.

Cultural Understanding

Participants felt that cultural differences between facilitator and participant were not much of an issue. Facilitators felt participants were comfortable with them joining in the discussion.

Impact of Program Observation

Facilitators noted that being able to watch others, sometimes more experienced facilitators, at work delivering the curriculum was the key to continual improvement in the program. One facilitator mentioned the ability to learn from the interactions with students as integral to improvement. Another mentioned the opportunity for self-reflection on their own thinking processes.

HO2W's phase 2 examined the effectiveness of the R&R2: FGYW curriculum on participants who completed level 1. HO2W is based on the idea that by reducing cognitive deficits and increasing prosocial thinking, the women will produce prosocial behavior that will further enhance the completion of levels 2–5. Those levels will be infused with CBT elements to reinforce previous learning. The women's investment in their cognitive skill building process enables them to use these new tools in other life areas (e.g., employment, family relationships, finances, and community).

Data collection included a variety of assessment measures. For the purposes of this chapter, here are preliminary findings based on a thirty-five-item pre- and post-test survey specifically designed to assess the participant's knowledge of the R&R2: FGYW skills, components, and curriculum expectations. Results showed minimal but meaningful change in prosocial decision making.

Out of thirty-five survey questions, eight were in the predicted direction (showing participant improvement) and achieved (4) or approached (4) statistical significance at the (p=.05) level. Questions included the following:

- Have you ever used an emotions chart?   (p=.000)
- Do you know how to curb your anger?   (p=.05)
- Have you ever used an anger diary?   (p=.001)
- How often do you use positive self-talk?   (p=.023)
- Do you know your own personal strengths?   (p=.041)
- Is it important to know and learn body language?   (p=.055)
- Are you a problem-solver?   (p=.082)
- What is the likelihood that you think of other alternatives? (p=.023)

It is anticipated that longer-term, more detailed analyses of the effects of HO2W will be conducted. In addition to program completion and prosocial decision making, this research will examine recidivism, relapse to substance abuse, and employment outcomes using control or comparison groups. Plans are also being made to make HO2W a nonprofit organization. It is my hope that HO2W will translate into foundational knowledge that can inform scholarship and best practices for future research and program effectiveness in women returning from prison.

CONCLUSION

Over the past forty years, the United States has witnessed an extraordinary growth in the number of women behind bars, which resulted in women becoming the fastest-growing incarcerated population in the country. Most of these women are mothers. Based on the escalation of imprisoned women, adverse consequences have had a major impact on the familial bond between mother and child.

Addressing the needs of incarcerated women can come about through new programs that reduce the marginalization these women face and the negative consequences for their immediate families. HO2W provides an example of such a program. By focusing our attention on programmatic reforms, lawmakers, judges, and other stakeholders will be able to provide a lasting foundation for imprisoned women and the restoration and reunification of the mother and child.

NOTES

1. Sentencing Project, "Fact Sheet: Trends in U.S. Corrections," June 26, 2017, www.senten cingproject.org/publications/trends-in-u-s-corrections/; and Danielle Kaeble et al., *Correctional Populations in the United States*, Bureau of Justice Statistics, December 2015, www.bjs.gov/index.cfm?ty= pbdetail&iid=5519.

2. E. Ann Carson, *Prisoners in 2014*, Bureau of Justice Statistics, September 2015, www.bjs.gov/ content/pub/pdf/p14.pdf; and Sentencing Project, *Incarcerated Women and Girls, 1980–2016*, May 10, 2018, www.sentencingproject.org/publications/incarcerated-women-and-girls/.

3. Sentencing Project, *Incarcerated Women and Girls.*

4. Robynn J. A. Cox, "The Impact of Mass Incarceration on the Lives of African American Women," *Review of Black Political Economy* 3, no. 2 (June 2012): 203–12, https://doi.org/10.1007/ s12114-011-9114-2; and National Research Council, *The Growth of Incarceration in the United States: Exploring Causes and Consequences* (Washington, DC: National Academies Press, 2014).

5. Clemens Bartollas and Frank Schmalleger, *Juvenile Delinquency*, 2nd ed. (Boston, MA: Pearson, 2015).

6. Carson, *Prisoners in 2014*; Aleks Kajstura, *Women's Mass Incarceration: The Whole Pie 2017*, Prison Policy Initiative, October 19, 2017, www.prisonpolicy.org/reports/pie2017women.html; and Torrey McConnell, "The War on Women: The Collateral Consequences of Female Incarceration," *Lewis & Clark Law Review* 21, no. 2 (2017): 493–524.

7. Kajstura, *Women's Mass Incarceration.*

8. Ram Subramanian, Kristi Riley, and Elizabeth Swavola, *Overlooked: Women and Jails in an Era of Reform*, Vera Institute of Justice, August 2016, www.vera.org/publications/overlooked-women-and -jails-report.

9. Subramanian, Riley, and Swavola, *Overlooked.*

10. Kajstura, *Women's Mass Incarceration.*

11. Kajstura, *Women's Mass Incarceration.*

12. Carson, *Prisoners in 2014*; and Sentencing Project, *Incarcerated Women and Girls.*

13. Carson, *Prisoners in 2014*; Sentencing Project, *Incarcerated Women and Girls*; and McConnell, "The War on Women."

14. James A. Inciardi, *The War on Drugs IV* (Boston, MA: Allyn & Bacon, 2007); and National Research Council, *The Growth of Incarceration.*

15. Inciardi, *The War on Drugs IV*; National Research Council, *The Growth of Incarceration*; and James Robert Lilly, Francis T. Cullen, and Richard A. Ball, *Criminological Theory: Context and Consequences* (Thousand Oaks, CA: Sage, 2011).

16. McConnell, "The War on Women."

17. Kathleen Daly, "Women Pathways to Felony Courts: Feminist Theories of Law Breaking and Problems of Representation," *Southern California Review of Law and Women's Studies* 2 (1992): 11–52.

18. Daly, "Women Pathways to Felony Courts"; and Merry Morash and Pamela J. Schram, *The Prison Experience: Special Issues of Women in Prison* (Prospect Heights, IL: Waveland Press, 2002).

19. Daly, "Women Pathways to Felony Courts"; and Morash and Schram, *The Prison Experience.*

20. Sentencing Project, "Fact Sheet: Trends in U.S. Corrections."

21. Bartollas and Schmalleger, *Juvenile Delinquency.*

22. Cox, "The Impact of Mass Incarceration on the Lives of African American Women."

23. Stephanie Sherry, "When Jail Fails: Amending the ASFA to Reduce Its Negative Impact on Children of Incarcerated Parents," *Family Court Review: An Interdisciplinary Journal* 48 (2010): 380–97; and Cox, "The Impact of Mass Incarceration on the Lives of African American Women."

24. McConnell, "The War on Women"; and Dorothy E. Roberts, "Prison, Foster Care, and the Systemic Punishment of Black Mothers," *UCLA Law Review* 6 (2012): 1474–1500.

25. Rebecca Covington, "Incarcerated Mother, Invisible Child," *Emory International Law Review* 1 (2016): 99–133; Sylvia A. Harvey, "2.7 Million Kids Have Parents in Prison: They're Losing Their Rights to Visit," *Nation*, December 2, 2015, www.thenation.com/article/2-7m-kids-have-parents-in -prison-theyre-losing-their-right-to-visit/; and Katie Reilly, "*Sesame Street* Reaches out to 2.7 Million American Children with an Incarcerated Parent," Pew Research Center, June 21, 2013, www.pewre search.org/fact-tank/2013/06/21/sesame-street-reaches-out-to-2-7-million-american-children-with-an -incarcerated-parent/.

26. Marian S. Harris, "Incarcerated Mothers: Trauma and Attachment Issues," *Smith College Studies in Social Work* 87, no. 1 (2017): 26–42.

27. Harvey, "2.7 Million Kids Have Parents in Prison."

28. Kathi L. Harp and Carrie B. Oser, "Factors Associated with Two Types of Child Custody Loss among a Sample of African American Mothers: A Novel Approach," *Social Science Research* 60 (2016): 283–96.

29. Lorie S. Goshin et al., "An International Human Rights Perspective on Maternal Criminal Justice Involvement in the United States," *Psychology, Public Policy, and Law* 23, no. 1 (2017): 53–67; and Joann Wu Shortt et al., "Project Home: A Pilot Evaluation of an Emotion-Focused Intervention for Mothers Reuniting with Children after Prison," *Psychological Services* 11, no. 1 (2014): 1–9.

30. Covington, "Incarcerated Mother, Invisible Child," 99–133; Lisa R. Muftic, Leana A. Bouffard, and Gaylene S. Armstrong, "Impact of Maternal Incarceration on the Criminal Justice Involvement of Adult Offspring: A Research Note," *Journal of Research in Crime and Delinquency* 53 (2015): 93–111.

31. #cut 50: A Dream Corps Initiative, "Dignity for Incarcerated Women," www.cut50.org/dignity; and Elizabeth Kiefer, "Senators Cory Booker & Elizabeth Warren Demand 'Dignity' for Women behind Bars," *Refinery29*, July 12, 2017, www.refinery29.com/2017/07/163017/dignity-incarcerated-women -act-prison-reform-bill.

32. Cory Booker and Elizabeth Warren, "Booker & Warren: Women in Prison Deserve Dignity," CNN, September 5, 2017, www.cnn.com/2017/09/05/opinions/female-prisoners-dignity-act-booker -warren-opinion/index.html; and #cut 50: A Dream Corps Initiative, "Dignity for Incarcerated Women."

33. #cut 50: A Dream Corps Initiative, "Dignity for Incarcerated Women."

34. #cut 50: A Dream Corps Initiative, "Dignity for Incarcerated Women."

35. Stephanie S. Covington, "The Relational Theory of Women's Psychological Development: Implications for the Criminal Justice System," in *Female Offenders: Critical Perspectives and Effective Interventions*, ed. R. T. Zaplin (Gaithersburg, MD: Aspen Publishers, 1998), 113–31.

36. Stephanie S. Covington and Barbara E. Bloom, "Gender-Responsive Programming and Evaluation for Females in the Criminal Justice System: A Shift from *What Works?* to *What Is the Work?*" (paper presented at the 51th Annual Meeting of the American Society of Criminology, Toronto, Canada, November 17–20, 1999).

37. Covington, "The Relational Theory of Women's Psychological Development."

38. Brandi E. Cihlar, "The Trauma Recovery and Empowerment Model: A Trauma-Informed Treatment Program for Female Offenders in the Community," US: ProQuest Information and Learning, 2014.

39. Stephanie S. Covington and Barbara E. Bloom, "Gendered Justice: Programming for Women in Correctional Settings," American Society of Criminology, November 2000, http://stephaniecovington. com/assets/files/11.pdf.

40. Covington and Bloom, "Gender-Responsive Programming and Evaluation.*"

41. Michael S. Gazzinga and Todd F. Heatherton, *Psychological Science*, 5th ed. (New York: Norton, 2015); and Dennis Greenberger and Christine A. Padesky, *Mind over Mood: Change the Way You Feel by Changing the Way You Think*, 2nd ed. (New York: Guilford, 2015).

42. Stephanie A. Ainsworth and Jennifer Lerch, "Cognitive-Behavioral Therapy (CBT) for Higher Risk Offenders," *Perspectives* 36, no. 3 (2012): 32–36; and Grant Duwe and Valerie Clark, "Importance of Program Integrity," *Criminology & Public Policy* 14, no. 2 (2015): 301–28.

43. L. S. Goshin, "The Ex-Prisoner's Dilemma: How Women Negotiate Competing Narratives of Reentry and Desistance," *Journal of Family Theory & Review* 7, no. 4 (2015): 525–29; Randy Shively and Rose Ricciardelli, "Gender-Specific Reentry: Pathways to Recovery," *Journal of Community Corrections* 25, no. 3 (2016): 7–28; and Natalie J. Sokoloff, Jay Sherr, and Catherine Stephens, "Women in Prison Today: Alternative Directions, Inc., Women's Imprisonment in U.S. and Maryland," https://natalieSokoloff.wordpress.com/publications-2/women-in-prison-today-alternative-directions-inc-womens-imprisonment-in-u-s-and-maryland/.

44. National Research Council, *The Growth of Incarceration.*

45. Sherri Doherty et al., "Finding Their Way: Conditions for Successful Reintegration among Women Offenders," *Journal of Offender Rehabilitation* 53 (2014): 562–86.

46. Sokoloff, Sherr, and Stephens, "Women in Prison Today."

47. Robert Ross, Yvonne Gailey, Wendy Cooper, and James Hilborn. R&R2 for Girls and Women: A Prosocial Competence Training Program (Cognitive Centre of Canada: Ottawa, Canada, 2008).

8

The Importance of Work

Will Heaton

In 2007, I pled guilty to conspiracy charges for my actions related to a congressional scandal. Until that time, I had enjoyed a meteoric rise in my professional career. Just months after graduating from college, I obtained a position in the Office of the Speaker of the United States House of Representatives, and two years later I was the chief of staff for a prominent member of Congress. Then, not seven years later, my aspirations for a prominent career on Capitol Hill vanished.

My felony conviction has greatly impacted my life. I had never thought much about the criminal justice system's impact on this country, but all of that changed when I walked out of court that day. After leaving Capitol Hill, I began researching the impacts of our criminal justice system on men, women, and children and was shocked. I was quickly learning that a criminal record and incarceration had far-reaching consequences and affected many more Americans than I imagined.

Today, more than ten years later, my life and career stand in stark contrast to the large majority of others affected by the criminal justice system. For example, I received a sentence of only two years of probation, one hundred hours of community service, and a $5,000 fine. This is nothing compared to the years of incarceration and extended supervision that many other people receive—sometimes for lesser offenses. I've rebuilt my life and career because of access to opportunities despite the barriers that accompany a conviction.

I dedicate much of my time to abolishing many of these employment barriers and creating a reentry system that opens doors to opportunity—as opposed to eliminating them. I'm fortunate to have worked at the Center for Employment Opportunities (CEO), a New York City–based nonprofit organization started in the 1970s, to help change a system that hinders people's success. CEO helps thousands of formerly incarcerated people each year find and retain employment despite their criminal history. By creating opportunities for work, it opens pathways for each of its clients to build the confidence and skills necessary to succeed in the workforce.

In this chapter, I explain the extreme difficulties of the reentry process and the multitude of barriers faced by people with criminal records. I then offer policy recommendations that can eliminate some of the unnecessary burdens currently embedded in the reentry process today. Throughout the chapter, I draw upon CEO's employment services model and my own

125

experiences to explain why work must play a central role in the reentry process if we hope to end the cycle of incarceration in this country.

AMERICA'S REENTRY CHALLENGE

Reforming America's criminal justice system is a multifaceted challenge that requires significant structural reform. In 1980, there were a little more than five hundred thousand people incarcerated in American prisons and jails and roughly 1.3 million people under community supervision. By 2015, those numbers had skyrocketed to 2.25 million and 4.6 million people, respectively.[1] Beginning in the 1970s, government leaders began implementing and enforcing a series of increasingly punitive and harsh criminal justice policies to strengthen public safety and wage a war on drugs. The result was a criminal justice system fraught with racial and economic inequities that was costing taxpayers billions of dollars with little return on their investment.

The increasing number of incarcerated people also meant that a growing number of people would be returning home to their communities after serving their sentence. According to the latest Bureau of Justice Statistics (BJS) numbers, approximately 630,000 people return home from prison annually—a rate that will most likely increase with sentencing reforms.[2]

Unfortunately, far too many of these individuals will return to prison. Within three years of release, more than two-thirds of individuals in state prison are rearrested, more than half are reconvicted, and more than 40 percent had a parole or probation violation or arrest that led to imprisonment.[3] Worse, 76 percent of people who were under the age of twenty-five when released from prison were rearrested within three years, and 84 percent were rearrested within five years.[4]

This is why organizations such as CEO that create employment opportunities for returning citizens must become the norm. Originally founded in the late 1970s as a demonstration project to study the effects of employment on recidivism, CEO has replicated its program in eighteen cities in New York, California, Colorado, Ohio, Oklahoma, and Pennsylvania, with further expansion efforts under way. Today the organization serves more than five thousand people annually and has made more than twenty-five thousand job placements since becoming an independent nonprofit in 1996.

Research shows employment can help reduce recidivism among even the most high-risk individuals.[5] But America's criminal justice system offers few resources to help returning citizens find a job and stay employed. CEO's focus on employment offers an effective model for lawmakers seeking to reform a critical component of the criminal justice system and give taxpayers a better return on their investment.

THE COSTS OF A FELONY CONVICTION

The costs of incarceration and recidivism are far reaching. An analysis by the Center for Economic Policy Research estimates that, in 2008, the United States lost as many as 1.7 million workers due to employment barriers for people with criminal records—resulting in a staggering 0.9-percentage-point reduction in the nation's employment rate. The analysis estimates the resulting loss in gross domestic product to be as much as $65 billion per year.[6] Some research also indicates that removing barriers to employment for job seekers with criminal records would yield tremendous economic benefits through increased earnings, higher taxpayer revenues from employment, and avoided costs in reduced recidivism rates.[7]

Incarceration takes a human toll as well. Nationally, the number of kids who have a parent in jail or prison at some point in their childhood hovers around 5.1 million—a conservative estimate.[8] Losing a parent who is also the primary source of income leaves families scrambling to cover basic needs along with legal and other court fees. When a father is incarcerated, family income can decrease by as much as 22 percent.[9] Regarding men in general, incarceration depresses the total earnings of white males post-release by 2 percent, Hispanic males by 6 percent, and black males by 9 percent.[10] Homelessness is another problem.[11]

Finding steady employment that pays a living wage is extremely difficult when saddled with a felony conviction. At the same time, employment is one of the most critical factors to help people avoid recidivating because it refocuses individuals' time and efforts on prosocial activities, making them less likely to engage in riskier behaviors and to associate with people who do.[12] The chance to work provides hope and motivation for people involved in the criminal justice system, as we have learned that stable employment is an important predictor of successful reentry and desistance from crime.[13]

WORK'S CRITICAL ROLE IN REDUCING RECIDIVISM

We need to address a number of factors to effectively reverse the reentry crisis. Arguably, the most important will be creating a system in which people with a criminal history have opportunities to develop the skills, work experience, and networks necessary to succeed in the workforce. Research indicates that once an individual has stayed crime free for three to four years, that person poses no more risk of committing a new crime as would a member of the general public without a criminal record.[14] However, while a person's chances of recidivating may decrease significantly after three or more years, most people stumble within the first year.

The Bureau of Justice Statistics' last comprehensive recidivism study reported that more than one-third (36.8 percent) of all released state prisoners who were arrested within five years of release were arrested within the first six months, with more than half (56.7 percent) arrested by the end of the first year.[15] Conversely, only 13 percent of those not arrested by the end of year four were arrested in the fifth year after release.[16] Studies have also shown employment is associated with lower rates of reoffending, indicating that effective employment services should be a key aspect of governments' reentry services.[17]

These dire recidivism rates justify the need for more employment service programs such as those offered by CEO, which targets men and women within three months of their release. For instance, just one week after starting the program, our clients begin earning a daily paycheck that provides them with a vital source of income and stability. CEO's provision of a steady job and routine helps provide much-needed structure as these men and women begin the reentry process.

Designing a reentry system that can help people navigate the earliest periods of reentry could have significant positive effects in reducing the recidivism rate as seen with CEO's own model.

An independent random control trial (RCT) evaluation conducted by MDRC found that CEO significantly reduced rearrests, reconviction, and re-incarceration within three years of release.[18] CEO participants with a higher risk of re-incarceration spent 30 percent less time in prison or jail than the control group—outcomes deemed rare in rigorous studies of this kind.[19] Furthermore, CEO had the largest impact on those who came to the program shortly after release (within three months). Among that subgroup, program group members were significantly less likely than control group members to be arrested (49 percent to 59 percent); convicted of a crime (44 percent to 57 percent); or incarcerated (60 percent to 71 percent).

These impacts represent a reduction in recidivism of 16 to 22 percent across the three outcomes.[20] A cost-benefit analysis of CEO's program conducted in conjunction with the MDRC study showed that every dollar invested in CEO saved as much as $3.30 in tax revenue due to decreased correctional costs.[21] MDRC's evaluation of CEO shows that designing an effective, scalable reentry system can have significant financial and social benefits for our nation. It will require a more sophisticated approach, however, that addresses returning citizens' unique needs and applies interventions at the right time.

Prior to the MDRC evaluation, CEO served returning citizens with a broader diversity of risk factors. Since the evaluation, CEO focuses its efforts more exclusively toward moderate to high-risk individuals recognizing the potential for a much greater impact and more efficient use of our resources. Government leaders must take a similar approach. Simultaneously, taxpayers must demand a better return on their investment spent on corrections and reentry because solutions do exist.

CENTER FOR EMPLOYMENT OPPORTUNITY PROGRAM MODEL

CEO's core model focuses exclusively on helping an individual develop work experience, essential workplace skills, and a positive attitude toward employment in order to succeed in the workforce. It consists of four phases during which participants progress at their own pace, enabling each person to focus on his or her own unique barriers to employment while adhering to CEO's evidence-based model.

The program is designed to develop and promote self-sufficiency through training, employment experience, cognitive-behavioral interventions, vocational skill training, assistance with all aspects of the employment application process, and retention once employed with businesses in the community. CEO focuses on serving individuals assessed at moderate to high risk of recidivism, with little (if any) prior work experience. As a result, nearly 50 percent of CEO participants are young adults ages eighteen to twenty-four.

The four phases of CEO's highly structured program are Pathway to Employment (P2E), transitional work, job coaching and job placement, and post-placement retention services.

Pathway to Employment (P2E)

The process of preparing participants for full-time employment begins with a week-long class taught by a qualified instructor at CEO's offices. CEO staff assist each participant in assembling all necessary work documents (e.g., state ID, I-9 compliance) and ensure eligibility for the Supplemental Nutrition Assistance Program (SNAP) and other available resources. Then staff prepare individuals to enter or reenter the workforce with interactive sessions in which participants learn crucial workplace practices. They create a résumé, learn to fill out job applications, and practice answering interview questions, specifically questions regarding their criminal history.

P2E also incorporates Cognitive Behavioral Interventions (CBI). A CBI is a nonclinical intervention that relies on a cognitive behavioral approach to teach participants strategies to manage risk factors, placing heavy emphasis on skill-building activities to assist with cognitive, social, emotional, and coping-skill development.[22] CEO uses a specially designed curriculum called Cognitive Behavioral Interventions for Employment (CBI-EMP) that was developed in partnership with the University of Cincinnati Corrections Institute, one of the leading institutions studying criminogenic behavior.

Transitional Work

After graduating from P2E, participants move immediately into paid transitional work. Examples include providing crew-based maintenance, landscaping and entry-level skilled services for CEO customers such as cities, state departments, and community colleges. CEO secures contracts with these partners, allowing these agencies to hire quality labor services for an affordable price while also providing jobs that help returning citizens gain workplace experience and develop positive workplace habits.

Participants typically work three to four days per week on transitional work crews and receive on-the-job training and coaching from their site supervisors. CEO provides transportation to and from the worksite, and at the end of every shift, participants are paid and given feedback using CEO's performance assessment tool Passport to Success (PTS). On average, participants spend two to four months on CEO transitional work crews before being placed in unsubsidized employment.

Job Coaching and Job Placement

During their time in the transitional job phase, participants receive a full suite of vocational services. For instance, job coaches help participants become "job start ready" through mock interviews, assistance in creating résumés, guidance in the job search, and referrals to additional support services. Meanwhile, business account managers (BAMs) build relationships with local employers and refer participants based on an employer's specific needs and a participant's skills and interests. A participant is then hired into a full-time position by the employer and begins earning unsubsidized income.

Job Retention

For one full year following placement into an unsubsidized job, CEO participants receive personalized job retention services, which include workplace counseling, crisis management, and career planning. Retention services offer a continuity of support once an individual has been placed into a full-time job—establishing a long-term connection to the labor force. In addition, CEO offers "Rapid Rewards" incentives that provide monthly bonuses to individuals who meet progressive employment retention milestones.

ECONOMIC OPPORTUNITY INITIATIVE

In the last few years, CEO has made a deep commitment to helping participants stay employed and build a career through the Economic Opportunity Initiative. It integrates a research-driven approach to developing skills-training modules into CEO's core program. Based on a study from the Brookings Institution that focused on the characteristics of good jobs that led to upwardly mobile career opportunities and the skills needed to perform well in these jobs, CEO is offering trainings that enable participants to qualify for these types of positions. This helps participants develop the skills that lead to new career pathways and long-term financial stability.

POLICY RECOMMENDATIONS FOR REDUCING RECIDIVISM

Lawmakers should focus reentry reform efforts in two key areas to achieve better returns on the taxpayers' investment: (1) increase workforce opportunities for people with criminal histories and (2) replicate and expand proven workforce development and skills-training services.

Increase Workforce Opportunities

As cited previously, a majority of returning citizens are unemployed more than a year after release. But regardless of whether a person has been incarcerated, a criminal record creates barriers to employment. Decreasing the high rates of recidivism will first require creating an environment where people with criminal histories, especially those who have been incarcerated, have workforce opportunities that can help them attain self-sufficiency. This will require eliminating many hiring practices and stigmas that currently limit or outright prohibit these individuals from even entering the labor market, let alone pursuing a career.

Job seekers currently on probation, parole, or with a criminal history are more likely to be refused consideration for a job.[23] In a study conducted in New York City, a criminal record reduced the likelihood of a callback or job offer by nearly 50 percent (28 percent for applicants without a criminal record versus 15 percent of applicants with one). The effects were even worse for black applicants.

The penalty for having a criminal record for black applicants was nearly twice as severe as the penalty suffered for white applicants with criminal records.[24] Given the large number of black and Hispanic men and women who are affected by the criminal justice system, the corresponding barriers associated with a criminal record affect these communities more drastically.[25]

Background checks also serve as a significant barrier to employment and have grown significantly as technology makes them easier and less costly. Nearly 87 percent of businesses conduct background checks as part of their employment applications.[26] Other surveys indicate that background checks may be decreasing but are still quite prevalent.[27]

Nevertheless, in 2016, the Federal Bureau of Investigation released around seventeen million background checks for employment purposes, a sixfold increase from the decade before.[28] These checks have become so commonplace that they create a wide-reaching, prohibitive barrier to employment for people with criminal histories as employers screen people out for past offenses—offenses that, in some cases, happened years earlier.

A second employment barrier is occupational licensing bans. While many occupations require a state license in order to work, a significant number of these occupations ban anyone with a criminal record from applying and working in the field. The American Bar Association's inventory of penalties against those with a record has documented 27,254 state occupational licensing restrictions as of 2016.[29]

For citizens reentering their communities, these outright restrictions create significant hurdles for finding employment. Even entry-level or self-employed positions often have blanket bans that can last a lifetime or are "mandatory disqualifications" for which a licensing agency has no authority to grant a license even if they deem a person qualified to do the job.[30]

Occupational licensing is much more prevalent in the US economy now than it has ever been. According to the Bureau of Labor Statistics, nearly one-quarter of all employed workers reported having a license in 2015 as opposed to only 5 percent in the 1950s. Licenses can be difficult to obtain, and costly as well, but they remain necessary for many occupations, including self-employed occupations that are often the best employment route for people with criminal convictions. Here is one example.

The fields of barbering, hairdressing, and cosmetology offer paths to financial security and are expected to add 70,500 total positions between 2016 and 2026.[31] However, in twenty-four states any felony conviction can serve as grounds for denial of a barber's license.[32] The reality that even a qualified individual cannot obtain a license simply because of a criminal offense severely limits employment opportunities when so many positions require a license.

To ease the path of reentry, government at all levels will need to decrease the number of regulatory bans that prevent people with criminal convictions from pursuing gainful employment. Granted, certain bans are necessary for certain occupations, but, by and large, removing many of these bans, and the stigmas associated with them, can open up a path to economic self-sufficiency for many formerly incarcerated people and the families for which they provide. Our legal and regulatory system should not restrict entrepreneurism and economic opportunity. Instead, it should open up opportunities for people to find gainful employment and lead fulfilling lives.

Tailor Workforce Development and Skills-Building Programs

Creating more workforce opportunities will not guarantee success. An increasing body of research indicates that merely matching someone to a job will neither ensure their success nor help them avoid rearrest or a return to incarceration.[33] Nevertheless, we must work hard to create a workforce development system that accounts for the unique needs of people with a criminal history and addresses those needs appropriately.

These men and women do not lack talent, but they have too often been barred from accessing opportunities that would help them succeed. For instance, formerly incarcerated men and women, regardless of gender, race, and ethnicity, earn substantially less prior to their incarceration than their non-incarcerated counterparts of similar ages (see table 8.1).[34] Incarcerated individuals also have lower education levels and skills training than the general population (see table 8.2).[35]

Table 8.1. Median Annual Incomes for People Prior to Incarceration and Non-Incarcerated People*

	Incarcerated People (prior to incarceration)		Non-Incarcerated People	
	Men ($)	Women ($)	Men ($)	Women ($)
All	19,650	13,890	41,250	23,745
Black	17,625	12,735	31,245	24,255
Hispanic	19,740	11,820	30,000	15,000
White	21,975	15,480	47,505	26,130

*Median annual incomes for incarcerated people prior to incarceration and non-incarcerated people ages twenty-seven to forty-two, in 2014 dollars, by race/ethnicity and gender.

Source: Bernadette Rabuy and Daniel Kopf, *Prisons of Poverty: Uncovering the Pre-Incarceration Incomes of the Imprisoned*, Prison Policy Initiative, July 2015, accessed October 29, 2017, https://www.prisonpolicy.org/reports/income.html.

Table 8.2. Education Attainment Level Comparison of Incarcerated People versus the General Public

Highest Level of Education Attainment	US Prison (%)	US Household (%)
Graduate or professional degree	1	11
Bachelor's degree	1	17
Associate's degree	4	9
High school credential	64	50
Below high school	30	14

Source: Marsha Weissman, *The Use of Criminal History Records in College Admissions—Reconsidered* (Syracuse, NY: Center for Community Justice, 2009), i, accessed October 23, 2017, http://www.communityalternatives.org/pdf/Reconsidered-criminal-hist-recs-in-college-admissions.pdf.

Homelessness and food insecurity plague many returning citizens. Research shows that approximately 10 percent of people released from prisons and jails—a percentage that could be as high as 50 percent in large, urban areas—face homelessness.[36] This is true for CEO participants as well.

A survey of CEO's participants found that 41 percent had run out of food and lacked the resources to secure more since being released from prison. Forty-three percent reported that running out of food was a "major concern." The concern was amplified among those who had served longer sentences—more than 60 percent of individuals who had been incarcerated ten or more years reported food insecurity.

Altogether, returning citizens earn less before and after serving time, lack education and skills training essential for succeeding in the workforce, and oftentimes confront homelessness and food insecurity. Viewed in this context, should we be surprised that so many people who leave prison eventually return? Even one of these barriers could limit any individual's chances of pursuing a productive life. When combined, a person's chances for success are significantly diminished. Without access to proper employment and educational services, we begin to clearly see why the reentry process is so challenging for so many people after serving time.

Reforming the criminal justice system won't fix America's education challenges or ongoing struggle with poverty. But reforms, especially to the reentry process, can give returning citizens and others with a criminal history a much better opportunity to find employment and begin earning a living. Eliminating unnecessary and overly punitive employment regulations will open up more workforce opportunities. Creating more evidence-based workforce development and training programs will ensure more formerly incarcerated people have access to opportunities that can help lift them out of poverty.

REAL-WORLD CHALLENGES

Antisocial attitudes, beliefs, and personality patterns of program participants, for example, can affect how a person returning from incarceration might perform in the workplace. Individuals with these characteristics tend to have more negative attitudes about working, less stable employment histories, and an unwillingness to take low-paying jobs when they could earn more income by resorting to criminal activity again.[37]

Effective workforce development programs must address these attitudes and behaviors before placing someone into a job, or ensure that the job is combined with case management services. Therefore, workforce development and skills-building programs must first assess an individual's needs and then provide the appropriate level of treatment and services.

Research underscores the importance of identifying and understanding the difference between two types of needs: the needs of an individual with deeply entrenched criminal thinking, and the needs of an individual with less deeply entrenched criminal thinking. This difference is important to identify in order to sustain a system that can help returning citizens achieve income security and lifelong stability while desisting from future criminal activity.[38]

The type and intensity of job readiness, as well as the presence of barriers to employment, will affect the types of services a program should deliver to an individual in addition to when and how they should be provided.[39] Lawmakers, program administrators, and community-based organizations should prioritize replication of evidence-based practices that account for these differences and structure services accordingly. Failing to do so will only perpetuate long-standing recidivism challenges.

For example, CEO focuses its services toward a very specific portion of the overall population of formerly incarcerated people. CEO's more intensive program model works most effectively with men and women assessed with the highest risk to recidivate. In MDRC's RCT evaluation of CEO, the results showed that individuals with higher risk actually achieved better outcomes than people with lower risk.

Placing people with low-risk factors in intensive programs can be counterproductive because research has clearly demonstrated that when we place lower-risk individuals in more intensive programs (usually with people assessed with higher risk), we often increase their failure rates (and, thus, reduce the overall effectiveness of the program).[40] CEO works closely with corrections agencies to ensure that parole and probation officers prioritize referrals of individuals with high-risk assessments to our program in order to provide the right treatment to the right person. But the CEO model is not perfect.

MDRC's evaluation highlighted its weaknesses, too. For example, CEO's impacts on overall employment occurred early in the first year of the study period, when the increases in employment were driven mainly by the transitional jobs themselves. The impact faded as program group members left the transitional jobs. In other words, participants were benefiting from transitional employment after completing CEO's program, but unemployment increased as more time passed post-program completion. Since the evaluation, CEO has invested considerable resources to bolster its job retention and training services to better prepare participants for success in securing better jobs and building careers.

As government leaders consider criminal justice reforms, they must acknowledge that employment services programs should provide a blend of job readiness training, work experience, and shorter-term certification and skills certification courses. Then, as an individual builds confidence and obtains employment, program resources should be dedicated toward navigating ongoing barriers and provide ongoing services to progress further in a career.

CONCLUSION

Not a day goes by that I don't wake up thankful that I'm employed and can provide for my family. Work gives me a sense of purpose and reinforces my belief that I'm needed and am contributing to society. Without my job, many necessities and comforts in life—home, health, and happiness—would not be achievable. But not a day goes by when I also don't think about how my felony conviction has, and still may, hinder my professional career.

Having the opportunity to find work quickly during and after my court hearings is a key factor of my success today. Initially, I struggled to find a job due to the notoriety of my crimes.

As the publicity faded, finding work became easier. A large majority of people affected by the criminal justice system never find stable employment after incarceration. In many cases, they are already at a significant disadvantage before ever getting arrested and convicted—incarceration and a criminal history just exacerbate those conditions. The stigma never fades, and opportunities never appear.

Public- and private-sector investments inherently required for a more effective reentry system will not be small. However, if we invest resources wisely, they can generate cost savings that can offset that spending. Effective models such as CEO's already exist. Government and community leaders must now take action to expand these models on a much larger scale. Then my own story of redemption could become the norm instead of the exception.

NOTES

1. Danielle Kaeble and Lauren Glaze, *Correctional Populations in the United States, 2015*, US Department of Justice, Bureau of Justice Statistics, December 2016, https://www.bjs.gov/content/pub/pdf/cpus15.pdf.

2. E. Ann Carson and Daniela Golinelli, *Prisoners in 2012: Trends in Admissions and Releases*, US Department of Justice, Bureau of Justice Statistics, September 2014, https://www.bjs.gov/index.cfm?ty=pbdetail&iid=4842.

3. Allen J. Beck and Bernard E. Shipley, *Recidivism of Prisoners Released in 1983*, US Department of Justice, Bureau of Justice Statistics, April 1990, https://www.bjs.gov/content/pub/pdf/rpr83.pdf; Patrick A. Langan and David J. Levin, *Recidivism of Prisoners Released in 1994*, US Department of Justice, Bureau of Justice Statistics Special Report, June 2002, https://www.bjs.gov/content/pub/pdf/rpr94.pdf; and Matthew R. Durose, Alexia D. Cooper, and Howard N. Snyder, *Recidivism of Prisoners Released 30 States in 2005: Patterns from 2005 to 2010*, US Department of Justice, Bureau of Justice Statistics Special Report, April 2014, https://www.bjs.gov/content/pub/pdf/rprts05p0510.pdf.

4. Durose, Cooper, and Snyder, *Recidivism of Prisoners Released 30 States in 2005*.

5. Cindy Redcross et al., *More Than a Job: Final Results from the Evaluation of the Center for Employment Opportunities (CEO) Transitional Jobs Program*, Office of Planning, Research and Evaluation, Administration for Children and Families, US Department of Health and Human Services, January 2012, www.acf.hhs.gov/sites/default/files/opre/more_than_job.pdf.

6. John Schmitt and Kris Warner, *Ex-Offenders and the Labor Market*, Center for Economic and Policy Research, November 2010, www.cepr.net/documents/publications/ex-offenders-2010-11.pdf.

7. Office of the Deputy Mayor of Philadelphia for Public Safety, *Economic Benefits of Employing Formerly Incarcerated Individuals in Philadelphia*, Economy League of Greater Philadelphia, September 2011, http://economyleague.org/uploads/files/712279713790016867-economic-benefits-of-employing-formerly-incarcerated-full-report.pdf.

8. Annie E. Casey Foundation, *A Shared Sentence: The Devastating Toll of Parental Incarceration on Kids, Families and Communities*, April 2016, 2–3, www.aecf.org/resources/a-shared-sentence/.

9. Annie E. Casey Foundation, *A Shared Sentence*, 3.

10. Bruce Western and Becky Pettit, *Collateral Costs: Incarceration's Effect on Economic Mobility*, Pew Charitable Trusts, 2010, www.pewtrusts.org/-/media/legacy/uploadedfiles/pcs_assets/2010/collateralcosts1pdf.pdf.

11. Sarah Knopf-Amelung, "Incarceration and Homelessness: A Revolving Door of Risk," *In Focus: A Quarterly Research Review of the National HCH Council* 2, no. 2 (November 2013): 1–5, www.nhchc.org/wp-content/uploads/2011/09/infocus_incarceration_nov2013.pdf.

12. Le'Ann Duran et al., *Integrated Reentry and Employment Strategies: Reducing Recidivism and Promoting Job Readiness*, Council of State Governments Justice Center, September 2013, 2, http://csgjusticecenter.org/wp-content/uploads/2013/09/Final.Reentry-and-Employment.pp_.pdf; and Joe Graffam

et al., "Variables Affecting Successful Reintegration as Perceived by Offenders and Professionals," *Journal of Offender Rehabilitation* 40, no. 1/2 (2004): 147–71, www.ncjrs.gov/App/Publications/abstract.aspx?ID=209131.

13. Christy A. Visher, Laura Winterfield, and Mark B. Coggeshall, "Ex-Offender Employment Programs and Recidivism: A Meta-Analysis," *Journal of Experimental Criminology* 1, no. 3 (2005): 295–316; and John H. Laub and Robert J. Sampson, "Understanding Desistance from Crime," *Crime & Justice* 28, no. 1 (2001): 17–24.

14. Alfred Blumstein and Kiminori Nakamura, "Redemption in the Presence of Widespread Criminal Background Checks," *Criminology* 47, no. 2 (2009): 331, www.ncjrs.gov/pdffiles1/nij/226872.pdf.

15. Durose, Cooper, and Snyder, *Recidivism of Prisoners Released 30 States in 2005.*

16. Durose, Cooper, and Snyder, *Recidivism of Prisoners Released 30 States in 2005.*

17. Ellen Houston and Jared Bernstein, *Crime and Work: What We Can Learn from the Low-Wage Labor Market* (Washington, DC: Economic Policy Institute, 2000); and Bruce Western and Becky Pettit, "Incarceration and Racial Inequality in Men's Employment," *Industrial and Labor Relations Review* 54, no. 3 (2000): 3–16.

18. Redcross et al., *More Than a Job.*

19. Redcross et al., *More Than a Job.*

20. Redcross et al., *More Than a Job.*

21. Redcross et al., *More Than a Job.*

22. University of Cincinnati Corrections Institute, "Changing Offender Behavior," n.d., www.uc.edu/corrections/services/trainings/changing_offender_behavior.html.

23. Scott H. Decker et al., *Criminal Stigma, Race, Gender, and Employment: An Expanded Assessment of the Consequences of Imprisonment for Employment*, National Institute of Corrections, January 2014, 52, www.ncjrs.gov/pdffiles1/nij/grants/244756.pdf.

24. Devah Pager and Bruce Western, *Investigating Prisoner Reentry: The Impact of Conviction Status on the Employment Prospects of Young Men*, National Institute of Justice, October 2009, www.ncjrs.gov/pdffiles1/nij/grants/228584.pdf.

25. Leah Sakala, *Breaking Down Mass Incarceration in the 2010 Census: State-by-State Incarceration Rates by Race/Ethnicity*, Prison Policy Initiative, May 28, 2014, https://www.prisonpolicy.org/reports/rates.html.

26. Society for Human Resource Management, "Background Checking—the Use of Criminal Background Checks in Hiring Decisions," July 19, 2012, 2, www.shrm.org/hr-today/trends-and-forecasting/research-and-surveys/pages/criminalbackgroundcheck.aspx.

27. CareerBuilder, "More Than 1 in 4 Employers Do Not Conduct Background Checks of All New Employees, according to CareerBuilder," November 17, 2016, www.careerbuilder.com/share/aboutus/pressreleasesdetail.aspx?ed=12/31/2016&id=pr975&sd=11/17/2016.

28. Madeline Neighly and Maurice Emsellem, *Wanted: Accurate FBI Background Checks for Employment*, National Employment Law Project, July 2013, 8, www.nelp.org/content/uploads/2015/03/Report-Wanted-Accurate-FBI-Background-Checks-Employment.pdf.

29. Michelle Rodriguez and Beth Avery, *Unlicensed and Untapped: Removing Barriers to State Occupational Licenses for People with Records*, National Employment Law Project, April 16, 2016, www.nelp.org/content/uploads/Unlicensed-Untapped-Removing-Barriers-State-Occupational-Licenses.pdf.

30. A search of nationwide "permanent" offenses resulted in 19,786 restrictions in occupational and professional licenses and business licenses categories in the ABA Inventory, and a search for "mandatory/automatic" offenses resulted in 11,338 restrictions. ABA Inventory (accessed March 24, 2016). Definition of *mandatory* provided in ABA Inventory, User Guide, Question and Answer 2. See Rodriguez and Avery, *Unlicensed and Untapped.*

31. Occupational Outlook Handbook, "Barbers, Hairdressers, and Cosmetologists," Bureau of Labor Statistics, last modified April 13, 2018, www.bls.gov/ooh/personal-care-and-service/barbers-hairdressers-and-cosmetologists.htm.

32. Rodriguez and Avery, *Unlicensed & Untapped.*

33. Duran et al., *Integrated Reentry and Employment Strategies.*

34. Bernadette Rabuy and Daniel Kopf, *Prisons of Poverty: Uncovering the Pre-Incarceration Incomes of the Imprisoned*, Prison Policy Initiative, July 2015, www.prisonpolicy.org/reports/income.html.

35. Holly Xie and Stephen Provasnik, *Highlights from the U.S. PIAAC Survey of Incarcerated Adults: Their Skills, Work Experience, Education, and Training*, US Department of Education, National Center for Education Statistics, US Program for the International Assessment of Adult Competencies, November 2016, 5, https://nces.ed.gov/pubs2016/2016040.pdf.

36. John Jay College of Criminal Justice and the Fortune Society, *In Our Backyard: Overcoming Community Resistance to Reentry Housing*, 2011, http://johnjay.jjay.cuny.edu/fles/TOOL_KIT_1-NIMBY_FINAL.pdf.

37. Edward J. Latessa, "Why the Risk and Needs Principles Are Relevant to Correctional Programs (Even to Employment Programs)," *Criminology & Public Policy*, no. 4 (2011): 973–75.

38. Latessa, "Why the Risk and Needs Principles Are Relevant to Correctional Programs (Even to Employment Programs)," 975–76.

39. Latessa, "Why the Risk and Needs Principles Are Relevant to Correctional Programs (Even to Employment Programs)," 974–75.

40. Latessa, "Why the Risk and Needs Principles Are Relevant to Correctional Programs (Even to Employment Programs)," 973.

9

Entrepreneurs, Innovation, and New Opportunities to Reform Criminal Justice

Thomas G. Stewart

Criminal justice reform is an important topic that has major implications for American society, but it is very difficult to evaluate. After writing a dissertation at Harvard University on the topics of poverty, prisons, and inner cities in the early 1990s, I left the experience distraught and seriously questioning whether the US criminal justice system generally, and prisons in particular, could be reformed. Twenty years have passed since I last thought deeply about prisons and how they affect millions of individuals, families, and communities. Quite frankly, I feared the same conclusions were inevitable based on two fundamental assumptions.

The first assumption is about returning citizens. With the exception of a small percentage of incarcerated individuals who have received life sentences without the possibility of release, the vast majority of incarcerated individuals will return to civil society one day. We cannot afford the current rates of incarceration and recidivism, and we must explore cost-effective ways to help returning or transitioning citizens thrive once released.

The second assumption involves technology and entrepreneurship. There are only a small percentage of innovation-driven governors, legislators, mayors, or police chiefs; therefore, the majority of solutions to in-prison education and job training for reentry services will require a partnership with entrepreneurs in the technology and nonprofit sectors. Our economy cannot afford to invest $80 billion annually into the carceral state without a demand from society that it use twenty-first-century strategies to obtain a better return on investment for returning or transitioning citizens: both inside and outside of prison.[1]

This chapter compares and contrasts lessons learned about in-prison education and reentry opportunities and challenges facing prisoners and criminal justice reformers twenty years ago versus what the present generation of reformers are up against. Here is why.

On a personal note, my younger brother was incarcerated for nine years, beginning in the late 1980s through the mid-1990s. Since his release nearly twenty years ago, he has completely transformed his life. For example, he has held management and leadership roles at Ann Taylor, Mexx, and, most recently, 7-Eleven. He is an upstanding resident of Virginia with a wife and four children, and he sincerely appreciated regaining many of his civil rights as a result of Governor McAuliffe's Restoration of Rights Policy.

However, the stigma of incarceration continues to haunt him and his family in many other ways.[2] For instance, his youngest son is a star peewee league football player in his community, and many of his son's football games are played on fields located on a federal military installation near their home—but he is prohibited from entering military installations because of his past record.

From a professional perspective, I am the former president of Patten University (Patten), a regionally accredited higher education institution located in Oakland, California. Patten sought to use technology to offer greater access and more affordable postsecondary opportunities to adult learners, and it offered an associate's degree to inmates at San Quentin State Prison through a partnership with the Prison University Project (PUP). Our team watched guys walk across the stage every graduation ceremony full of pride. Yet even with a college degree, they will experience hidden barriers and obstacles to enjoying the rights and privileges of full citizenship.

Fortunately, there are people working every day to make truly extraordinary advancements as criminal justice reformers.[3] This is why the exploration of the work of five talented entrepreneurs in Northern California—specifically people and reform efforts that are grounded in the San Francisco Bay Area—is used as a case in point. Understanding how entrepreneurs in the tech and nonprofit sectors are thinking about prison reform and reentry from an ecological perspective is one of the objectives of this chapter. The interviews explored the following questions:

- How did these entrepreneurs become involved in criminal justice reform?
- What are the common barriers facing transitioning citizens?
- What products and services are necessary to change the outcomes for transitioning citizens?
- How is technology being used more effectively to address the salient challenges facing transitioning citizens?
- How can policy makers, funders, and other interested stakeholders help create eco-friendly environments for transitioning citizens?
- How do these criminal justice entrepreneurs measure success, and what outcomes are associated with their work?

GETTING OUR MINDS AROUND EDUCATION, TECHNOLOGY, AND NEW POSSIBILITIES

Many promising programs and initiatives address the salient challenges returning and transitioning citizens face upon release. The average transitioning citizen has multiple support needs, ranging from mental health and/or substance abuse counseling to assistance with employment, housing, relationship counseling, and family reunification. Rarely can these transitioning individuals find a one-stop holistic or comprehensive solution to their needs. This is where technology and innovation can potentially have the most significant impact.

In light of the technology-rich world that we live in today, reformers must ask themselves: How can we use technology to help incarcerated and transitioning citizens address the challenges associated with learning and earning? The first big step to writing this chapter involved identifying people researching, writing about, or implementing best practices associated with helping adults learn and earn in today's social-economic environment.

Each of the tech and social entrepreneurs interviewed in this chapter are attempting to advance or create innovative strategies to help transitioning citizens transform their lives. Of the many people interviewed for the chapter, five were selected to help illustrate the three critical elements involved in creating a pathway to success: (1) transitioning citizens committed to personal transformation, (2) a new breed of entrepreneurs and criminal justice reformers, and (3) the efficient use of new and emerging technology.

KENYATTA LEAL, PROGRAM COORDINATOR AT ROCKETSPACE—TRANSITION IS POSSIBLE

In 1994, at the age of twenty-five, Kenyatta Leal was handed a sentence of twenty-five years to life in California because of the "three-strikes law"—a law that mandated lengthy sentences for repeat felons. In its original form, a person with a prior conviction for a serious felony received a prison sentence twice the length typically given for a second offense, and a third criminal conviction yielded at least twenty-five years to life. The excessive sentencing stemming from three-strikes is an example of the draconian approach to criminal justice that was very common at that time.

Kenyatta was one of nearly seven thousand men per year in California who fell victim to the three-strikes law. His situation begs the question: How does one endure prison for at least twenty-five years and not lose hope? In an attempt to answer this question, Kenyatta sought advice from an older inmate—a "lifer" who had been incarcerated for more than twenty-five years. Despite the harsh conditions of the prison, this lifer was known for his grace and high moral character, and many inmates before and since Kenyatta had sought his guidance and advice about "doing time while not losing hope."

As they walked the perimeter of the San Quentin yard one afternoon, the older inmate advised Kenyatta to write down the ten things he valued most in life. He further instructed Kenyatta to ask himself, "What can I do every day, in and out of prison, to prioritize and realize the things most important to me?"

Kenyatta quickly recognized that until that moment he had no priorities, no clear sense of purpose, and he was spending his time before and during prison aimlessly. Moved by the recommendation of the "lifer" turned mentor, he spent the balance of his prison time at San Quentin building a foundation that would help him find meaning and purpose. Also, he began to nurture relationships with other men who were focused on healing, transformation, and making a difference in the lives of others.

He became motivated to take advantage of the more than eighty programs available to inmates at San Quentin, including PUP, which allowed him to earn an undergraduate degree from Patten. He augmented his undergraduate education with business knowledge and experience as a member of The Last Mile program.

Kenyatta served nineteen years in prison before California passed Prop 32 in 2012. This law changed the way future crimes were classified for inmates like him. As a result, he was resentenced to seven years and was immediately released in 2013. When asked to describe life after prison—notably, what it means to potentially gain full citizenship—he said, "It's a process, and you have to believe it will pay off. I had no illusions about how hard it would be given my prior offenses."[4]

He went on to add, "Finding viable employment was the single most important aspect of my success because it allowed me to be self sufficient. I'm now committed to expanding educational opportunities that prepare men and women for employment opportunities that give them hope while incarcerated."

When asked who was one of the first people to give him an opportunity to learn about technology, Kenyatta credits Duncan Logan, founder and CEO of Rocketspace, which provides support to tech start-ups. Logan gave Kenyatta the support needed to develop his skills as a technology entrepreneur, as well as the opportunity to expand and scale employment opportunities for transitioning citizens. Kenyatta used these skills to become a founding member of "The Last Mile" (TLM) to expand software development and coding classes in prison.

In 2014, TLM, through a partnership with the California Department of Corrections and Rehabilitation, launched the nation's first curriculum for coding inside a prison. The program has more than two hundred graduates, and thirty have been released. Of the thirty men who have been released, all are gainfully employed and none have committed an offense. This includes one gentleman who was making 25 cents per hour while in prison. After his release, he was hired by Chan Zuckerberg and is presently earning a six-figure salary.

The Last Mile launched the first software and coding program in a California institution for women, and Kenyatta is directly involved in helping teach incarcerated men and women software development skills, paying them the $16 per hour (the highest prison wage anywhere in the country), and assisting with job placement with tech companies. Of the fifty people who completed their program and have been released, there has been zero recidivism.

This program is currently operating in six corrections facilities in California—three for men and three for women—and it educates approximately 340 people. Over the next year, the plan is to expand into four new facilities. This assumes at least forty people per facility and partnerships with fifty facilities across the country, including one thousand people over the next five years. With an estimated shortage of one million software engineering jobs by 2020, as TLM notes on its webpage, Kenyatta and his team are playing an important role in the delivery and diversity of the talent pipeline for America's software industry—from inside prison walls.

JOHN DEASY, CHAIR OF THE BOARD OF THE RESET FOUNDATION—REACHING THE GOLD STANDARD

Assuming a transitioning citizen is highly motivated and committed to personal transformation, as Kenyatta demonstrated, the glaring challenge before sentencing, or after incarceration, is the dearth of alternative placement options available to judges and district attorneys. House arrest, home detention, or other alternatives to prison that do not address the potentially counterproductive influences within the home and community are problematic. Alameda County in California, for example, has a dire need for alternatives to prisons, and one unlikely social entrepreneur, John Deasy, is working aggressively to fill this gap.

As a career-long K–12 educator, administrator, and former urban superintendent, John was often frustrated by the number of students who disappeared from his classrooms and schools, only to later reappear on the rolls of various jails and prisons. The arrest and conviction of his students was particularly acute in the Los Angeles Unified School District (LAUSD), where John most recently served as superintendent. After retiring from LAUSD a few years ago, John relocated to the San Francisco Bay Area and committed the balance of his career to helping better serve young adults who often become trapped in the criminal justice system.

In 2013, John stepped in to lead the Reset Foundation, which aims to break the cycles of poverty, incarceration, and unemployment. The ultimate goal of Reset is to help young men, most between twenty-one and twenty-four years of age, secure "full-participation in the community," which potentially includes having their criminal record expunged. Reset initiated a small pilot program in San Francisco in 2014, and a full-fledged residential program started in 2016. The residential program began with five men, and John has plans to grow the Alameda-based program to a maximum of sixty young men while replicating it in high-needs communities across the country.

It is a high-touch residential program that reflects California's attempt to explore alternatives to incarceration. Five counties in California were selected to pilot "deferred delayed sentencing," and Alameda County was the first jurisdiction to take advantage of this opportunity. At its core, Reset demonstrates the complexity and potential value of sentencing options that seek to help transitioning citizens, in John's words, "achieve full participation in their community without the lingering effects of incarceration."

Essentially, the program gives judges the discretion to convict but then delay or avoid sentencing that requires incarceration. Judges, district attorneys, and other key stakeholders must collectively support recommending candidates for Reset. For example, a simple request for financial support by a family member is often communicated or interpreted as a crisis that has to be addressed immediately and potentially at the expense of other important obligations such as showing up at work on time or honoring a curfew.

After observing John's close interaction with these young men, he explained how to discern tangible and incremental signs of success. "Something seems to magically happen along the journey for those who turn things around," he responded. "After accumulating enough small victories with employment, housing, etc., [the men] gain the ability to see another way to live as a reality. There are a couple of young men who come immediately to mind; they have the talent and are now gaining the confidence to one day take my job."

His comments beg the question: Is it possible to scale a solution that helps transitioning citizens reach "the gold standard" (or what others refer to here as full citizenship)? Time will tell.

TIFFANY SMITH, CEO OF TILTAS—
CREATING A SEAMLESS PATHWAY TO EMPLOYMENT

Transitioning citizens have many needs as they attempt to secure self-sufficiency, but perhaps none is more important than employment. Demonstrating the capacity to secure and maintain employment, as well as generate consistent income, sets the foundation for all other possibilities. Advancing new technologies that address this issue will require social entrepreneurs like Tiffany Smith, and funders who are willing to back entrepreneurs like her.

Even while a full-time undergraduate at Howard University, Tiffany was able to help many of her friends and family members avoid or navigate the criminal justice system by assisting them with legal research and filing appeals—essentially acting as a virtual paralegal. These experiences reinforced for Tiffany the importance of education in her pursuit to make a difference in the lives of the people and communities near and dear to her heart. After securing her undergraduate degree in architecture, she acquired additional experience working for a construction firm in Washington, DC.

The District of Columbia (DC) has one of the highest rates of incarceration in America, and, based on the DC Office of Returning Citizen Affairs, there are approximately sixty thousand people living in the city with a criminal record. On average, eight thousand return to the city per year.[5] While working in Washington, Tiffany quickly gained additional insights into the challenges many transitioning citizens face when attempting to secure employment in the construction industry. "The stigma associated with incarceration," she noted, "makes it very difficult, if not impossible, for many of these men to secure the most basic entry-level positions in construction."

Armed with a deeper understanding of the barriers to employment facing these transitioning citizens, Tiffany enrolled in the Kellogg School of Management at Northwestern University with the sole purpose of developing the business expertise necessary to address a specific problem—helping transitioning citizens secure viable employment. After earning her MBA, she launched Chicago-based Tiltas Inc.—"a web-based platform that aims to provide transitioning citizens with an online community to support their transition back into society."[6]

Tiffany recently won the People's Op Tech Competition sponsored by Oakland, California–based Kapor Capital.[7] She is using the prize money to beta test a software application. However, despite winning this competition in 2017, she feels raising venture capital is one of the highest obstacles facing female social entrepreneurs interested in building criminal-justice-focused businesses.

"Most VCs [venture capitalists] are not willing to provide us the level of funding needed to build businesses that focus on transitioning citizens," Tiffany said. "Given the time needed to assess, prepare, and find employment for a transitioning citizen, I can't meet the time demands most VCs are looking for in early-stage companies," or, essentially, move a company like hers from start up to profitability at an unreasonable pace.

When asked what policy makers, funders, and other stakeholders could do to help her grow her business, she identified the need for support from individuals and organizations that can help provide research and empirical data about the needs and behaviors of transitioning citizens.

JOE KWONG, CEO OF SPROKIT—
GAMING THE CRIMINAL JUSTICE SYSTEM

Though employment is arguably the single most important aspect of successful reentry, the reality is that transitioning citizens have two or more other critical needs. The ideal solution would help them secure a bundle of services such as those offered by the Reset Foundation. Additionally, software or applications capable of capturing all the many incremental or baby steps a transitioning citizen takes to demonstrate commitment toward transformation is needed.

Joe Kwong is a forty-something Asian American male living in the Bay Area. Joe began his career as an Emmy Award–winning filmmaker who had one foot in the entertainment industry and the other in the gaming industry as a game designer. He never fathomed the possibility that he would one day become an entrepreneur in the education-technology sector, focused on improving the life chances of people transitioning from prison to mainstream life. But that is precisely where he is and what he does today.

Joe's journey began when he received an unsolicited request from the Corporation for Public Broadcast (CPB) to design an interactive American history course for high school students. A representative from CPB explained to Joe that American history is one of the most disliked courses among high school students. With a small grant from Congress, Joe received a crash course on how to use his background in entertainment, technology, and gaming to motivate and engage young adults.

This opportunity led to another engagement that focused on developing web-based tools for adjudicated young adults, and in doing that work, he quickly learned that the needs of this population were much different from those of traditional high school students. As he gained a deeper understanding of the challenges facing young adults tangled in the criminal justice system, but who are attempting to turn their lives around after incarceration, he realized that he needed to change his approach.

In 2015, Joe (along with Jeff Fino) established SPROKIT, which stands for "Successful Prisoner Re-entry = Opportunity and Knowledge Interactive Tools." SPROKIT is "a mobile app for re-entering prisoners that connects them to social services, parole/probation, employers, family & friends."[8]

As Joe made the transition from serving traditional high school students to transitioning citizens, he had to design an application that was compatible with smartphones and could be used as a tool to transcend multiple jurisdictions and end users. Equally as important, he had to factor into the equation the importance of connecting the discrete needs of transitioning citizens—namely, the social services and other supports they need. "When everything syncs up," he emphasized, "we have a beautifully effective process."

Joe believes his greatest insight and breakthrough involved creating a game-like component that keeps all users engaged. "If there is not an effective entertainment component," he noted during the interview, "you can't retain the returning citizens. 'SPROKITed' individuals can stay in touch with their probation officer and enjoy other benefits that can truly help them."

Joe is excited about his accomplishments, though when asked what has been his most significant challenge, he noted, "My biggest challenge has been attempting to disrupt an institution [jails and prisons] that focuses exclusively on punishment. There is no rehabilitative component in or out of prison. Attempting to change that paradigm has been difficult. We need to find a more humanistic approach to helping returning citizens succeed after they are released."

Most jurisdictions, like Alameda County, measure success by a single digit. Reducing recidivism from 75 to 70 percent would be such a measure. But through SPROKIT, Joe is looking for bigger numbers. He believes that, by helping transitioning citizens rebuild their social capital and form stronger support networks, SPROKIT can produce double-digit outcomes.

Today, the Alameda County Department of Corrections is his largest client, and he is working with them to create a cohesive approach to serving the needs of transitioning citizens. He is developing an application that connects transitioning citizens to rides, clothing, and other vital services and supports creating an unprecedented system of collaboration in Alameda County. SPROKIT does not share user numbers by jurisdiction as a matter of policy. However, generally speaking, they currently serve less than two hundred people, and they expect to serve more than two thousand in the next year. They plan to scale to more than twenty thousand end users in the next five years.

The criminal justice system often considers a 5 percent reduction in recidivism a tremendous success. SPROKIT believes it can exceed this number in most jurisdictions where it operates. More important, it has other benchmarks for success. In Alameda County, California, for example, they define success by changing the attitudes and behavior of probation officers.

Also, because SPROKIT's gamification involves corporate responsibility units (ride shares, food privileges, internships, apparel, etc.), success is determined by community involvement from corporate sponsors, increased employment opportunities, and a desire by other public institutions to participate within the SPROKIT network. This includes police, courts, and a variety of nonprofit organizations.

CHRIS GREWE, CEO OF AMERICAN DATA MANAGEMENT SYSTEMS—PROVIDING PRISON-BASED EDUCATION SOLUTIONS

Chris Grewe has been an entrepreneur all his life. He embarked upon his first venture at the age of nineteen, and he has consistently explored ways to improve student instruction using technology as an intervention tool and business development strategy. His entrepreneurial efforts exist at the intersection of instruction, remediation, and technology. However, he had no idea that his career path would lead him to a place where he is now committed to radically transforming the criminal justice sector, with a goal of "transforming prisons for good."

Early in his career, Chris began analyzing student retention data and quickly drew one conclusion: "If a student doesn't graduate from high school on time, they are eight times more likely to end up incarcerated, and 70 percent of the people we incarcerate don't have a high school diploma." After further investigation, he began researching the education needs of incarcerated adults, which included a visit to a local jail in Southern California.

He gained many helpful insights from the jail administrator who gave him a personal tour of the facility. He was particularly struck by the lack of educational resources available to those prisoners, as well as the administration's dependence on antiquated instruction. The jail, for example, had three classrooms and a makeshift library that barely served a small fraction of the more than three thousand inmates housed there.

More important, he recognized that there was a need for remedial support and workforce development training. "Prison walls," Chris noted, "create a man-made digital divide between incarcerated individuals and enormous advances in technology that are unfolding in the broader society." He quickly turned to the warden and said, "If I can identify a low-cost and innovative solution that does not threaten 'jail security,' would you consider it?" This experience was the impetus behind American Prison Data System (APDS), which was founded by Chris during the summer of 2013, and it operates as a certified public-benefits corporation.[9]

APDS began by looking closely at the range of safety and operational concerns faced by jails and prisons. Once identified, the team developed a tablet that can be assigned to individual inmates. The idea is to leverage technology used in most educational settings by making it accessible to people in secure environments.

In addition to the tablets, APDS partners with K–12 and postsecondary content providers to help inmates secure their GED or other credentials. Much like a guardian who places parental controls on their child's access to undesirable websites on the internet, inmates only have access to curated educational content and learning resources.

APDS appears to be growing rapidly. The organization has grown from Chris and a few trusted family members and friends to more than twenty-four employees. To date, they have delivered educational services to more than fifty thousand incarcerated learners.

APDS's preliminary educational outcomes are promising. They are witnessing a 63 percent pass rate on High School Equivalency Testing for those using their solution versus a 42 percent pass rate for those who do not. They are also finding that jails and prisons that deploy the tablets are witnessing a sharp reduction in violent behavior. Because inmates are spending a larger portion of their time studying and engaged in constructive activities, they have less idle time. Through the use of their programmatic solution, APDS has recorded a reduction in violence of between 88 and 100 percent in units using their customized solution.

KEY LESSONS LEARNED

Some salient findings were commonly shared by these unique entrepreneurs and the initiatives they are leading. First, each of them shared one fundamental belief—returning citizens are capable of personal transformation, and the products and services they are developing can make a tangible difference. From Kenyatta Leal's personal experience with incarceration to Tiffany Smith's direct encounters with returning citizens, they all have witnessed success on a small scale and believed they can have a greater impact.

Second, there is a fine line between inmates and corrections officials—namely, corrections and parole officers. This observation was made by fiction writer Kurt Vonnegut and prophetically articulated in his 1990 novel *Hocus Pocus*. Vonnegut fictitiously describes a society in which countless numbers of Americans are incarcerated, and the greatest threat to prison security is the unity between inmates and prison guards. The solution, offered in the book, is to outsource the management of US jails and prisons to Japan and other foreign countries because of the language barrier between the new guards and their charges.

As far-fetched as Vonnegut's story may seem, the contemporary tension between corrections personnel—namely, corrections officers—and inmates is more acute than the public realizes. For instance, many corrections personnel reside in low-income neighborhoods; have achieved at best a high school diploma; and, like inmates, are overly exposed to the depressing effects of the prison environment. Chris Grewe noted, "Very early during one of our deployments, guards questioned why they aren't eligible for some of the educational services the inmates are receiving at their facility."

As a result, APDS, as well as Joe Kwong at SPROKIT, have factored providing services to corrections and parole officers into their business models. For example, APDS provides corrections officers at Rikers Island, New York City's main jail, access to the same educational programs as the inmates. Rikers has a long-standing reputation for neglect and abuse of inmates. However, the efficient use of new and emerging technologies that address security concerns, and the needs of corrections personnel, represent a major breakthrough in criminal justice reform.

In addition to promising advancements, there were two glaring gaps. First, with the exception of APDS, which is in the early stages of launching a longitudinal study, nearly all the outcomes reported here are based on anecdotal or informal observations. Most of the entrepreneurs acknowledged a need for empirical research that can be used to refine, replicate, and scale their initiatives. However, none of the initiatives includes a robust and independent research component.

Also, two of the entrepreneurs' forays into education began at the K–12 level, and it is not clear that they understand the critical distinction between traditional and nontraditional students at the postsecondary level. There is a growing body of research motivated by the scholarship of Jeremy Knowles that distinguishes *pedagogy*—the art and science of teaching and learning for young people to young adults or traditional students—from *andragogy*—the art and science of teaching and learning for adults or nontraditional students.

Nontraditional students—adults around twenty-four to fifty years of age—often pursue a postsecondary credential because of a downturn in the economy, or because their skills are obsolete within the current knowledge economy. Some of them discontinued their education because of military services, childbirth, or other significant life events. For these reasons, reentering citizens resemble nontraditional students in the following ways:

- financially independent
- desire full-time employment while in school
- responsible for supporting dependents
- part-time or flexible enrollment is most convenient

Despite these characteristics, returning citizens are treated more like traditional students. Developing and implementing viable educational products and services for this unique student population must acknowledge their differences.

CONCLUSION

As noted at the onset, the purpose of this chapter was to compare and contrast prison reform and reentry opportunities and challenges facing returning citizens and criminal justice reformers today versus two decades or so ago. Simply put, there is a growing and positive shift in the way the country is thinking about reentry and recidivism.

From a historical perspective, there has never been a time in our history more conducive to criminal justice reform in and outside of prison than today. During the late 1960s through the 1970s, there was a liberal movement that expanded civil rights and liberties of prisoners in most federal and state institutions. The two decades covering the 1980s to 1990s included a dramatic increase in the number of incarcerated people and a dramatic reduction in rehabilitative services—namely, substance abuse support, educational opportunities, and post-incarceration employment services.

Over the last five years, starting with the Obama administration, there was a growing realization that the United States cannot sustain the high cost of prison growth. That understanding appears to be shared by the Trump administration, and there are bipartisan efforts under way led by Senator Brian Schatz (D-HI), who introduced the "Restoring Education and Learning" (REAL) Act in February 2018. The bill seeks to reinstate Pell Grant eligibility for incarcerated individuals to reduce the cycle of recidivism, save taxpayers money, and improve safety.

In California, some promising signs are emerging from a funding perspective. Organizations like the California Workforce Development Board (CWDB) and California Wellness Foundation are forming a public-private partnership that will provide entrepreneurs and community-based organizations new sources of funding, notably "workforce accelerator" dollars. CWDB has pledged to provide funding to help prepare more than two hundred thousand California citizens for jobs of the future, with particularly focus on returning citizens. Their plan anticipates sentencing reductions and early release for nonviolent offenders, and they are committed to providing comprehensive supports during both pre- and post-release periods.

Though jails and prisons are ubiquitous institutions in the United States, the pendulum appears to be swinging from a strictly punishment approach to more liberal efforts to offer rehabilitative supports. Findings from interviews with technology and social entrepreneurs strongly suggest there is a burgeoning ecosystem of criminal justice reformers with the commitment, knowledge, and capacity to reverse or improve outcomes for returning citizens.

NOTES

1. Using more precise terminology creates an opportunity to more thoroughly develop progressive ways to think about and measure success after incarceration. A review of the contemporary literature, including many of the chapters written here, revealed an emphasis on the use of the term *returning citizens*, and a focus on reducing recidivism as the ultimate metric for success.

The term *returning citizens* is commonly used today instead of *ex-con*, *formerly incarcerated*, and other terms that perpetuate a stigma commonly associated with prisons. Efforts to help prisoners shed the disgrace commonly associated with incarceration are movement in the right direction. These are fundamental shifts from the discourse about prisons in the 1990s. However, it is misleading to assume that ex-offenders will be recognized as "returning citizens" when, in fact, they will be denied most of the basic rights associated with full citizenship.

We should consider using a more precise term like *transitioning citizens* to better capture the journey from losing one's freedom (incarceration) to partially regaining privileges and rights upon release to the restoration of all civil liberties (full citizenship). It is important to acknowledge each of these critical phases of reentry to completely understand the challenges and opportunities facing transitioning citizens.

2. Michelle Alexander, *The New Jim Crow: Mass Incarceration in the Age of Colorblindness* (New York: New Press, 2010).

3. Joyce Arditti, "Families and Incarceration: An Ecological Approach," *Families in Society: The Journal of Contemporary Social Services* 86, no. 2 (2005): 251–60.

4. The quote from Kenyatta was obtained during an interview with the author on October 25, 2018. The additional interviews in this chapter with John Deasy, Tiffany Smith, Joe Kwong, and Chris Grewe took place on October 9, 2017; September 22, 2017; October 5, 2017; and January 3, 2018, respectively.

5. Clinton Yates, "'Returning Citizens' Are Still One of D.C.'s Most Marginalized and Motivated Groups," *Washington Post*, January 16, 2015, https://www.washingtonpost.com/news/local/wp /2015/01/16/returning-citizens-are-still-one-of-d-c-s-most-marginalized-and-motivated-groups/?utm_ term=.1af616cc10cc.

6. Jeff Schmitt, "2017 MBS to Watch: Tiffany Smith, Northwestern (Kellogg)," *Poets & Quants*, August 7, 2017, https://poetsandquants.com/2017/08/07/2017-mbas-to-watch-tiffany-smith-north western-kellogg/.

7. Kapor Capital is an Oakland, California–based venture capital fund that places an emphasis on backing minority-led start-ups.

8. SPROKIT homepage, http://www.sprokit.net/.

9. Public-benefits corporations are a specific type of entity that places the public benefit before the traditional corporate goal of maximizing profit for shareholders.

10

Student Voices

Karen Jones, Brian Amaro, Salih Israil, Marcus Lilly, and Michelle Jones

Despite reformers' emphasis on improving conditions and opportunities for the incarcerated, the voices of the incarcerated are almost always left out of public policy conversations. To shed light on what it is like to attend school in prison, appreciate the value education programs offer the incarcerated, and better understand the challenges facing the incarcerated as they attend school behind bars, this chapter features five essays authored by the incarcerated or formerly incarcerated.

Their stories and accounts provide a rare view into the lives that these programs impact, and what policy makers and educators can do to improve, sustain, and expand quality programs in prison.

THE AUDACITY OF COLLEGE IN PRISON—BY KAREN JONES

Handcuffed in the back of an obscure blue van, I spent the hour-long drive to the Maryland Correctional Institution for Women (MCIW) praying and crying. Nothing could have prepared me for the culture shock that was my Starbucks-to-shackles life. I can never forget pulling up to a dismal building and the driver graciously allowing me to "get it all out." I scream-cried. Ugly-face cried. But I had to get out of the van.

The first thing I noticed was the stench: a combination of hot garbage and what I would soon learn was perpetually grey food. Starting that first day, the six and a half years that I spent behind that barbed-wire fence broke me. I like to think that I have put the pieces back together, but if I am honest, parts of me are broken still. Fortunately, we live in a world of balance and, even within the desolate existence of prison where dehumanization is standard, there are silver linings.

Mine came in the form of education. My first year at MCIW felt like an out-of-body experience; I walked around, a shell of a person clinging to the desperate hope for the miracle of deliverance that would never come. Eventually the fog started to clear when an opportunity arose to take classes from a local community college. I immediately signed up, but not without judgment: "This is going to be watered down." Even so, I took every class available.

Being in class became the only time I felt like a human being. Suddenly, I had a voice. My opinions mattered. I could ask hard questions and contemplate complicated answers. For those hours in class, there was no one telling me to squat and cough, no one counting me like cattle, and no one putting me down because their brass badge dictated they could.

After two years, the prison transitioned from community college classes to courses through the Goucher Prison Education Partnership (GPEP). GPEP is a division of Goucher College that offers a liberal arts education to incarcerated students. Those who complete the requisite coursework are eligible to receive a bachelor's degree. I approached this new phase of my prison experience with the same characteristics that carried me through: judgment and skepticism.

I was, by now, too proud to let anyone make me feel like a charity case, too stubborn to obey the rules enforced by people who went home to their families every night, and too much of a skeptic to believe that the education provided would be legit. The fall semester started, and within the first week, I had to eat humble pie. The workload was surreal. Each class added to the stack of papers to read and assignments to write.

GPEP professors provided us with the academic materials we needed to produce quality work, eliminating our ever-popular prison excuse of not having access to anything. With each new assignment, our professors stretched our intellectual boundaries, challenging our thoughts and perceptions, and demanding text-based evidence to back up our claims. GPEP thought of everything, came prepared, and took no prisoners. Pun intended.

Over time, I learned that I wasn't a charity project. I was being served by people who live a life of service and instill that value in those whose lives they touch. The wall of stubborn suspicion that had built up over the past three years began to wear away, and I soon learned that the vigorous work schedule was necessary for success. To my surprise, I was no longer a skeptic. I began to realize that I was being given the same education offered at the main campus.

I was being entrusted with the same responsibilities and expectations as the students attending classes on campus. My mind was being challenged, and it felt like I was coming up for air. For the first time in a long time, I felt hope. This time it wasn't hope for the miraculous deliverance; my hope was in the redemption that an education offered. My time wouldn't be spent etching tally marks into the concrete for each day that passed. Education gave me some of my control back, and I decided that the atrocity that is prison wasn't going to be the end of my story.

Most people, myself included, go to prison because we violate the trust given to us by society. On the inside, no amount of remorse opens the gates, and we are, essentially, warehoused. GPEP gave me the opportunity to invest in myself. I started my prison college experience a paradox of gratitude and cynicism and finished a more whole version of my-self. After years of college, I finally felt empowered and redeemed. Some education comes in the form of books. But I learned, specifically in prison, some comes in the form of the restoration of humanization.

College in prison means belonging to a minority of people whose whole is greater than the sum of its parts. It is hard work in the face of persecution from officers and inmates alike who don't understand *the weight* of it. The weight of those who would come after me, pursuing an education that will change their lives. The weight of my immigrant parents who left their country for me to have an education, *not* a felony conviction.

On my first day at MCIW, I didn't see how I was going to survive. Through education, I found more than a desolate existence; I found purpose, and it gave me the grit to come out as a better woman and the determination to pay forward that which I can never pay back. Almost everything within our society tells us that college operating in prison is audaciously inappropriate. But if we could look past our ignorance toward the incarcerated, we would see that it makes sense.

It might be easy to pretend inmates don't exist while we are locked behind bars, but here is the thing: *we come home.* We sit next to you at work. We join the PTA. We strike up a conversation with you at Starbucks, and you have no idea that we have done hard time in an even harder place. If I could, I would challenge the American people, who notoriously love a comeback kid story, to invest in the very story they root for.

I am a comeback kid. I returned home, started and run my own business, and bought a house. I also work full time, raise my children, and advocate for criminal and social justice reform—and it's only been two years. My education gave me the strength and confidence I needed to achieve ambitious goals. Give me time, America. I'm worth the wait.

MY STORY—BY BRIAN AMARO

While awaiting trial for capital murder in the county jail, I was able to participate in a unique test (thanks to the intervention of a Christian group): helping a deemed violent offender receive a general education diploma (GED). This group handpicked me from a whole pod of inmates who were charged with violent crimes. I accepted, though mainly because I wanted an excuse to get out of my cell. The education classroom on the top floor was specially fitted for me; they installed a small cage in the back of a class with room to fit one desk, as well as a slot to collect books and tests.

I received many stares from the class, who all pretty much had to take the course just to be released sooner. I had to arrive an hour before the rest of the class to be let into my cage, and I had to wait an hour after all had left to be let out, chained up again, and escorted back to my cell. I finished the course and earned my GED. Even though I was ecstatic to earn my GED, receiving it was a baby step on a very large journey, but it was a step in the right direction. This step led me to books, which have since become a passion of mine.

The more I read and learn, the more I hope, and the more I hope, the more I plan and envision a better life. A dysfunctional childhood, homelessness, and parentless teenage years . . . my past sounds like a very popular story within these gates. The most common ground us inmates share is a poor education, and in the Texas Department of Criminal Justice, education is *not* always easily accessible.

Easily accessible are the gangs and drugs that plague prisons, but I see and feel the difference in inmates who finally get to participate in an educational course. Even prison gangs respect the value of education. Having been in prison since the late 1990s—since my late teens—I know how prison gangs work, because I was actively involved in one[1] for more than a decade. Leaving a gang isn't always as easy as it was to join, but one of the most respected ways was when one of us got lucky enough to get involved in academics, because we all know that an education is vital for us to have any hope for a future.

Due to my conviction (murder) and the fact I had no money, it was nearly impossible to receive a sufficient education in "here." Budget cuts, limited space, and my twenty-year sentence were the reasons for the rejections for all my requests for any college-level courses. After four years of waiting, I was able to participate in an electrical vocational course—even though I asked for computer training.

I accepted because I didn't want to wait any longer, but I honestly don't remember any of the training, despite having one of the highest grades. It involved *very little* "hands-on" work.

It was mostly book work. I learn more from "hands-on." Once I finished that course, I was told by school counselors that I had achieved all that I would be allowed to academically while in prison. I still had fifteen more years.

I noticed that not just violent criminals but also most gang members are mostly followers and uneducated, so it's easy to see what they lack: a sense of self-worth, a vision of what they can offer, and the tools to create and lead for themselves. "Once a mind has been expanded, it is impossible for it to return to its original dimension." I read that somewhere and marveled at the meaning.

I had a wonderful sense of accomplishment when I passed and earned my GED, though further accomplishments have not been easy. Today I am not just ready to reenter society but also eager and prepared to contribute to my community and be a successful citizen. I have been fortunate enough to have been accepted in a program—a movement—called the Prison Entrepreneurship Program (PEP). I am part of a brotherhood that brings tears to my eyes just trying to explain how they have impacted my life and the brothers (inmates) around me!

I finally got my college-level curriculum that I was praying for, and the "hands-on" type of learning—in abundance! These were nine months of the hardest transition I ever had to endure, and I loved it! PEP took an ignorant and inexperienced inmate—and made a business-savvy man out of him! Not too bad of a dancer, either. I learned how to create a solid business plan and was even able to present it to a room filled with real-life executives.

The sense of accomplishment I felt when I walked on a stage wearing a graduation gown, receiving a certificate from Baylor University's Hankamer School of Business, is a memory I will always cherish. Nearly twenty years in prison, I honestly feel that delivering my business pitch in a room filled with hundreds of people was the scariest thing I had to face! I could go on forever explaining how vital this program was—is—for us, but here is the most profound point for me: PEP set the stage for me to reconnect with my family and make them proud of me.

The training we were given had our heads spinning, but we are better men for it. We now have a definition of what an *authentic man* is—and a plan to live our lives as one. PEP has helped us find our "why." My "why" is my future, because I plan to live and thrive there! Our success is easy to see, and I pray that PEP flies even higher—across the nation—so every inmate has an opportunity to live between our wings!

THE AWAKENING—BY SALIH ISRAIL

"I'm twenty-seven years old with fourteen years left on a twenty-to-forty-year sentence," I told the executive director of Bard Prison Initiative (BPI), Max Kenner, during my admissions interview at Eastern Correctional Facility in New York in 2003. I was responding to the question about why I wanted to apply to BPI and participate in a liberal arts education. Although at that time I believed a liberal arts education consisted of learning to paint or playing an instrument, I knew BPI's presence at Eastern represented a unique opportunity, and I wanted in.

The only problem was there were two hundred other applicants who felt the same way, and BPI was only accepting sixteen of us. To say the admissions process was highly competitive would be an understatement, and I was both thrilled and relieved when I learned I had been accepted. Looking back, I knew there were potential economic advantages to going to college, but I had no idea I was about to embark on a fourteen-year journey that would totally transform how I understood and related to myself, others, and the world around me.

I had very simple expectations as I entered my first semester: taking courses meant acquiring credits; acquiring credits meant earning a degree; and earning a degree meant a world of possibilities after I was released. Those expectations were grounded in the idea that my *work* as an accepted college student would consist of consuming information, retaining that information, and taking tests that measured how well I retained that information.

Instead, I found myself enrolled in courses that not only introduced me to the complex and nuanced ideas of innovative thinkers such as Immanuel Kant, Ralph Ellison, Thomas Paine, and Jean-Jacques Rousseau but also challenged me to identify and articulate my understanding (or lack thereof) of those ideas. Every text I encountered represented a new opportunity for me to critique, rethink, or enhance my ideas and values.

As I moved along my educational journey, I realized my access to a college education wasn't something I was given or something I did. Rather, my college education was something I experienced, and there were three major dynamics that proved essential in ensuring it was a life-altering and transformative experience.

The first dynamic was the cultivation of shared learning spaces where I and fourteen to twenty other men of various ages, backgrounds, and cultures willingly struggled to make sense of new and complex ideas.

At times, this shared struggle required a certain level of vulnerability: an openness to being critiqued and corrected, as well as a vulnerability that was crucial to creating pathways to growth and mature thought. In other words, what I experienced through a college education was a shared experience, and this shared experience was just as vital to my ability to grasp complex ideas in texts like Jean-Jacques Rousseau's *The Social Contract* as it was to my determination to struggle through these texts when they seemed confusing.

The second dynamic was the discursive nature of the collective coursework offered in a given semester. To illustrate, in my third semester I took five courses ranging across five disciplines: anthropology, sociology, literature, mathematics, and philosophy. Imagine reading Peter Berger's *Sociological Imagination*, F. Scott Fitzgerald's *Tender Is the Night*, and selections from Benjamin Whorf's *Language, Thought, and Reality* while simultaneously working through the underlying moral implications of the notion of informed consent.

Initially, each text, each course, seemed a mountain unto itself. Then I began to acknowledge that, although there were distinct differences between the disciplines, each carried concepts, theoretical frameworks, and critiques that provided context and insight through which to engage others.

The third, and probably most important, dynamic was an overwhelming sense of commitment and purpose, and by that, I mean a collective sense of commitment and purpose that morphed into a network of support and encouragement among my cohort. My fellow college students and I regularly discussed the significance of having access to a college education and the importance of engaging it to the fullest.

Thus, although I was solely responsible for fulfilling the requirements of each course, I was fully aware that I was only one of a group of college students participating in the college-in-prison program at Eastern. Slowly but surely, my experience of college education evolved into it being about more than just me. I embraced the idea that on many levels my engagement with BPI directly and indirectly impacted incarcerated people who didn't have access to a college education, who did have access to a college education, and who could have access to a college education in the future.

In the end, my experience of college education accomplished three unexpected feats: (1) it challenged and encouraged me to critique, evaluate, and alter the kind of narrow-minded thinking and values that permitted me to participate in the criminal behavior that led me to prison; (2) it created opportunities for me to learn and grow to respect and value the ideas and positions of others; and (3) it inspired me to continually evaluate how my decisions and behavior impact the rights and autonomy of others.

And yes, it also increased my chances of acquiring gainful employment—I was hired as a data analyst with the Brooklyn Community Bail Fund within three weeks of my release. In fact, my experience of college education fulfilled not only the combined goals and aims of every other program available at Eastern but also the rehabilitative goals and aims articulated in the mission statement of the New York State Department of Corrections and Community Supervision. So why aren't prison officials across the country working diligently to extend access to such a tried and proven program?

Unfortunately, many of them are so concerned about a potential backlash over an infringement upon the preconceived notions of exceptionalism and privilege generally associated with the term *college* that they simply refuse to acknowledge the large body of research that suggests access to college education is arguably the most viable option for achieving rehabilitative outcomes and drastically reducing recidivism.

SINS OF OMISSION—BY MARCUS LILLY

The majority of the human beings confined in prison cells will return to their communities hopeless. If not properly educated, they will recidivate. The same youth offenders who are regularly suspended from correctional educational schools are the same repeat gun offenders who return to society to shoot innocent bystanders. This is what I call the "Spider-Man Effect" because Peter Parker's uncle, an innocent bystander, would still be alive had Spider-Man used his power to stop a robber from committing an act that harmed his uncle. This may be a scene from a Marvel Comic movie, but it is also observational learning.

If this country fails to truly rehabilitate its incarcerated citizens, then it indirectly contributes to crime in American communities. Prison intensifies the criminal mentality instead of eradicating it. Therefore, to some degree, the inaction of those in society who fail to act—but who have the resources to make a difference—is almost equal to the illegal acts that will increase recidivism. The two are intertwined. Incarcerated citizens suffer from sins of ignorance while policy makers suffer from sins of omission.

The prison environment in the nineteenth century fostered a moral compass. Actually, the word *penitentiary* is derived from the word *penitence*, which means to atone for one's wrongdoings. Thus, the purpose of prison during those times was to discourage criminal behavior and encourage rehabilitation. This seems rather indifferent on behalf of the policy makers because they are ultimately choosing recidivism over education.

What Should Policy Makers Know Regarding Why Education Is Critical to Reducing Recidivism?

According to reports, "on average, inmates who participated in correctional education programs had 43 percent lower odds of recidivating than inmates who did not."[2] In addition, other studies suggest that "Every inmate who leaves the system saves that state an average of $25,000 per year. . . . Former inmates with jobs also have less need for public assistance and contribute to society, in the form of taxes and purchasing power."[3] Although these statistics certainly convey the numbers, they cannot describe the impact education has on human lives.

For example, that same youth offender who received a prison-based college education now has the resources to work toward a career. Instead of selling heroin in his community, thus adding to the epidemic, he can become an entrepreneur. Moreover, he will have higher self-esteem and will more likely be a better father to his son. No amount of statistics can account for this sort of transformation.

Policy makers may argue that punishment should trump education. However, even punishment has its limitations, which can lead to negative outcomes. Moreover, it does not encourage desirable behavior. I know of many prisoners who still think that crime pays after decades of incarceration. Others argue that law-abiding citizens are not getting a free education, so why should "criminals" acquire one? Albeit, the rehabilitative effects of education are well documented.

Also, if we know most ex-offenders are likely to recidivate, aren't we indirectly aiding and abetting in their future crimes if we do not help educate them? It makes more sense to invest in human capital to break the cycle of recidivism. This "nothing works" philosophy was started roughly forty-two years ago by sociologist Robert Martinson. Ironically, he contradicted his own findings four years later by admitting that some programs are effective. So, why are we still stuck in the past?

What Was Challenging about Attending College while Incarcerated?

Progress can be very difficult when everyone else in your environment is purposely held at a standstill. Sometimes I feel a sense of "survivor's remorse" when people ask me to assist them in getting into the college program. I can see that they have the desire to learn, but there aren't enough programs that provide education. That being said, gaining access to these programs is an issue. For instance, the same nonaccredited college program that helped pave the way for me to get into the University of Baltimore has been terminated. This leaves around 150 students left to fend for themselves in an environment that breeds ignorance.

In addition, the majority of the correctional officers treat prisoners who are pursuing an education as if they do not deserve to be in college. Ironically, these are the same officers who complain about inmates idling their time away. This leaves us twirling in a cycle where incarcerated citizens are judged harshly for improving their education but also blamed for not doing so. Finally, education has always been challenging to me.

I failed the third and fifth grades because of comprehension issues. I was horrible at math and could barely read. I dropped out of high school in the ninth grade, and I hardly passed my GED test. For this reason, not only was college-level work an arduous task, but learning how to use a laptop was completely foreign to me. As a result, I am somewhat unequipped to reenter a society that is now governed by technology.

How Has This Program Benefited Me?

This program has helped me broaden my perception of self. I now feel confident enough to sit in an auditorium packed with professors and politicians and be the one to elevate the conversation. I have the knowledge to mobilize my community and link micro assets to the macro environment. I can now be a better father to my son and inspire him to go to college.

I can now be the one who can reach the "thug" out there on the corner. Maybe my advice can prevent him from robbing someone's mother. Most important, returning back to prison isn't a thought in my mind.

In closing, I grew up knowing that I would go to prison before I would go to college. Now, as a college student in prison, I know that I will walk across the stage and earn my degree, with no worries of walking into a prison cell where I will not be free.

DO WHAT MAKES SENSE: THE VALUE OF HIGHER EDUCATION PROGRAMS IN PRISON—BY MICHELLE JONES

Equally the doorway and the door, the incarcerated and post-incarcerated's access to a higher education operates as a counterweight to the stigma and the taint of criminality that pervade our lives. It is leverage the post-incarcerated can use to defend against an indelible taint, the "forever-a-criminal" that is our proverbial bumper sticker. Existing, much less studying, in prison is not easy.

Even the most benevolent of prisons are still cordoned off, secretive, and heterotopic spaces of crisis.[4] These are places that, to one degree or another, remake you. Normative behaviors such as sharing goods, giving hugs, and waving "hello" are subject to disciplinary sanctions in most prisons. The noise, interruptions (count times, fire drills, and suspended movement), and constant and often arbitrary changes of bunk mates, staff, and custody and facility rules produce chaotic experiences. Imagine being in college and struggling with no paper clips, staplers, rubber bands, or three-ring binders. Are you wondering how we hold ourselves or anything together?

True story: I once made a Trapper Keeper out of three cheap pocket folders, purloined tape, and shoe strings. Being a college student means overcoming personal feelings of inadequacy, the fear of failing, and the horrible discovery of just how far behind one really is. It also means countering faculty's preconceived notions and prejudices about incarcerated people. Being a college student is a call to go above and beyond one's perceived limitations and tap one's own potential despite the limitations. Earning a degree in prison is a testament to more than just a desire for good grades; it is a testament to the unquenchable power of the spirit to revive and rise.

For us, access to a higher education is the following:

1. an accomplishment under great pressure wherein we can do something great;
2. evidence we are not worthless or damned, but that we are smart and capable of making a meaningful contribution;
3. a demonstration to our children and families that we are valuable members of the group and they should not give up on us; and
4. a present goal, which could include a reduction in time served—a goal to give ourselves over to as opposed to dwelling in/on our past mistakes full of their recrimination and mental torture.

My access to a higher education represented a key component of my current success. When I started college at the Indiana Women's Prison (IWP) in 1998, students worked all day and attended classes at night. College programs in the Indiana Department of Correction (IDOC) were funded with state dollars. Students could attend Martin University or Ball State University.[5] I chose Martin University because I knew about its history of serving predominantly poor and African American communities.

Martin faculty challenged me to competently read, write, and speak across their curriculum. In the classroom, I didn't feel bound. I found freedom in the world of ideas and easily jumped into English composition with the same enthusiasm as political science. I'd always liked school as a child, but now with my fractured past and internal brokenness with all of the accompanying losses, college was my refuge and escape, one of the prominent paths I took to rebuild myself.

By law, incarcerated students in Indiana were given eight semesters to complete a four-year degree. I had just finished my junior year with Martin University when the IDOC terminated its contract with Martin, leaving Ball State as the sole provider. I had funding for only one more semester in 2001. Martin's departure and the question of transferable credits to Ball State left me wondering whether I would ever graduate.

Ball State ultimately took less than half of Martin's credits. I became a sophomore again. Gratefully, one Ball State faculty member's scholarship fund—and some Franciscan monks—provided the rest of my tuition so I could graduate in 2004. Because of their kindness, when I stood on the podium and accepted my degree, I cried grateful tears.

My bachelor's degree has served me in countless ways since. A four-year theological seminary program started at the prison and, at that time, accepted students with bachelor's degrees only. I now have a lay ministerial certification from the University of the South. It served me well in the leadership and other intellectually and creative areas of my life.

In 2012, all state funding for higher education programs in prisons across the state ended. We were devastated and mourned like a death occurred; in many ways, it had. Yet hope arrived a year later when Dr. Kelsey Kauffman—with the support of our then superintendent, Stephen McCauley—created the Higher Education Program (HEP). HEP provided precollege, college, and graduate education for women at every stage of their educational background.

Most important, when HEP searched the facility looking for those with bachelor's degrees to participate in the Indiana Women's Prison (IWP) History Project, I was able to participate. Charged with researching and writing the history of the first fifteen years of our prison, my incarcerated colleagues and I have had the very unusual opportunity to engage in and present research at local, regional, and national conferences. Our findings are challenging dominant narratives about the origins of women's prisons and connecting the inherent violence of prisons to our contemporary incarceration.

In the process, I've served as a spokesperson for incarcerated women nationally, highlighting the perils of labeling incarcerated people as *prisoner, felon, inmate,* and *offender,* as well as exposing the consequences of imposing an indelible taint of criminality upon the post-incarcerated's access to opportunity and regaining full citizenship, including civil and social death and criminal justice debt.[6]

Today, I am a PhD student at New York University and spent a year as a research fellow at the Harvard University Warren Center. The IWP History Project's scholarship is now under contract with New Press for publication, in no small part because I was able to take advantage of the opportunity to earn an offered higher education. No one would refute that the possession of a higher education has indeed changed the trajectory of my life.

One of my goals is to change how the post-incarcerated scholar is viewed by academia.[7] Very often, released scholars seek to further their education but find themselves blocked by cosmic exclusionary practices that further the collateral consequences of incarceration.[8] Moreover, the post-incarcerated scholar is often devalued. I holistically refute our presumed disposability.

There are scholars coming out of mass incarceration who are able to interpret the lived experience of incarceration, as well as historicize and synthesize its individual impact and societal consequences to academia and the world. I believe I am one of them, but I am by no stretch of the imagination the only one. Thousands of men and women in prison today are brilliant, talented, and worthy people who simply need access to opportunity to realize their innate potential.

Prison higher education programs across this country, whether fledgling or fully funded, are providing the means for men and women to be more despite family fragmentation, collateral consequences of criminal conviction, and negative self-definition. The stakes are too high to do less. Given that recidivism is reducible by 40 percent when incarcerated people have access to a higher education, and education is commonly a path to self-sufficiency and sustainability in employment, we must do more.

A responsible and responsive community can do more. The question is, what kind of community do we have in America today? There needs to be a pathway to a higher education in every prison. The time of indifference and inaction has long passed. There are those who scoff and say that their children didn't have access to a free education, so why should we educate incarcerated people? My response is simple. Ninety-five percent of incarcerated people return to the community, and a higher education is a method to ensure that the overwhelming majority stay out of prison. It is a worthy cost to pay, considering the alternative.

The facts speak for themselves: Seventy million Americans have criminal records overall, 80 percent of African American men in some cities have criminal records, and checking the box on an employment application is often an automatic exclusion. Millions, literally millions (mostly people of color), face legalized discrimination, cosmic employment exclusion, and precarious economic sustainability because of their involvement with the criminal justice system. In a recent follow-up study, the Bureau of Justice found that five out of six people (83 percent) were re-incarcerated within nine years of release.[9] Yet nearly every state in the nation spends more incarcerating people than educating its elementary and secondary school students.[10]

Let us do what makes sense. Can we do what makes sense?

NOTES

1. Orejon is a mostly Hispanic-dominated gang, also known as "Tango," with more than ten thousand members.

2. Lois M. Davis et al., *Evaluating the Effectiveness of Correctional Education: A Meta-Analysis of Programs That Provide Education to Incarcerated Adults* (Santa Monica, CA: RAND Corporation, 2013).

3. David Skorton and Glenn Altschuler, "College Behind Bars: How Educating Prisoners Pays Off," *Forbes*, March 25, 2013, https://www.forbes.com/sites/collegeprose/2013/03/25/college-behind-bars -how-educating-prisoners-pays-off/#6b2bd8d22707.

4. Michel Foucault, "Des Espace Autres," March 1967, translated from the French by Jay Miskowiec as "Of Other Spaces: Utopia and Heterotopias," *Architecture/Mouvement/Continuité*, October 1984, 5–7. Michel Foucault's concept of *heterotopias* describes spaces, real or imagined, existing everywhere in which undesirable, disposable, and criminalized "deviant" persons are tucked away, out of sight of normative spaces and "respectable" people. There are two kinds of *heterotopias*: One is the "space of crisis," for individuals who find themselves in temporary spaces of exclusion, like prisons or mental hospitals. The other is "space of deviance," which are spaces intended for those who operate outside of accepted social norms. Prisons are both. By their very nature, they are secretive places; they are not open or transparent, and within them, the incarcerated experience violence.

5. Ball State University offered associate's degrees and bachelor's degrees. Martin University offered only bachelor's degrees.

6. Michelle Jones, "From Debt to Debt: The Realities of the Post-Incarcerated" (Session Title: We Have No Home in This Place: Prisons, Debt, Gender and Health), American Studies Association Conference, Denver, Colorado, November 18, 2016, http://www.indiana.edu/~video/stream/launchflash.html?folder=video&filename=American_Studies_Assn_Panel_20161118.mp4; "Distrusting the Narrative: Women's Prison History and Ethics," *Examining Ethics*, Prindle Institute of Ethics Podcast, October 26, 2016, http://www.examiningethics.com; and "Rewriting the Sentence: College behind Bars," American Public Media, American Radio Works, National Public Radio, September 9, 2016, http://www.apmreports.org/story/2016/09/08/prison-education [30:08–52.09].

7. Jody Lewen, "Academics Belong in Prison: On Creating a University at San Quentin," *Publication of the Modern Language Association of America* 123, no. 3 (May 2008): 684–95. Lewen asserts, "Within the various disciplines, students acquire conceptual vocabulary with which to interpret and articulate personal and community experiences. . . . They also discover intellectual and professional worlds and being to visualize careers through which they might make positive contributions" (692).

8. John B. King, *Beyond the Box: Increasing Access to Higher Education for Justice-Involved Individuals*, US Department of Education, 2016, 5–7, https://www2.ed.gov/documents/beyond-the-box/guidance.pdf. The US Department of Education has recently addressed the discriminatory practices colleges and universities deploy to exclude students from postsecondary education. This report highlights how "the admissions process is one of the many barriers that justice-involved people face, particularly people of color, who are disproportionately represented in our nation's justice system" (5). However, as important as undergraduate education is, everyone is forgetting about those of us who have already earned an undergraduate degree, whether in or out of prison, and are ready for graduate school, which exposes a whole different level of carceral gatekeeping judges. See also Katti Gray, "How 'Collateral Consequences' Complicate Life after Prison," *Crime Report*, February 6, 2017, https://thecrimereport.org/2017/02/06/how-collateral-consequences-can-still-hurt-after-prison/#; and Margaret Colgate Love, Jenny Roberts, and Cecelia Klingele, "Collateral Consequences of Criminal Convictions: Law, Policy and Practice," *Thompson Reuters Westlaw/NACDL Press* 10, no. 2014-48 (2013).

9. "2018 Update on Prisoner Recidivism: A Nine-Year Follow-Up Period (2005–2014)," press release, Bureau of Justice Statistics, accessed July 18, 2018, http://www.bjs.gov/index.cfm?ty=pbdetail&iid=6267.

10. "Education vs. Prison Costs," *CNN Money*, accessed August 1, 2017, https://money.cnn.com/infographic/economy/education-vs-prison-costs/.

Conclusion

Gerard Robinson and Elizabeth English Smith

Prisoner rehabilitation through postsecondary education and reentry programming serves as one of the most contested topics in American criminal justice reform today. At the center of this national debate about crime and punishment are 230-year-old questions about the role prisons should play in a democratic society. Are our prisons designed for corporal punishment, human improvement, or a combination thereof? Throughout the twentieth and twenty-first centuries, the US government has provided conflicting answers to the American public.

To address how to reform our criminal justice policies by better preparing individuals to successfully reenter society after serving time, this volume features the voices of prominent national figures pushing for reform. They include current and former students who have benefited from an education program in prison, those teaching or managing educational programs in prisons, and entrepreneurs, researchers, and policy influencers. This diversity demonstrates the breadth of this policy conversation and how our criminal justice system touches many other facets of American life: education, family, work, faith, and civil society.

For instance, Max Kenner, Andrea Cantora, and Renita Seabrook remind us why education itself—the power of the classroom—matters to criminal justice reform, and how the resurgence in prison education, due in part to the Second Chance Pell Pilot Program, is the latest articulation in a decades-old pursuit of using education to rehabilitate the incarcerated. The legal pursuit to secure educational rights for the incarcerated is similarly ongoing, as Ames Grawert outlines.

Daniel Shoag, Stan Veuger, and Will Heaton address the economic and workforce challenges and successes associated with formerly incarcerated men and women reentering the labor market. At the same time, Thomas Stewart explains why entrepreneurs matter in improving outcomes in the criminal justice system, and Linda Gibbs offers valuable insight into an innovative public-private partnership she helped lead in New York City. Nancy La Vigne explains why implementation fidelity and thinking outside the box on implementation science are important ingredients to addressing what works, why, for whom, and under what circumstances in evaluating reentry programs. We round out the book by hearing the stories of those whose lives have been directly benefited from educational programs behind prison walls.

Still, the positions communicated in this volume are not without critics. "The fairness doctrine" provides one example. Some ask whether it is fair for working-class families in

California, Ohio, or New York to take out a loan to pay for their child's college tuition while an inmate is awarded a free college degree. Where is the fairness for a Louisiana grandparent who is responsible for raising a granddaughter whose dad was murdered by someone who is learning a trade that is paid for by taxpayers? Is it fair to millions of college students saddled with nearly $2 trillion in debt while prisoners are not? The "soft on crime" theme is another criticism. The list goes on.

Each critique has merit. And though this volume does not provide a definitive answer to each, and possibly introduces more questions, it does offer insight into the richly textured complexity of the role of prison in society: to both punish past actions and prepare individuals for the future. While this is an uncomfortable conversation, it is a necessary one.

Adopting an "education for liberation" framework is important to this conversation for several reasons. First, "education for liberation" is more than a sound bite—it is a social thought experiment in reimagining the purpose of prison. While prisons were once viewed as *penitentiaries*—places where individuals went to receive help and become rehabilitated—that mind-set changed over time as politicians sought to make prisons more unbearable in an effort to deter crime and intensify punishment. Yet, over the years, some research has shown that the strictly punitive approach to prison does not work; it only creates professional criminals. As more politicians now recognize these inefficiencies, our mind-set is again shifting back to a greater emphasis on rehabilitation.

Second, "education for liberation" is not soft on *crime*; it is smart about *time*. If we care about advancing opportunity and reducing recidivism, investing in effective prison education and workforce reentry supports on the front end—instead of spending thousands of dollars to re-incarcerate an individual each year on the back end—is a wise choice.

Third, "education for liberation" is not beneficial for the incarcerated alone but also for their families, communities, and society as a whole. Investing in education and reentry supports for the incarcerated reduces recidivism, producing more law-abiding citizens, stable families, and safer communities.

Fourth, it is important to note that our "education for liberation" theme does not cheer-lead every aspect of our nation's current correctional education system. We think substantial improvements are necessary. Too many existing programs are not of high quality, and too few require an evaluation, which often makes it difficult to discern what is truly working and what is not. The field is not perfect, and one of the goals of this volume is to build momentum around the important conversations that must take place among correctional officers, state agencies, educators, inmates, and scholars to create the most rigorous, evidence-based models of correctional education in state and federal prisons across the nation.

Fifth, "education for liberation" embraces all learning models: Adult Basic Education, a GED, vocational and technical training, community colleges and universities, and programs that lead to a certificate, licensure, or credential. We also believe correctional staff are key stakeholders in this process and, thus, should have access to educational programs.

Finally, the phrase "education for liberation" implies that every individual is worthy of the opportunity to turn his or her life around if they so choose.

Despite the growth of the array of correctional-based education programs, coupled with a burgeoning interest from states and foundations in supporting them in recent years, many in the criminal justice and education fields—who too often work in silos—have no clear place to turn for evidence of their success, their implementation challenges, and possibilities for the future. We hope that this volume helps fill this void.

Index

About the Editors

Gerard Robinson is the executive director of the Center for Advancing Opportunity (CAO), a Washington, DC–based research and education initiative created by a partnership with the Thurgood Marshall College Fund, the Charles Koch Foundation, and Koch Industries. The mission of CAO is to develop evidence-based solutions to the most pressing education, criminal justice, and economic mobility issues in fragile communities throughout the United States by working with faculty and students at historically black colleges and universities (HBCUs) and other postsecondary institutions.

Prior to CAO, Robinson was a resident fellow at the American Enterprise Institute (AEI), where he worked on education policy issues, including choice in public and private schools, regulatory development and implementation of K–12 laws, the role of for-profit institutions in education, and the role of community colleges and HBCUs in adult advancement. Robinson has served as commissioner of education for Florida and secretary of education for the Commonwealth of Virginia, where criminal justice was part of his portfolio.

Robinson has a master of education degree from Harvard University, a bachelor of arts degree in philosophy from Howard University, and an associate of arts degree from El Camino College.

Elizabeth English Smith is a policy analyst at the Council of State Governments Justice Center, where she provides technical assistance to states, localities, and nonprofits that are recipients of Second Chance Act grants. Previously, she was the manager of external affairs for domestic policy studies and a research associate at the American Enterprise Institute (AEI), researching and writing about prison education/reentry, early childhood education, and K–12 education policy.

She has authored and coauthored several op-eds and reports about prison education and reentry programs, and her work has appeared in outlets such as *U.S. News and World Report*, *Real Clear Policy*, and *National Review*. She serves on the advisory board of the Texas-based Prison Entrepreneurship Program (PEP) and the advisory board of the Petey Greene Program, which provides tutoring to incarcerated individuals. She has a bachelor of arts in political science and Spanish from the University of Michigan and a master of public policy from George Washington University.

About the Contributors

Andrea Cantora is an assistant professor in the School of Criminal Justice at the University of Baltimore. Cantora has worked as a researcher at the John Jay Research and Evaluation Center and the Vera Institute of Justice's Center on Sentencing and Corrections. She specializes in qualitative research and program evaluations, with a primary focus on prisoner reentry and urban crime prevention. Her work has been published in the *Journal of Offender Rehabilitation*, the *American Journal of Criminal Justice*, and *Criminal Justice Studies.* Cantora has also worked directly with incarcerated populations since 2005, including on the development of a women's reentry program in New York City.

Since 2014, Cantora has taught college-level courses at Maryland's Jessup Correctional Institution in the JCI Scholar Program. Most recently, she developed and is overseeing the implementing of the University of Baltimore's Second Chance College Program at Jessup Correctional Institution. This new program is part of the US Department of Education's Second Chance Pell Grant Experiment. Cantora earned a BA in criminal justice and psychology, respectively, and an MA and PhD in criminal justice from John Jay College of Criminal Justice in New York.

Linda Gibbs is a principal at Bloomberg Associates and a senior fellow at Results for America. Previously she served as New York City deputy mayor of Health and Human Services from 2005 to 2013. Supervising the city's human service, public health, and social justice agencies, she spearheaded major initiatives on poverty alleviation, juvenile justice reform, and obesity reduction. "Age Friendly NYC," a blueprint for enhancing livability for older New Yorkers, and "Young Men's Initiative," addressing race-based disparities facing black and Latino young men in the areas of health, education, employment training, and the justice system, are two of the collaborative efforts she shaped to address significant social challenges.

Gibbs also improved the use of data and technology in human service management, contract effectiveness, and evidence-based program development. During her tenure, New York City has been the only top-twenty city in the United States whose poverty rate did not increase while the national average rose 28 percent. Prior to her appointment as deputy mayor, Gibbs was commissioner of the New York City Department of Homeless Services and held senior

171

positions with the Administration for Children's Services and the Office of Management and Budget. She is a graduate of SUNY Buffalo School of Law.

Newt Gingrich was the Speaker of the United States House of Representatives from 1995 to 1999. Gingrich was first elected to Congress in 1978, where he served Georgia's 6th Congressional District for twenty years. Today, he is a Fox News contributor and the author of thirty-six books, including fifteen fiction and nonfiction *New York Times* best sellers. He has also been an adviser to President Donald Trump during both the 2016 campaign and his presidency. Gingrich received his bachelor's degree from Emory University and his MA and PhD in modern European history from Tulane University.

Ames C. Grawert is senior counsel and John L. Neu Justice counsel in the Justice Program at the Brennan Center for Justice. In that position, he advocates for a fairer, more effective criminal justice system and leads a team dedicated to exploring and documenting the collateral costs of mass incarceration. Prior to joining the Brennan Center, Grawert was an assistant district attorney in the Appeals Bureau of the Nassau County District Attorney's Office and an associate at Mayer Brown LLP. Grawert is a graduate of New York University School of Law and Rice University.

Will Heaton serves as vice president of policy and government affairs at Just Leadership USA (JLUSA), a national nonprofit organization dedicated to cutting the US correctional population in #halfby2030. In this role, he managed JLUSA's Washington, DC, office, guiding the organization's federal strategy and helping to expand JLUSA's growing national impact. Prior to joining JLUSA, Heaton served as the director of policy and public affairs at the Center for Employment Opportunities (CEO), a national nonprofit dedicated to providing immediate, effective, and comprehensive employment services to formerly incarcerated men and women. In this capacity, he led CEO's policy and advocacy efforts to increase workforce opportunities for formerly incarcerated individuals and end the dehumanization of individuals affected by the justice system. He has also served as the vice president of member relations and chief of staff at the Council on Foundations, one of the largest philanthropic networks in the United States. Heaton began his career in the US House of Representatives as a legislative aide in the Office of the Speaker, and then he served as chief of staff for an Ohio congressman. He holds a bachelor of arts in history and government from the College of William and Mary. He has experienced aspects of the criminal justice system firsthand after a deferral felony conviction more than ten years ago and has dedicated his career to ending the inequities that the criminal justice system perpetuates in the United States.

Van Jones is a CNN political contributor and host of the recurring CNN program, *The Van Jones Show*. A graduate of the University of Tennessee and Yale Law School, he was a special adviser to the Obama White House and is the author of three *New York Times* best sellers. Jones founded the social justice accelerator, the Dream Corps, and has led numerous social and environmental justice enterprises, including the Ella Baker Center for Human Rights, Color of Change, and Green for All. In 2014, Jones cofounded #cut50, a bipartisan initiative to make communities safer while reducing the number of people in our prisons and jails.

Max Kenner is the founder and executive director of the Bard Prison Initiative (BPI), one of the leading college-in-prison programs in the United States. He created BPI as a student volunteer organization when he was an undergraduate at Bard College in 1999. After gaining the support of the college and cooperation of the New York State Department of Correctional Services, Kenner oversaw the growth of the program into a credit-bearing and, subsequently, degree-granting program in 2001.

Today, BPI enrolls more than three hundred incarcerated women and men full time in a curriculum spanning the breadth of academic disciplines, which offers 70 courses a semester and has conferred 550 degrees to incarcerated students. BPI is home to the national Consortium for the Liberal Arts in Prison, which establishes and cultivates college-in-prison programs across the country with partners that include the University of Notre Dame, Wesleyan University, Washington University in St. Louis, and Goucher College.

Nancy La Vigne is a vice president at the Urban Institute, where she directs the Justice Policy Center. La Vigne publishes research on prisoner reentry, criminal justice technologies, crime prevention, policing, and the spatial analysis of crime and criminal behavior. Her work appears in scholarly journals and practitioner publications and has made her a sought-after spokesperson on related subjects. Before being appointed director, La Vigne was a senior research associate at Urban, directing groundbreaking research on prisoner reentry.

Before joining Urban, La Vigne was founding director of the Crime Mapping Research Center at the National Institute of Justice. She later was special assistant to the assistant attorney general for the Office of Justice Programs within the US Department of Justice. She has also been research director for the Texas Sentencing Commission, research fellow at the Police Executive Research Forum, and consultant to the National Council on Crime and Delinquency.

La Vigne was executive director for the bipartisan Charles Colson Task Force on Federal Corrections Reform. She chairs the board of the Crime and Justice Research Alliance and serves on the board for the Consortium of Social Science Associations. She testifies before Congress on prisoner reentry and criminal justice reform and has been featured on NPR and in the *Atlantic, New York Times, Washington Post*, and *Chicago Tribune*. La Vigne holds a BA in government and economics from Smith College, an MA in public affairs from the LBJ School at the University of Texas at Austin, and a PhD in criminal justice from Rutgers University.

Renita L. Seabrook is an associate professor in the School of Criminal Justice and the director of the Nonprofit Management and Community Leadership Program at the University of Baltimore. Her research interests include program development and evaluation as well as offender reentry and rehabilitation—specifically female offenders. Her publications have appeared in various journals, books, and social media outlets, including *Race, Ethnicity, and Law: Sociology of Crime, Law, and Deviance*, the *Daily Record*, the *Journal of Public Management & Social Policy*, and *Maryland's Criminal Justice System*.

Seabrook is on the editorial board for the *Journal of Prisoners on Prisons*. Prior to her work in academe, Seabrook worked as a research assistant for the Administrative Office of the Courts in the New Jersey Intensive Supervision Program, as a program development consultant for the Georgia Department of Corrections, and as a research coordinator/instructor for the Georgia State Board of Pardons and Paroles.

Seabrook is a 2014 community fellow for the Open Society Institute–Baltimore, in which she founded the Helping Others 2 Win Program—an experiential learning program that affords women in transition from prison viable reentry services. Seabrook earned a BA from Purdue University and an MA and PhD from Rutgers University–Newark.

Daniel Shoag is an assistant professor of public policy at Harvard Kennedy School of Government and an affiliate of the Taubman Center for State and Local Government. His research focuses on state and local government finance, worker signaling and the hiring process, and regional and urban economics. Daniel's research has been published in major academic journals such as the *Journal of Royal Society Interface*, the *Quarterly Journal of Economics*, and *American Economic Review P&P*.

Shoag has worked as a visiting scholar at the Federal Reserve Bank of Boston and as a visiting professor at Tel Aviv University; he also was selected as a rising new scholar by the Stanford University Center on Poverty and Inequality. He cofounded and now cochairs the HumTech conference (which counts more than two hundred as participants) in Boston, and he is a coeditor of the annual peer-reviewed conference proceedings volume. Shoag received his BA and PhD in economics from Harvard University.

Thomas G. Stewart is president of John F. Kennedy University Online, a regionally accredited institution located in Pleasant Hill, California. He has extensive experience working with social enterprise organizations that serve nontraditional and marginalized groups, with particular expertise in the areas of qualitative research, coalition building, and business development.

Stewart has been involved in numerous entrepreneurial, civic, and volunteer activities, including senior executive and board memberships with the Black Alliance for Educational Options, the SEED Public Charter School of Washington, DC, and the World Organization of Resilient Kids. He has authored numerous articles and reports and coauthored a book about families and school reform in 2014.

Stewart is a US Army veteran and holds a BA with honors from the University of the District of Columbia and a PhD in government from Harvard University. His dissertation title is "Urban Poverty and Prisons: The Political Socialization of Inner-City Males."

Stan Veuger is a resident scholar at the American Enterprise Institute (AEI), where his research is in political economy and public finance. He is also the editor of *AEI Economic Perspectives*, a visiting lecturer of economics at Harvard University, a Future World fellow at the IE School of International Relations' Center for the Governance of Change, and an extramural fellow at Tilburg University's Department of Economics. His research has been published in leading academic and professional journals, including the *Journal of Monetary Economics*, the *Quarterly Journal of Economics*, and the *Review of Economics and Statistics*.

Veuger is the editor, with Michael Strain, of *Economic Freedom and Human Flourishing: Perspectives from Political Philosophy* (2016). He also writes frequently for general audiences on economics, politics, and popular culture. His writing has appeared in *Foreign Affairs*, the *Los Angeles Times*, the *National Interest*, the *New York Times*, and *USA Today*, among others. Veuger serves as the chairman of the Washington, DC, chapter of the Netherland-America Foundation.

Veuger received a PhD and an AM in economics from Harvard and an MSc in economics from Universitat Pompeu Fabra. He completed his undergraduate education at Utrecht University and Erasmus University Rotterdam.